Callin's from a Star

MERRELL FANKHAUSER

Typeset by Jonathan Downes,
Cover and Layout by SPiderKaT for CFZ Communications
Using Microsoft Word 2000, Microsoft Publisher 2000, Adobe Photoshop CS.

First published in Great Britain by Gonzo Multimedia

c/o Brooks City,
6th Floor New Baltic House
65 Fenchurch Street,
London EC3M 4BE
Fax: +44 (0)191 5121104
Tel: +44 (0) 191 5849144
International Numbers:
Germany: Freephone 08000 825 699
USA: Freephone 18666 747 289

© Gonzo Multimedia MMXIV

ISBN: 978-1-908728-38-8

To my parents Milt & Evelyn Fankhauser.

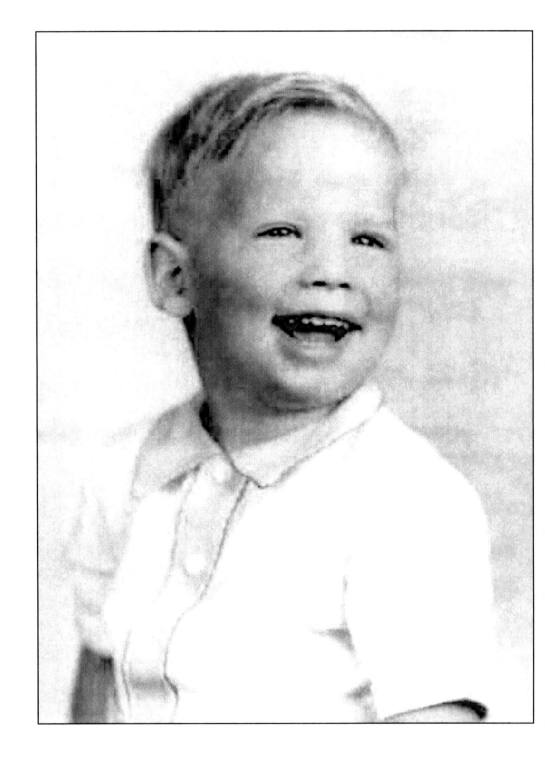

CHAPTER 1
Life begins in Kentucky

I was born Merrell Wayne Fankhauser in Louisville, Kentucky at 11:45am on December 23,1943, under the sign of Capricorn.

My Dad's name was Milton Carl Fankhauser, born in Penfield, NY. His Dad, Ruben Fankhauser, who was the son of John Fankhauser and the grandson of Nicholas Fankhauser, helped settle one of the first Swiss townships in Powhatan, Ohio. His relatives, Nicholas and Daniel Fankhauser left their village near Trub, Switzerland, in 1819. Their long journey started out in Bern, where with eight other Swiss families they embarked on a flatboat and moved down the Aer River to the Rhine and then down the Rhine to the city of Antwerp. After some delay they set sail from Antwerp on a three-masted French vessel named, *The Eugenius*. A few days after their departure, Mrs. Daniel Fankhauser gave birth to a baby boy who was named Jacob Ocean Fankhauser, due to the circumstances surrounding his birth.

Near the Forty-Ninth Parallel, the ship encountered a heavy storm; after this experience Nicholas remarked that he would not be a sailor for all the wealth in the world! Following several days of fog, land was sighted on the morning of July 20th.

After disembarking in New York, the Fankhausers, along with five other Swiss families, went to Perth Amboy, New Jersey where they purchased four oxen and two wagons. Upon one wagon they loaded the baggage and on the other the women and children. They began their six hundred mile journey westward, passing through Bethlehem, Reading, Lebanon, Bedford and Washington, where they continued on through Pennsylvania and Wheeling, West Virginia. Here they took a boat on the Ohio River and landed some twenty miles downstream near what is now known as Powhatan Point, Ohio. They were informed that there was plenty of government land nearby in Monroe County, so the Fankhauser families and several others decided to settle in what is now Switzerland Township.

The above information was taken from *Lest We Forget*; a book written by Nicholas Fankhauser and published in 1915 by F. A. Scherzinger. My grandfather, Ruben, died of blood poisoning when my Dad was only fourteen. My Dad's mother's name was Nellie Tyo, who was full blooded Canadian Indian, possibly from the Wyandot Tribe. Her classic Indian features have been passed down through the generations. Not much was known about her or how she met Ruben Fankhauser, but I can remember her when I was a child as a very strong and willful person with piercing eyes.

My mother's maiden name was Evelyn Paldena Weixalbraun and she was born in Bremen, Germany. Her father, Frank Weixalbraun was a stout Austrian, who in his younger years was a wrestler and later became a German soldier. Her mother was a hard working German lady and her maiden name was Anna Marie Warnecke, also born in Bremen. They left Germany and came to America in 1924. They first settled for three years in Ashland, Nebraska; a small town near Omaha. There they found work in a meat packing company. When my mother arrived in America she couldn't speak a word of English, yet in eight short weeks she was reciting poetry in perfect English!

After three years they moved to Louisville, Kentucky, where Frank found work in a stone yard. They saved their money and in 1932 they opened a restaurant that became very successful. My mother worked in the restaurant with her sister, Ann, up into her teens. She used to sing in the kitchen, into a pot, pretending that she was on stage holding a microphone. She later landed a job with a big band and was soon traveling to outer areas singing, much to her strict Austrian father's dismay! I remember well, when I was a child, hearing her tell the story of the flood of 1936, when the Ohio River overflowed onto its banks and how the family had to be rescued from the restaurant in a row boat!

My mom and dad met at Churchill Downs where the Kentucky Derby is held. My dad was in the Army in Patton's Tank Division. After only a few weeks my dad was telling his friends, "That's the girl I'm going to marry".

Both my mom and dad had a musical background. My dad played guitar in a Dixieland band and he loved those old Jimmie Rodgers Railroad songs. He taught me to whistle when I was ten months old and my musical career began. My dad was quite a guy, he was a very good machinist and a fairly well known race car driver in the 40s and early '50s. He raced at Indianapolis in 1948. In the '50s he appeared in a motion picture titled *To Please a Lady*, starring Clark Gable and Barbara Stanwyck. It was a story about a race car driver who went on to win in the

Indy 500. He also appeared in a movie titled *The Big Wheel* which starred Mickey Rooney. In both of the films he drove in the race scenes and his car was recognizable because of its pear shaped front grill. The race cars that he drove were his own creations, he built everything from the ground up and he even built his own engine! I remember as a youngster watching him take a sheet of aluminum and make a beautiful race car body out of it. He actually developed one of the first torsion bar suspensions for race cars!

There was always music in our house, everyone sang and danced. By the time I was three years old I had made my first record on Santa Claus' lap in a department store, singing *Zip a de do da!* When I went to visit my German grandmother she would always put on those great old Viennese Waltzes, how I loved those waltzes and the stories that she would tell me about the Black Forest.

As I grew up in Kentucky, most of my time was spent hunting and fishing, or searching for mysterious things in the woods near the creek at the end of our street. I can remember trying to catch frogs and crawdads. Many times I'd fall into the swamp and come home looking like the creature from the Black Lagoon! Mom would very calmly undress me on the back porch and then hose me off, Man, that water was cold! I went to school at the five room Adair Street School that was about a quarter of a mile from our house. I can remember cold snowy winter mornings walking to school and we would pretend to ice skate - in our shoes - on the frozen sidewalk in front of the school.

Then in 1950 along came my sister, Linda Ann, and what a cute little papoose; she was born with a full head of dark hair. Nurses at the hospital called her 'Little Minehacha'. She immediately showed her talent as a dancer and before long she was twirling and tapping all over the floor! I still remember many nights when we would all be singing and clapping and she would be doing the Jitterbug. Boy did we have fun!

Linda Fankhauser

I also remember going across the railroad tracks where the black folks lived and watching two old guys, who had been eating cornbread and drinking wine. They put a broken wine bottle neck on their fingers and played guitar with it and it really made an impression on me. I must have been about ten years old at the time.

We got our first TV and I would race home on Friday nights to see the latest adventure of *Superman* and *The Lone Ranger*.

With the increasing cold winters in Kentucky, my dad began filling our heads with dreams of California and warm sunshine. In the winter of 1952 we left for our first visit to California. I can remember the excitement of packing things and loading up the unfinished new race car that Dad was building and then heading out on the highway for that golden state. Yah hoo! I was looking for Indians everywhere and I couldn't wait to get to the mountains and desert. I was sure there would be a whole tribe waiting around the next bend, and maybe they would let me have a pony to ride, and some real bows and arrows!

We finally reached some desert and because of some license or document problem they didn't want to let us through the toll gate to the next state. So we went back and waited until night and when it was dark, dad made a dash for it. He wound that old Ford up like we were going down the straightaway at Indianapolis; we blew right through the check station doing a little over ninety miles an hour! That was moving pretty fast for those days. We didn't sleep that night and we drove all day and into the next night until we found a motel.

The following day we got up and went to breakfast and my dad was checking the maps to find a way around the next checkpoint and he found a road that went around the checkpoint alright and it was right smack dab in an Indian Reservation. All right, *now* we're talking!

We left the highway in a cloud of dust on a dirt road that soon turned to nothing but a trail. My imagination was running wild, what would we see? Maybe they would attack us; we might need Roy Rogers and Gene Autry to help us. We drove over the bumpy trail for miles and didn't see anything, then all of a sudden there was a real live Indian sitting on a horse looking at us like we were from outer space! We kept on driving, it was about mid day now and the sun was pretty hot, we stopped and took a drink of water. We made sure that we had plenty of water, my mom always had a cooler full of ice and we would have jars of ice water. We had only stopped for a few minutes when we noticed that there were a lot of Indians around us, looking very curious about the race car that we were towing. I asked my dad if he could talk Indian to them? Before he could answer me my mom said something to a squaw who was sitting on a horse, but all the squaw did was grunt. My dad tried to ask one of the men which way the highway was and he pointed in the direction of a valley between two hills. We continued on and I could tell by the look on my mom's face that she was worried. "Oh Milt," she said, "Why did we do this?" I could tell that my dad was enjoying the adventure and he kept driving.

Finally we reached the valley between two hills and it looked like a wagon trail going up a rather steep hill. We started up the hill and lost traction and had to back down slowly. My dad got that look in his eyes that I had seen many times before, just like when the flag was coming down at the beginning of a race. Once again he revved up the Ford and away we went. Yippee! We made it to the top of the hill and from there we could see telephone wires and a shiny ribbon of highway in the distance. It was almost Sunset by the time we made it to the highway and we had to go through several barbed wire gates, and at last there we were back in modern man's world. It had been like a trip back into time and I was sorry to see the Indians disappear in the distance. We checked into a motel that was real western looking with a buckboard in front and the rooms had rustic wooden furniture with pictures of cowboys and Indians on the walls, this was great! My last thoughts were

that Heaven couldn't be as good as this, as I fell asleep somewhere in Arizona.

We awoke early the next morning and I couldn't stop thinking about the trip through the Reservation the day before, I couldn't wait for us to finish breakfast to find out what adventure was waiting for us today.

We stopped around noon by some big boulders and had tuna fish sandwiches that my mom had made and my dad got out his 8mm movie camera and filmed my sister and me, along with my mom and shots of the race car. I went over the hill and gazed off into the distance at the wide expanse of hills dotted with Cactus. Not one human being was in

sight for as far as I could see, I was always armed with my Boy Scout pocket knife and ready for action. I could hear Mom calling my name from off in the distance. "Milt, where has he gone?"

I came running and jumped off a small boulder Indian style, just like in the movies. I didn't want to get back in the car, but they convinced me that it was time to go and that there was plenty more up ahead to see. I kept asking my dad if he knew where Roy Rogers lived and would we see him? He said to keep a sharp eye out sonny, and you never know. He always called me sonny until I was about twenty years old!

I remember stopping to eat dinner and I fell asleep, later I woke up and it was pitch black. I noticed that we were up on a hill looking down at a lot of lights. I asked what it was and my dad told me it was Needles. I told him not to fall off or we might get poked and everyone laughed. He told me that was the name of the town, I said "oh." We drove for quite a ways and we were all drifting off when my dad yelled, "Yah hoo!" He often did this when it was late and we were having a hard time staying awake. Hearing that blood curdling yell while we were have asleep would sometimes scare us all, I think he would do it to keep himself awake too!

CHAPTER 2
Welcome to California

It was the middle of the night as we entered California, no big fan fare, no golden gates, and still no sign of Roy Rogers or Gene Autry!

We rented a little apartment in Bellflower, California, near the garage where my dad would be finishing the race car with his friend, Lou Maddis. I was enrolled in school and it was quite different than the rural school house I went to in Kentucky. The kids talked different than I did, as I had a fairly strong southern accent. They asked me where I came from and I told them I was an Indian from the woods of Kentucky. One kid told me that his dad told him that there was no such thing as a blonde Indian, so therefore I couldn't be one! Never the less, I stuck to my story that I was indeed a blonde Indian from Kentucky and I lived in the trees. I did have a tree house that I would hide in when I heard that my mom was cooking liver for dinner!

We stayed in California for five months, the race car was finished and it was time to go back to Kentucky. My dad had to get ready for the coming racing season. After a stretch of races my dad came home very tired; he would drive practically all night to get to a race and sleep in the truck, get up to race and then head out to another track. It wasn't an easy life and sometimes something would break on the car and then it was either a fast repair, or he might miss the next race and any prize money. He suffered a mild heart attack sometime in 1953, the doctor ordered him to stay in bed for a month and gave him some blood thinning medication. He stayed in bed two weeks and was back up working again, and took a job in the engine development division of International Harvester in Louisville. By this time he had pretty much decided that his days of driving race cars were over.

In 1954 we made the decision to move to California permanently. We sold the house with the big garage in the back yard, packed everything up that we owned and loaded up old #23, his last race car, onto the trailer and back we went to sunny California.

We rented an apartment in Lakewood and we lived there for about a year. Dad opened a body shop, where he did a lot of customizing, the custom hot rod scene, and the James Dean era had begun. Dad would come home and say, "Sonny, you wouldn't believe what these guys want me to do to their cars, they want me to shave off the door and trunk handles and lower the cars

down so low that they can't even drive over a driveway!" At that time I thought that those cars were just the coolest things I ever saw, with those fancy scalloped and flame paint jobs! My dad had gotten a pilot's license and a Flight Instructor Rating while we still lived in Kentucky and had bought a little two seat Taylor craft that we would occasionally fly. I remember how he would take me up and demonstrate every maneuver the plane could do until I would beg him to land! But then I would want to go back up and do it all over again. He had done some metal work on a high performance sailplane called the "Jenny Mae". I thought it was just about the most beautiful flying machine that I had ever seen, with its long slender wings and vee tail. The designer told my dad about a glider port that was coming up for lease in the more southern part of California at a place called Lake Elsinore. So one Sunday we went out to Lake Elsinore to meet the owner of the airport and look the place over. I can remember rounding a turn in this valley and seeing all these palm trees, and I was thinking that this must be paradise; there were gliders, airplanes and a lake that I could fish in! When we got there it was a nice little town, but the lake was a mere puddle, apparently the under ground springs that fed the lake had covered over with silt some years ago and the lake had gone dry. The little town could never quite raise the money to dredge the lake and hopefully unplug the springs that could once again fill the lake up. The town had once been a popular vacation spot and the mineral springs were quite an attraction for celebrities and movie stars.

The little house at the airport was a bit run down but it was cozy. My dad made the deal and we moved in sometime in 1955. There was a lot of repair needed to both the house and hangar and there was a partially built building attached to the hangar that was going to be a restaurant, the dreams and plans we had for that place were endless. I spent a lot of time with my dad learning carpentry and interior finish work, and we made a nice little operation out of the place. My dad spent the weekends towing gliders from early morning till sunset, some days he would make over two hundred dollars,

which was pretty good back in those days. My mom would be busy selling hot dogs and her delicious homemade barbeque hamburgers. I would make fifty cents for running the wing tips of gliders while they were taking off and then retrieving the tow lines after my dad dropped them over the field after towing a glider up to altitude. The thermals were plenty and a good sailplane could stay up all day riding the up currents in the valley, it was a beautiful sight to see all these various designs of gliders soaring around in the clear blue sky. Every once in awhile, I would get a ride in a two place glider and received flight instruction and I learned to fly. During the week my dad was teaching me to fly the Piper Cub and I could land it and take off with no problem, but I was still too young to get a license to fly a powered airplane. I got real interested in aircraft design and I would build models of my favorite planes and sometimes they would fly away, never to be seen again; sucked up in a thermal in the blue California sky.

On my eleventh birthday I got a ukulele and Dad showed me some chords and I learned a few little songs and started experimenting. I used to listen to a radio station near San Diego, whose call letters were XERB (Wolfman Jack later broadcast from there). They played all the hits of the day and I would try to learn them on my ukulele.

The winter months slowed down a little with the glider flying and my dad took a job flying for the national weather research. He was flying quite a bit in Florida, Montana and New Mexico. I remember one time he came back from the East coast and said, "Hey Sonny, have you heard of this guy named Elvis Presley?" I said, "Elvis who?" and I laughed! A few weeks later everybody in school was singing *Hound Dog* and *Don't Be Cruel*. I couldn't believe it! So I learned those songs on my ukulele and I spent many nights singing in the airplane hangar because it had a great echo that sounded almost like a record.

I went to school in the little town of Lake Elsinore for the seventh, eighth and ninth grades. Upon graduating to the ninth grade, little did I know what awaited me? A thing called Freshman Initiation! After getting my class assignments they notified us that the following

Wednesday we had a choice of clothing and hair styles that we had to wear. The choices were; a shower cap, curlers in our hair, a scarf, a woman's robe, a woman's nightgown, etc. I would like to see them try to make some of the kids of today do this. If you tried to avoid this humiliation by staying home that day, the seniors had all sorts of torture planned for your next arrival at school that could go on for days, including removing your pants and running them up a flag pole and then making you climb up and get them! My mother helped me get my outfit together for school that day; there I was standing on the road waiting for the school bus with my hair up in curlers wearing a ladies robe! When I got to school I was anointed with garlic and eggs in my hair, the end of the day culminated in a tug of war between the freshman and seniors, they won. That was a day that I will never forget.

One night I was alone at home in the little house on the glider port, my mom and dad and sister, Linda, had gone shopping to the larger town of Riverside, which was about twenty miles away. I heard a car drive up and I looked out the window to see a car that resembled our 51 Ford, but a closer look revealed it was a 49 Ford Coupe. The door opened and it was my friend, David Devor, who I had met while living in Lakewood. David was like a James Dean,/ Marlon Brando kind of guy and being a few years older than me, I looked up to him. I asked him if that was his car? His response was, "No, I lifted it." I asked, "What?" and he told me that he had stolen it in Bellflower, and decided to come out and visit me. He said that it was overheating and needed gas, so we pushed it down to the hangar and I pumped some aviation fuel out of a fifty five gallon drum into the car, while David filled the radiator with water. Just then I saw some lights coming down the long driveway to the hangar and I told David to hide in the back of the hangar behind one of the gliders. It was Charles Ray, the Chief of Elsinore police, who often patrolled the area. He saw me and I went over to his car and he said hi and asked what I was doing out there in the dark? I told him that I had heard a noise and was just checking the hangar. I guess he mistook David's car for my parent's car and asked where my parents were? I told him they were in the house watching television, he said okay and to have a nice evening and then drove off.

David came out of hiding and told me that I did a good job of getting rid of the cops; it was a scene right out of a '50s juvenile delinquent movie. I told David that my parents would be coming home soon and that he'd better get going. He had a hard time starting the old Ford and chugged up the long driveway to the highway. My mom and dad and sister arrived shortly after that and asked what I had been doing and I politely said that I was doing some homework. A few minutes later Police Chief, Charlie Ray, was knocking on our door, explaining that they found a stalled car up on the highway and upon checking the license plate they discovered that the car had been stolen and there was an all points bulletin out for it. Charlie said that he had seen the car here earlier and he asked me if I knew anything about it? My dad gave me *that* look and I knew I'd better come clean! I told them it was David Devor from Lakewood and that he had stolen the car to come out and see me. My mom couldn't believe what she was hearing. Charlie Ray gave me a stern warning not to ever lie to the police again and he went off into the night with another officer to look for David. They found him the next morning walking along the highway on the outskirts of town, hitch-hiking. They took him to jail and called his parents, who were very angry and had to drive a long way to the police department in Lake Elsinore to get him.

Mom took me to town to see him in jail so that I would see what it would be like if I ever decided to break the law. David told me that he was actually hiding on top of our house all night and was listening through a vent while Charlie Ray was questioning me! He said, "I heard you give me up!"

That was the last time that I ever saw David Devor. Years later in 1971, his mom saw me on TV with my band, Mu, and somehow got my phone number and called me. She told me that David had moved to San Francisco and had become a hippy.

She added, "By the way, your music is a little strange and off beat. I think you are going to have to do better, if you plan to make it."

All in all I had a pretty good time living at Lake Elsinore, I had two horses, a flock of pigeons and airplanes, it was a great place for a young person to grow up .I can remember on clear full moon nights at the airport, looking at the stars with my dad and talking about what's out there, how did we get here and when are the flying saucers going to land! My dad was very open-minded about things, but yet with a scientific attitude, he really taught me a lot.

At that time my dad had a dream to have the International glider contest at our glider port in Lake Elsinore, unfortunately it never happened. The lease ran out near the end of 1958 and business was slow, so we decided to move on to greener pastures. Before we moved the city was able to dredge the lake, there was also a strong rainfall, in addition to a release of water from Railroad Canyon Dam that partially filled the lake. The town saw their hoped for dream fulfilled. Today the lake has water, but it's still not up to the level that it once was. I was sorry to say goodbye to Lake Elsinore, but we were on to a new adventure!

Our adventure took us on a trip up the coast of California, where we looked at small towns with airports, a place where my dad could get a job as a flight instructor and charter pilot. We went as far north as Clear Lake, we came back down the coast and stopped at a little city known as Santa Maria. It seemed to be a nice area and dad had a good offer at the airport, so there we decided to stay.

Merrell and Bill Dodd

CHAPTER 3
Hello Central Coast

Once my dad accepted the job offer at the Santa Maria airport he went to work immediately, and mom and I went looking for a house to live in. We ended up driving twelve miles further up the coast to the little village of Arroyo Grande. There we found some brand new houses at the very reasonable price of thirteen thousand dollars! The houses were surrounded by strawberry fields and there was a cool breeze coming in off the ocean, which was only two miles away. The first job I got was picking and stemming strawberries in the fields with the Mexican workers, it was hard work in the sun all day and the wages were very low.

One summer I managed to save enough money to buy my first guitar, and later on I bought an amplifier and a microphone. My dad had been teaching me chords on the guitar, which had gotten me very excited and opened up a whole new world for me. My mom saw the excitement in my eyes, and I got some guitar instruction books and started studying. Around this time I got a job at the local Fair Oaks theatre as an usher and clean up person. One day I was practicing my guitar in the theatre and the manager heard me. He said, "Boy, I think you have some talent and you sing pretty well too". I used to have an act myself and I was pretty well known on the East Coast as Happy the Clown. Why don't we do some shows together?" I thought, "Wow, this is it. I am going to be in show business!"

The first show was booked for a Saturday afternoon, in between a double feature at the theatre. My mom made me a silver and white shirt, when I walked out on that big stage I really felt like a star. I think the first song that I sang was *Poor Little Fool*, by Ricky Nelson, the kids went nuts! Then I followed that song with *Blue Suede Shoes*, by Elvis Presley, and the place really went crazy! In between all of this, Happy the Clown was doing his jokes and running into the audience, giving the kids balloons and candy.

I went out front in the lobby at the end of the show and I was mobbed by screaming teenage girls wanting my autograph. This was great and I was getting paid twelve dollars a show too!

Now it was time to explore the sea. I started surfing and skim boarding, and I also spent a lot of time fishing and probing the tide pools for sea life. I once caught a fairly good sized octopus with my friend, James Keen. Jimmy took the octopus home and tried keeping it alive in a wash tub in his parent's garage, needless to say it died in a few days and the stink was terrible! His mom sure wasn't happy about that.

Jimmy and I became good friends and we both got our driver's licenses about the same time. At the time the big deal was to see who could burn the most rubber; if you could get second gear rubber you were really cool! He got a 38 Chevy and I got a 40 Ford Coupe. How I loved that car, it was maroon, with gray and white tuck and roll upholstery. By this time I was working at the local 76 Union gas station and I was able to save enough money to put a Corvette engine in my 40 Ford, and it would fly! We became real involved with drag racing and it's a wonder that we both survived through those years without having a serious accident.

One time we went down to Santa Maria and raced a guy who had a new 61 Ford and we beat him off the line and through the gears, but when I hit third gear the entire bottom of the transmission blew out on the highway. The car would still drive, but I couldn't shift gears. By the time we reached home the floor board was so hot that we couldn't keep our feet on the floor.

I continued to play the theatre concerts with Happy the Clown booking our show at other theaters; we traveled to San Luis Obispo, Morro Bay, Atascadero and Santa Maria. After a few months I made friends with a shy guitar player at school named Bill Dodd. He was getting pretty good at playing lead and we worked up some tunes and I asked him to join the act, I had to take a cut in pay, but it was worth it. We became a team and made ten dollars per show. We started doing talent shows and dances as a duo and later on we added a bass player and a drummer and called our first band *The Orbits*. Bill's cousin, John Oliver, came in on bass and Bill and I pretty much taught him everything, he ended up being a fine bass player.

We went through a few drummers in a small area where there weren't many players to choose from, Rock 'n' Roll music being played by small combos was still a fairly new thing. One time we played a dance for the annual Arroyo Grande Harvest Festival, it was a quite a big event and would draw a couple thousand people. The city blocked off the main street of the little village and we had our band on a flatbed truck at one end of the street, while a Country Western band played at the other end. We were really hot and people were dancing up a storm and having a blast. We ended up drawing everybody down to our end of the street and the Country & Western band had no one left to play to! Then they came down to see us, they were bigger and older guys and they gave us some pretty nasty looks.

We took a break and their guitar player came up to me and asked, "Why don't we play together"? That sounded good to me, so on the next set we merged the two bands and tore into some down and dirty rockabilly, and everyone loved it! It was the talk of the town for some time to come!

Bill Dodd and I became good friends with the guitar player, Lucky Rogers, we even took lessons from him for a few months and he gave our band some good pointers. Bill and I bought an old 1932 Ford roadster without an engine that was previously used as a jalopy racer.

We decided to make a drag racer out of it and bought a Mercury Marauder police car V8 engine from my boss, Bob Wheat, owner of the local Union Oil Gas Station where I worked. We adapted the big V8 engine to a 39 Ford three speed floor shift transmission, drive shaft and rear end. I had to build my own custom headers to fit around the steering box and other obstacles to fit the small roadsters frame. I had become a pretty good welder from aeronautics classes that I was taking at Hancock College in Santa Maria.

We put two big racing slick tires on the back for maximum traction. I even painted it a Honduras maroon color that matched my 1940 Ford Coupe. We found out right away that you couldn't take off in first gear because the engine had so much power that it would break the transmission. By now I was an expert at crawling through junk yards to find parts for these old transmissions and repair them. We found it was better to take off in second gear, we might be a little behind off the line, but when it revved up and you hit third gear all they saw was our dust!

Bill would sometimes forget to start off in second gear when he was racing somebody and he'd end up blowing the transmission. I kept reminding him not to forget to take off in second gear. One time he raced somebody and blew the transmission and had the roadster towed home to his house out in the country, where he thought he could fix it. I hadn't seen Bill or the roadster in a few days, so I decided to just pop in on him and see what was going on. I drove up and there was Bill with the floor boards out of the roadster, wailing on the transmission with a big sledge hammer! He had a crazy look in his eye and was sweating profusely and his hands were cut and bleeding. I asked him if he blew the transmission again? He answered, "Yeah. I've got to get it out to save my mind." He had the case completely beat away, but the jackshaft and main gears just wouldn't break. I convinced him that we had to unbolt the engine and pull it forward enough to get the transmission out and put the new one in. We sold the roadster and quit drag racing for awhile and concentrated on playing music.

We started playing high school and grammar school dances, store openings, or anything that we could get, we even won a talent contest. The group, *The Sentinels*, backed me up at one of the talent contests. Their drummer was Johnny Barbata, who went on to play with *The Turtles, The Jefferson Starship* and *Crosby, Stills and Nash*. The keyboardist of *The Sentinels*, Lee Michaels, later went on to a solo career. Bill and I went on performing together for a couple more years and then he was asked to join an R&B band called *The Biscaynes* and I joined the instrumental surf band, *The Revels*, for a short time, who had a hit record titled Church Key. I later joined *The Impacts*, who consisted of myself on vocal and lead guitar, Martin Brown on vocal and steel guitar, Steve Evans on rhythm guitar, John Oliver on bass, Steve Metz on drums, Joel Rose Jr. on sax and Jack Metz on sax and vocal. We played a mixture of Chuck Berry tunes and hopped up instrumentals that later became known as surf music. The first job *The Impacts* got was at a teenage hangout called *The Peppermint Twist West*. We played the entire summer there and it was usually for ten dollars each and also included a hamburger and a coke. There was no alcohol served.

The owner of *The Peppermint Twist West*, Pat Yeigh, had a stepdaughter named Terry, who sometimes worked behind the bar serving cokes and hamburgers and hot dogs. All the guys in the band tried to get a date with Terry, but they never succeeded. She lived in the Hollywood area and later became a teen starlet and changed her name to Darbi Winters.

One time she came up to the club with a manager and a writer named Earl Leaf and several other starlets and movie stars, Tommy Kirk and Tab Hunter were in the group. They were all out on the dance floor doing the Twist to the wild surf sounds of *The Impacts*. There was even an article written in the popular *Teen Magazine* about this fun filled night at *The Peppermint Twist West* in Pismo Beach, California. The sad part of the story is that Pat Yeigh had been drinking one night in Hollywood and Terry's mother wasn't home, Pat and Terry got into an altercation and he strangled her. It was a big shock and we never found out what really happened, Pat went to prison and the club closed.

CHAPTER 4
Wiped Out

D own the street from *The Peppermint Twist West*, the big dance hall *The Rose Garden Ballroom*, was packing them in with a mixture of Country and Rhythm and Blues bands. They served alcohol and the owner, Joel Rose Sr., soon had his fill of putting up with drunks and various problems, so he decided to drop the alcohol and have teen dances.

The Impacts got the job as house band and we began to play to packed houses every week-end and sometimes three nights a week during the summer. The Impacts quickly became the most popular band in the area! We developed an original sound and we were soon backing up all the stars of the day when they came through town. Theses stars included such big names as; Freddie Cannon, Brenda Lee, *The Righteous Brothers, The Coasters*, Little Anthony and Chuck Negron, who would later go on to be one of the singers in *Three Dog Night*. All the guys in the band got along fairly well and we had a lot of fun playing together. Martin Brown was probably the real rebel in the band, he had a habit of getting involved in a pinball game and then not getting back on stage in time. Jack Metz kept warning him and told him that the next time he was late he was going to be fired. Well we must have fired and hired him back a half dozen times, it was quite funny. Sax player Joel Rose Jr. had an old 1938 Dodge that we would cruise around in and one time after a gig someone showed up with some alcohol and Martin guzzled more than his share. The old Dodge had what was known as "suicide doors" on the back. They were hinged at the back and swung forward. We went around a corner and all of a sudden Martin just swung out, hanging on the door, and we were going at least fifty miles an hour, we just barely pulled him back inside!

The old Dodge was also good for hauling surf boards, as it was quite long and the surfboards of the day were appropriately called long boards. Joel and I went surfing and he had gotten bored as the waves were not very good that day and he was just sitting onshore watching me. I was sort of day dreaming, as I often did, and all of a sudden a giant set appeared out of nowhere. Before I could gain my composure a giant wave was taking me over the falls and the last thing I heard was Joel laughing and screaming ***"WIPE OUT!"*** Well after I came up and struggled to shore and got all of the sand and water out of my ears, I thought, "Hmm that would be a good song title!" I had already written a song in 1961 titled "Kick Out", so I just

Rose Garden Ballroom

changed the title.

Later in 1962 we were playing at *The Rose Garden Ballroom* and Norman Knowles, sax player from *The Revels*, was producing bands and he told us that he was looking for some good bands to record. If we were interested he would like to meet us at the ballroom on Sunday and he would bring a small reel to reel tape recorder and record us. We thought, Wow, this sounds pretty good and we might even get a record deal! The taping went very well and he said he wanted to take it down to Hollywood to the producer that he was working with; a Mr. Tony Hilder. We received a call about a week later and they wanted us to come down to Hollywood and record, so we followed Mr. Knowles down and we sort of caravanned down together. I was driving my 1940 Ford Coupe with the corvette engine in it, and of course I had to take the lead every once in awhile, just to show the guys how fast my car really was!

We arrived at the little studio about mid day, the engineer and owner was a man named Ted Brinson. He was very knowledgeable and had a new three track Ampex recorder and a very good reverb system. He worked as a postman during the week and recorded on weekends and his days off. He had built the studio in his backyard, attaching a new section to an already existing garage; it was built very well and had a great sound. He recorded quite a few known bands and artists including *The Olympics*, who had several hits, and the surf groups *The Challengers, The Sentinels, The Revels*, and many others.

The Impacts session began with us doing our original instrumentals live, just the way we did them at The Rose Garden Ballroom. We went through the songs very fast and everyone was amazed at how good we sounded and without any mistakes! We took a break and wolfed down some hamburgers during playback. We were very impressed at how we sounded with that heavy reverb, and every instrument was so clearly mixed. We went back to work on more new originals that hadn't been played live yet and a few of these took up to three takes. By the time we were done there was enough songs for an album, everyone was very pleased.

The songs recorded during this session were; *Wipe Out, Fort Lauderdale, Tears, Revellion, Blue Surf, Impact, Steel Pier, Tandem, Sea Horse, Beep, Beep, Lisa, and Church Key.* We also tried to record a vocal I wrote called *It's True,* but the vocal microphone had a short in it and we couldn't finish the song.

The recordings were taken to Del-Fi Records by Tony Hilder and Norman Knowles. The owner of Del-Fi Records, Bob Keene, signed the album for release immediately. Bob Keene was known for his releases of songs by Sam Cooke, Ritchie Valens as well as many other instrumental surf groups and later on, *The Bobby Fuller Four.*

Knowles and Hilder made the deal for *The Impacts WIPE OUT* album and received an undisclosed amount of front money and a contract for artist and publishing royalties from Del-Fi Records. Our band never found out how much front money Knowles and Hilder received? The Impacts recording session took place near the end of September 1962, the signing with Del-Fi Records took place in October. By the end of November 1962 *The Impacts WIPE OUT* album was released in mono and stereo and available everywhere and we noticed right away

DEAUVILLE **CASTLE CLUB**

1525 OCEAN FRONT SANTA MONICA

(Foot of Olympic Blvd.)

PRESENTS

MARCH 22– 23 – 24

SURF BATTLE

20 SURF BANDS

THE PERSUADERS	—	SURF NIGHTMARE
CHANTAYS	--	PIPE LINE
BREAKERS	—	SURF BIRD

IMPACTS
LIVELY ONES
GUEST DISC JOCKEYS

Rhythm Kings

Sentinels

Rhythm Rockers

Bob Vaught and the Renegades

Rhythm Crusaders

Jim Walter and the Delta's

The Charades

Horace Heidt Jr. and the Trade Winds

Dave Meyers and the Surf Tones

Dischords

Golden Nuggets

Sting Rays

Danny and the Sessions

SEE -- K.F.W.B. BATTLE OF SURF BANDS ON THE DELFI SURFING LABEL

SUNDAY MATINEE MARCH 24

2:00 PM TO? AGE 14-19 ONLY

SEE FREE SURFING FILMS IN COLOR

there was no songwriting credits listed on our album.

The Impacts went back to playing at *The Rose Garden Ballroom* and we played out of town quite often, due to the success of the album. With the whirlwind speed at which the recording and release took place, we somehow, in the excitement of it all, over looked the fact that the band had no actual contract with Del-Fi Records or anyone concerning artist and songwriting royalties!

During January of 1963, we received another call from Hilder and Knowles to come down and record some more songs and they wanted to re-cut my song, *Wipe Out*. Hilder thought that with a few changes in the arrangement it would be a good song to release as a single 45rpm record. We arrived later in the day, but we had to wait for *The Challengers* to finish their recording session first. *The Challengers'* drummer, Richard Delvy, went on to produce and manage several surf bands, including *The Bel-Airs*, who had a hit with an instrumental titled, *Mr. Moto* and later songs by *The Surfaris*. Delvy became quite a businessman, figuring out the complicated music publishing business and how to actually make money off of these recordings. He and many other sharp guys got a lot of songs from bands and artists without paying them anything!

We started recording in the late afternoon and we quickly went through a few instrumentals, such as Torchula, which was released on the Del-Fi compilation album *KFWB's Battle of the*

The Impacts L-R Steve Evans, Merrell, John Oliver Steve Metz, Jack Metz, Joel Rose, Martin Brown

Surfing Bands and Kon Tiki, which was released on the Shepherd compilation album Surf Wars. We then began the work of re-arranging my song, *Wipe Out*. Hilder had us listen to the drum roll from our song *Beep Beep* and he wanted us to repeat it every other verse, we thought that was a dumb idea and that it would never work. We asked him if we were ever going to get some form of a contract and that we really didn't want to go any further until we did. He said okay and sent his assistant Richard Delvy out to get some contracts.

Meanwhile we went back to working on the new version of *Wipe Out* and we started making mistakes on purpose, stalling for time and just plain being rebellious! We did one version with the guitar over dubbed on the old version, then another version with one drum solo in the middle and then another with drum solos all the way through, with no saxophone. We didn't

26

finish till Delvy came back with the contracts, Hilder rapidly filled out some publishing songwriting agreements for individual songs and had us each sign the ones we wrote solely on our own and together as a group. I wrote *Wipe Out, Sea Horse* and *Tandem* and co-wrote *Tears*. Hilder ran out of contracts and said he would get more, sign them and send them to us, but we never heard from him again. We still had no artist recording agreement, at that time we were only seventeen and we knew nothing about how to copyright a song. What we didn't realize was that we had just signed over the complete rights to our songs to Hilder. Hilder told us that money had to be exchanged to make it legal, so he paid us each a dollar! The date of our last session and the signing of the publishing agreements took place on January 28, 1963. A single version of our re arranged version of *Wipe Out* was never released and we never heard from Tony Hilder.

We just went on our way, playing our gigs and thinking that some money would eventually come in. One night almost a year later, we were all piled into Jack Metz' station wagon coming back from an out of town gig, when we heard a new song come over the radio titled *Wipe Out*, by a group called *The Surfaris*, we just about drove off the road! At first we thought it was one of our re-arranged versions, but later we decided that they had copied our song. Later we got all of our parents together for a meeting at *The Rose Garden Ballroom* and explained the situation. No one wanted to do anything about it except for my dad and Joel Rose Sr., Joel's father, who owned *The Rose Garden Ballroom*.

After some investigation they determined that it would take more money then we might make to start a case against Tony Hilder, Del-Fi Records and whoever else might be involved, so the idea was dropped! The album did go on to be a good seller for Del-Fi and would gross many thousands of dollars in later years.

The Impact's original version of *Wipe Out* was not exactly the same as *The Surfaris*, but my guitar part that is in the background was very similar and our chord progression fits *The Surfaris* version like a blueprint. Our version was copyrighted and filed with ASCAP in Tony Hilder's publishing company Anthony Music January of 1963, *The Surfaris* version was filed and released five months later with BMI in Richard Delvy and John Marascalco's publishing company's Miraleste & Robin Hood Music. Delvy had produced *The Surfaris* recording session for *Wipe Out* and *Surfer Joe*, and sold the songs to Dot Records who said they would like an entire album by the group. Delvy got some studio musicians and members of *The Challengers* together and recorded the rest of the songs needed to complete the album and sold it to Dot Records as The Surfaris! He learned the art of being a song shark very well!

DANCE TO The ExiLes "Please Be Mine"

JANE ReYNOLDS PARK, LANCASTER

SAT. MARCH 28

New RecorD ReLeAse AVAiLAble AT Dance

DoNATion #1·50

CHAPTER 5
Exiled in the Desert

Near the end of the summer of 1963, my dad got an offer to manage a flight school and charter business at Fox Field in Lancaster, California. We rented the house out in Arroyo Grande and once again the Fankhauser family was on the move, this time to the high desert area known as Antelope Valley.

My dad and I made the first trip over to the airport in Lancaster to look over the layout for the operation. We flew over in my dad's twin engine Piper Apache. The airport was about eight miles from town, out in the flat desert with nothing but sagebrush for miles. I can remember opening the door to the plane and feeling a rush of heat as though I'd stepped into a furnace. I was a bit shocked; it wasn't anything like I remembered from my childhood travels. I had become used to the lush greenery, the ocean and the California coastal lifestyle. There was no surfing, no fishing and no strawberry fields, what do they do here, I wondered? It didn't take me long to find out that drag racing, one A&W Root Beer stand and the drive in theater, was it!

I still had my 1940 Ford with the Corvette engine, so I decided to give some of these desert hot shots a go. The first few months I did pretty well till I went up against a new 426 Dodge Ram charger with push button automatic transmission. The guy blew me in the weeds; I didn't know which way he went, that was one fast car! I realized quickly that there was a new breed of factory built Hot Rods that were way ahead of the old street rods! My 40 Ford was a cute little car, but it was no match for these new muscle cars with their strong drive trains and quick shift transmissions. I retired my 40 Ford to a back corner of the airplane hangar.

Working at my dad's Chart Air Flight School gave me the opportunity to fly again. Having flown a J3 Piper Cub and sailplanes at the glider port previously, I felt very confident. With a few lessons in a new Piper Cherokee I was soon ready for solo, I just had to pass a radio and navigational test that my dad insisted on. I was more interested in flying, doing loops, spins and stalls, than operating a radio, my dad grew impatient with me one day and we had a head butting session over my learning correct radio procedure. I loved the Piper Cherokee; it was a very powerful airplane and could nearly climb straight up!

I had been going out with a girl in Lancaster and we returned to her house after a movie around ten thirty in the evening. Her parents were jovial people and asked if I would like a drink or a beer, even though I was only nineteen? I said "sure" and had rum and coke, chased with a beer. I said goodnight and roared off into the cool desert night in my new 1964 Dodge Polara. It was New Year's Eve 1963. I had a wild thought that I would like to go out to the airport and take a flight in the Piper Cherokee. I got to the hangar and quietly rolled the airplane out, got in and started it up and taxied to the end of the runway. I forgot all the preflight tests and pushed the throttle to the firewall and was soon airborne!

I flew around for awhile in the dark sky over the desert and soon found myself flying over the mountains toward Los Angeles. It was at that point that I came to my senses and thought, "What the heck am I doing?" I've been drinking and I am flying towards L.A. at over ten thousand feet." I turned around and headed back to the airport and thought I was lost for a moment till I saw the lights of the Lancaster Drive In theater and then I got my bearings and saw the landing lights of Fox Field off in the distance. I lined up on landing approach and made a fairly good landing, for being my first solo landing at night. I remember trying to turn off the runway a little too soon before the taxi apron and scaring some jack rabbits out of the sage brush. What I didn't know was that the night attendant at the administration building saw my dad's hangar door was open and one of the airplanes was gone. He knew that my dad was in town at a dinner with his partner and some other pilots, and he assumed that the airplane had been stolen and called the Sheriff. When I stepped out of the airplane I felt a firm hand grab my shoulder and arm, it was two sheriffs from the nearby station. They examined me and saw that I had been drinking and took me down to the station and called my dad.

Dad and Mom came to pick me up and my dad had that stern look on his face and my mom was very upset saying, "Merrell, what have you done? You could have been killed." I said, "I'm sorry, Mom. I just wanted to see what it would be like to be off the earth when the New Year came in." The next day, to my surprise, my dad wasn't that mad at me, but the FAA did put a waver on me so that I couldn't get my pilots license for ten months. That ended my flying for awhile.

I was in charge of the gas pumps and the airplane tie down area, making sure that the visitors were parked in the right place. I later went on to do aircraft maintenance, as I had studied that and aeronautical engineering for a year at Allan Hancock College in Santa Maria, California. I would sit in the hangar and practice my guitar when there was a lull at the airport. One day as I was playing, one of the county airport employees heard me and told me that his son was learning to play guitar and he asked if I would like to come over to his house and play with him? I told him yes, after not playing with anyone for about four months I was getting pretty itchy to jam with anybody! The airport employee turned out to be Ralph Cotton, Jeff Cotton's father. I arrived at their house one night after work to find this smiling little fourteen year old guy, Jeff Cotton, who would join me in the Exiles and then go on to become Antenna Jimmy Semens, in *Captain Beefheart's Magic Band*. Later, he would be the innovative slide guitar player in my group, *Mu*. I could tell right away that he had talent, I taught him the chords to my surf songs and my new experimental material, and after a few months of practice we decided to form a band.

We put an ad in the local newspaper for a bass player, drummer and sax player. We auditioned quite a few players and settled on Jim Ferguson on bass, Greg Hampton on drums, and Dan Stevens on sax. We spent a lot of evenings practicing in my dad's office after business hours at the airport, after a few months we decided we were ready for a gig. We did a mixture of Surf, Chuck Berry songs and originals. Jeff arranged for us to play an afternoon lunch concert at his high school and we went over with a bang, girls were screaming and the teachers were clapping along! After that we were the biggest thing in Lancaster, next we decided we should play somewhere we could make money. Someone mentioned that there was an auditorium at a park that you could rent for dances and it held almost six hundred people! We made a special trip to Hollywood to look for jackets, after quite a bit of shopping we decided on five light green Nehru jackets. They were called hoodlum priests back then and were collarless jackets with a little velvet trim around the neckline. They were similar to what *The Beatles* would later wear.

My mom inquired at the county parks department as to how we could go about arranging everything to rent the hall. We got permits and tickets and hired the required security guards, we also had to give a percentage to charity, which my mom did. So there we were - *Merrell and the Exiles*, ready to play our first paid gig, we were all concerned, we knew we had a following but would anyone come to hear us if they had to pay? All we had in the way of advertising was a few handmade posters and a small announcement in the local paper under the Parks Departments recreation schedule.

We got to the auditorium several hours before the doors were to open to set up the equipment. Much to our surprise there was already a small crowd milling around outside and several cars were cruising up and down the street. We set up the equipment and snuck out the backdoor and then went to Jeff's to change clothes and get ready.

Well, if we were surprised earlier when we went to the hall to set up the equipment, we were really surprised when we arrived to play! The place was packed to over the fire limit, and everyone cheered as we went back stage. Suddenly the entire band had stage fright, except for me, but I was a little nervous. Therefore I ended up being the coach; the older guy giving the pep talk to his men before they went into battle. I said, "Boys, we can do it we're rehearsed and we know all the songs, let's go out there and rock their socks off " and we did! It was almost as good as *The Beatles*, those boys from England who hadn't yet landed on our shores!

It was the winter of 1964 and *The Exiles* had conquered the town of Lancaster, California. Meanwhile, *The Beatles* were conquering the world! Before you knew it *The Beatles* were on the radio every half hour and they definitely affected the style of many, many groups to follow. Instrumental surf music had been replaced by this new style of beat music, even Elvis Presley was pushed into the background! *The Exiles* were playing at least once a month, either at the high school or at *The Jane Reynolds Park Auditorium.*

Our next step seemed obvious; make a record! Someone who had heard us told us about a recording studio and a small label called Glenn Records in Palmdale, eight miles away. We got the phone number and called Glen MacArthur, the owner, and arranged a meeting for the following Sunday, his daughter had seen us at one of the dances. We arrived and met Mr. MacArthur, a tall lean man who resembled actor John Carradine. We said that we wanted to rent some time to record two songs for a 45 single, after some discussion he said he would like to record us for nothing and see what we sounded like. So we came back the following Saturday and set up our instruments in the studio. We started warming up, at which time Glen told us we were just too damn loud and that he couldn't record us at that level, so we'd have to turn down. We kept turning down and turning down, and finally he said, "I think I am getting a sound on you now."

By then we had probably played the song a dozen times and our voices were getting tired sounding, so we took a break. The studio had a small control room and an area about as large as a two car garage for the band, but no ventilation or air conditioning. Glen had a modest two track recorder and a simple Altec mixing board and one reverb unit and an extra two track recorder that he would sometimes use for slap back echo. That was pretty much it for the equipment; he did have a few expensive microphones. Everything had to be recorded live on the spot; what you played was what you got!

We went back in after the break and in about three more tries Glen said it was sounding real good and that we better keep this one. We listened to the play back and we were pleased that everything was balanced, it had just enough reverb and the vocal was loud enough and you could hear all of the instruments clearly. We called it a take and *Too Many Heartbreaks,* our first original vocal recording, was in the can! I had written this song in Arroyo Grande when I played with *The Impacts,* but never had the opportunity to record it.

We were too hot and tired to go on, so Glen said that we'd do it again the following weekend at the same time and we said okay. We left feeling pretty good about our first recording session.

The following weekend we returned to the little Glenn Recording Studio, in Palmdale, to record the flip side of our proposed single, a song that I had written, called *Please Be Mine.* During one of my late night shifts working at the airport and gassing up an airplane, I had caught a cold that soon developed into a fever, I was sick, but never the less the recording must be done. We had to go through the song again at least a dozen times before Glen told us that he had a sound. We got it down but my vocal was strained, everyone, including Glen, thought it was good regardless. I never liked it until years later when I saw that it had a kind of young charm to it. Glen was excited and he said it was a hit and that it should be the 'A' side of the single. We got carried away with his enthusiasm; he later presented me with some publishing and recording contracts and said that he would like to put it out on his Glenn Records label. Everybody thought that this was it, instant stardom here we come!

I had a taste of the music business with The Impacts and the failure to make money from the *Wipe Out* album and I knew that it wasn't that easy. Up until now the Antelope Valley hadn't seen much in the way of Rock combos. Frank Zappa and Don Van Vilet's first band, *The Omens,* were the only ones who had performed in the Antelope Valley before us. At that time, the entire area of Lancaster and Palmdale had a population of approximately twenty thousand people. Most of them were aircraft workers at either Edwards Air Force Base, or Lockheed's plant in Palmdale. They built airliners, bombers and experimental fighter planes there. The area was growing and they were ready for Rock and Roll!

Sometime in March of 1964, Glenn Records released *"Please Be Mine"*, backed with *"Two Many Heartbreaks"*. It debuted at number 24 on the local radio station KUTY. The station covered the entire Antelope Valley; Lancaster, Palmdale, Mojave, Rosamond and it could even be picked up in parts of the San Fernando Valley! The next week the record jumped to number 9 on KUTY, above *The Beatles* song, *"She Loves You!"* Glen told us that our record was getting played in other states also and could be heard on KOMA, a powerful radio station in Oklahoma. Later we were thrilled when we heard our song on KRLA, one of the big stations in Los Angeles.

Glen made a second pressing of a thousand more of *"Please Be Mine"* and *"Too Many Heartbreaks"*, and he was shipping them out to distributors across the nation. The local stores couldn't keep them in stock and Glen was driving around in his Cadillac personally delivering the records. At one count he later told us that we had sold 2,500 records in the Antelope Valley alone! We started playing out of the area now due to the recognition with the record; we played a few teen clubs in the San Fernando Valley and Hollywood. There we met an agent who got us a job in Palm Springs. We were traveling in style with my 1964 Dodge Polara with a 383 high performance engine and four on the floor!

Jeff's mom and dad, Marge and Ralph Cotton, went to Palm Springs with us the first time and they helped bring some of the equipment. The PA system was furnished by the club, which made it easier on us. The club was a nice place called The La Paz Club, owned by a keyboardist named Al Anthony. We got free rooms and the club had beautiful grounds with palm trees and a pool, all we needed was Sandra Dee and Jayne Mansfield! The first weekend went very well and we made forty dollars each and we got to drink all the soft drinks that we could guzzle. Mr. Anthony had turned the club into a teen club and he was doing a good business, without any problems.

It was during that weekend that Jeff Cotton and I wrote *"Don't Call On Me"*. I can remember our excitement when we wrote the song in our room and we ran out and told the guys in the band to get out of the pool and come into the club and listen to the new song. We worked up a little arrangement for the song, where Jeff would do the guitar solo, which would later be his first recorded guitar solo. It had a great beat and we tried it out on the kids at the club that night and they liked it. We came home and told Glen that we had a sure fire hit with this new song , he said that we should hold off because the record we currently had out wasn't finished selling and getting air play and it was "still making some smoke". I knew that we needed a flip side for the record, so I started doing late night writing sessions by myself in the airplane hanger. During one of those late night writing sessions I was thinking about the California Coast and a little surfer girl I'd left behind, and I wrote *"Send Me Your Love"*.

I felt that this song was inspired and definitely good enough to back up *"Don't Call On Me"*. We had to go back to The La Paz Club in Palm Springs and this being our second time there, we got a rousing welcome. Mr. Anthony informed us that we would have a guest singer who he would like us to back up. We wondered who it could be, and would he be any good? It was a pleasant surprise when Joey Cooper walked in; he had blonde hair and looked like he could be my brother. He had a great voice and was a good rhythm guitar player. He later went on to play with a group called *The Shindogs* on a national TV show called *Shindig*, and did a stint in Leon Russell's band.

We had a terrific time playing with Joey; he had a great knack for harmony and arrangements. We did some Little Richard tunes and he was into the British sound that was just starting to really hit in America. We really brought the house down and Joey immediately had a lot of female admirers! Backstage, Joey came up to me and asked if he could borrow the backseat of my car for awhile? I said, "Ok, but don't mess it up." I thought he was kidding, the next morning at breakfast we found out that he wasn't kidding! He proceeded to tell us a story about him and his band in Hollywood, he used an explicit term that we had not yet heard. He said, "We met this hot chick and I balled her, and the next night the bass player and the drummer balled her, so I guess you could say the entire band had a ball!" He was telling this in a restaurant in a loud southern accent and the waitress was mortified! We were trying to tell him to be quiet, but we were in hysterics laughing so hard.

When the waitress came to our table Joey said, "Well hello honey, what are you doing tonight?" She ignored his question and went on about her business. We thought that we were going to get thrown out of there, but we managed to make it through breakfast and back to the club. We did some rehearsing and Joey said he was going over to Melissa's house, Dinah Shore's daughter, and that she would be coming to the club that night.

Meanwhile, Mr. Anthony had a promo scheme he wanted to do with us in the afternoon. He had some big banners made to attach to the sides of his Cadillac convertible advertising the appearance of *The Exiles* and Joey Cooper at *The La Paz Club* that night. We were riding around Palm Springs with him as he announced into a sound system in his car, "Come to The *La Paz Club* tonight and dance to *The Exiles* and Joey Cooper!" It was fun in the sun on a Saturday afternoon, waving and saying hello to everyone, it worked!

That night the club was packed. *Merrell and The Exiles*, along with Joey Cooper, rocked the place right up to midnight, but then it became a problem trying to get everyone to leave! Girls were staying and people were milling around outside talking, there were even a few people sharing a bottle of whatever they had brought to drink with others. It was turning into a real wild Palm Springs weekend, just like in the movies.

When Mr. Anthony finally got the place cleared out Joey decided to dare the guys in the band to go skinny dipping in the pool. Dan Stevens, the sax player, and Greg Hampton, the drummer, were the first to take him up on it, then Joey dove in also, but he got right out. Jeff and I were upstairs putting the guitars away and we heard all this commotion, so we looked over the railing just in time to see Mr. Anthony turn on the spot lights, there was Dan and Greg, buck naked! Mr. Anthony was very upset and he told them to get out of there and that he was afraid that they were going to get him shut down. He didn't want people to think that he had wild things going on at the club.

The next day before we left, Mr. Anthony told us that he would like to have us back again, but that we would have to restrain ourselves. We thanked him and assured him that we would. We said goodbye to Joey Cooper and he told us to give him a call sometime in Hollywood. Soon after, he wrote a big hit song called, *"I'm A Fool"*, for Dino, Desi and Billy.

Back In Lancaster, Dan Stevens set me up with a blind date with a girl named Josie Gray. She was aware of who I was because she had come to some of our dances. She was a real beauty, with blonde hair and blue eyes; the perfect California girl. People remarked that we looked like brother and sister. Her mom was German, like mine, and her mom still spoke with an accent. I fell for Josie.

Meanwhile we finally talked Glen into recording another single. We decided to drop Dan Stevens on sax, and we got a keyboardist named John Day. Then for some reason Gregg Hampton, the drummer, decided to take a break and we got Dan Martin to fill in for awhile. He ended up playing drums on the second *Exiles* single. The record took sometime to perfect, doing Glenn's method of playing it a dozen times, or more, while he got the sound right. Some of those sessions in that little studio in the desert were torture; we would really have to work to get those songs recorded. We would be wringing wet every time we finished a session, but we loved it!

Glen really liked this record and thought that it had better hit potential then our first single that was still selling. We recorded *"Don't Call On Me"* and *"Send Me Your Love"*. Again Glenn chose the backup song *"Send Me Your Love"* as the 'A' side and away he went to Hollywood to press up our second record.

We got an offer to play at the *Palmdale Roller Rink* where Frank Zappa and Don Van Vliet's band, *The Omens*, and many others had played. The show went over well and it led to a gig at the Palmdale high school. Jeff and I were writing more songs and we convinced Glen to let us come in once, or more, a month and lay down tunes that could possibly be used for an album someday. Glen's thinking of the day was that you didn't put an album out until you had a big hit single, to help sell the album. This formula mold would soon be broken by the psychedelic era that had a lot of groups experimenting with way out sounds. Record companies decided there was a market for this new style of music and the psychedelic sound was born. The advent of free form FM radio helped promote this new format. Some record companies decided to stick to the old format that you must have a hit song first before an album was released, and things should be in musical boundaries. This caused a lot of bands and artists to seek out alternative, and more adventurous, record companies to put their music out. Bubblegum music was popular, nice clean wholesome music for "teeny boppers". Every band's worst fear was that the producer, manager and the record company was secretly plotting to make a bubblegum band out of them! This drew lines of division; the establishment versus the non establishment. Many bands would rebel and cancel their contracts, only to be left in the dust and trampled by some other band ready to sell out to get a deal.

 We had a desire to create something that was musically wild and different. We had many different players move through the band, some which would later go on to play in Don Van Vilet's, *Captain Beefheart's Magic Band*. John French, on drums, came through, then Larry Willey, who would later join *The Exiles* permanently and go on to play bass in *Mu*. We tried some different things in Glen's little studio, but usually he would not understand what we were trying to do and he would put the songs on the shelf. Pretty soon we lost track of how many songs we had on the shelf?

Glen released *"Send Me Your Love"*, backed with *"Don't Call On Me"*, during the summer of 1964. It eventually made it to number four on the local radio chart and it also got radio play in other states. Glen was starting to get a few orders from distributors who he had sent a few records to, in England and Germany. That year we played the big Antelope Valley fair in Lancaster. We played in front of the grandstands for over five thousand people and this was the largest crowd we had ever played to. We were the High Desert's answer to *The Beatles*, and they loved us!

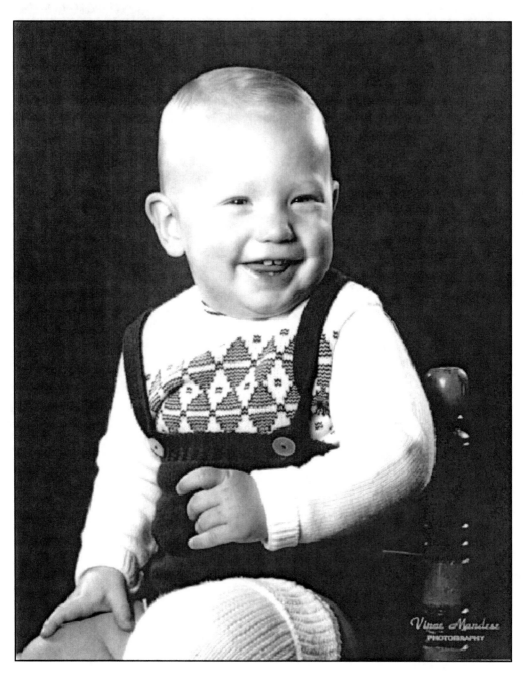

Tim Fankhauser

CHAPTER 6
Changes

After dating Josie Marie Gray for six months, we were married in Newhall, California on July 11, 1964. We rented a little apartment in Quartz Hill, California, which was about seven miles from the airport where I worked. It was a small town that had one store, a gas station and a restaurant and was nestled into the edge of the foothills that surrounded the valley. This was a time of change, as the guys in the band didn't feel I would be playing much, now that I was settling down to married life, so most of them abandoned ship. I just took an extended honeymoon, wrote songs and kept my job at the airport. Later, Jim Ferguson, the bass player, got married and moved into the apartment next to mine and we started jamming together and working on original songs to be recorded.

It was around this time that I wrote *Sorry For Yourself* and *I Saw Susie Crying*. Those sessions had me on guitar and vocal, Larry Willey on rhythm guitar and background vocal, John Day on keyboard, Jim Ferguson on bass and Greg Hampton was back on drums. We were all happy with these recordings and Glen was making plans to press The Exiles third single. Around this time, my dad met a well known arranger named George Tipton. George did music arrangements for Ed Ames, and later Jose Feliciano and Harry Nilsson. My dad flew George to some recording sessions in Las Vegas, Nevada, and he mentioned me to George. He gave my dad his phone number and I later made an appointment to see him at his office in Hollywood.

George was a nice guy and he really liked my songs and thought that I was a talented writer. He gave me some good advice and taught me some of the legal aspects of publishing and recording contracts. I met several people in the music business when I visited his office and on one of the visits I met Harry Nilsson. Harry was definitely a skilled songwriter who already had several songs recorded by other artists.

Meanwhile Jeff Cotton had started his own band called *Blues In A Bottle* and was playing a more blues style of music. Another young Lancaster guitarist named Jeff Parker joined him along with Don Geisen on bass. For awhile he had Greg Hampton and John French on drums, it was a good band but short lived. I put a new *Exiles* band together with Larry Willey on rhythm guitar and background vocals, Jim Ferguson on bass, and Mark Thompson on guitar and keyboard and at different times Greg Hampton, John French and Randy Wimer on drums. It was quite a revolving group of players and it later became hard to remember who had played on different recordings as

there were no notes kept. Most of these recordings would be lost on the shelf at Glen MacArthur's studio for over thirty years.

The summer of 1965 Glenn Records had decided to release *Merrell And The Exiles* third single, *Sorry For Yourself* backed with *I Saw Susie Cryin'*. He had milked everything he could out of the first two records that reportedly sold around five thousand copies. Not bad for the first releases of an unknown band on a small label that previously had only put out country records. Glen's claim to fame was that guitarist James Burton who played with Ricky Nelson and later Elvis Presley, and bassist Joe Osborne had jammed in his studio.

Glen had fifty or so radio stations and a few distributors and stores he would send each of his releases to. He was also getting an increasing amount of interest from Europe and more orders were trickling in.

Glen and I would make many trips to Hollywood looking for an agent or promoter to help push the records. We got several offers from other independent labels to take over my songs that were on Glenn Records. They all had the same story that we were only going to get so far on Glen's label with its small distribution and promotion. Glen always looked at these other labels as crooks that would just get control and steal everything, and never pay any royalties. I had a tendency to go along with his thinking in lieu of what happened with The Impacts Wipe Out album. I always thought there must be some honest labels out there like the bigger companies; they surely couldn't get away with ripping everybody off? We all had great hopes for *"Sorry For Yourself"* making it big, Glen sent the largest amount of promo records yet to radio and distributors. Then the orders and radio charts started coming in from all over California and as far away as Indiana and Ohio!

I told Glen that we needed to do more promotion, "we've got it going, it just needs more push". I talked him into sending the record to Dick Clark's *American Bandstand* television show. *Sorry For Yourself* was entered in the weekly 'rate a record' contest and won! Next we got a four star pick in *Billboard* magazine! I decided it was time to go to Hollywood and leave no stone unturned till we find an agent or promoter that will sign on for a percentage and get the record on the national Billboard charts. We went to The Hollywood Talent Agency and met an agent there named John Aragon who liked me and the record. Aragon told Glen that he wanted sixty percent of the records profit, Glen said he would think about it. As we were walking out one of the other agents said Aragon was being unfair and was asking way too much. We received a call a few days later from Aragon and he said he had big things lined up, and he had talked to national record promoter George Jay who liked the record and wanted to promote it. Aragon also had an offer to put me on one of the biggest television shows in L.A. called Ninth Street West! The show was hosted by KHJ radio disc jockey Sam Riddle, everyone watched the show and if you were on it you surely had made the big time! I was excited about doing the television show and felt I was finally getting a break. Glen and I went back down to Hollywood to a meeting with John Aragon and he said we needed to put *"Sorry For Yourself"* on a bigger label in view of the exposure we were getting, so we could sell some product. Aragon had a meeting set up with Al Levine who owned Interlude Records and a pressing plant that pressed a lot of independent label releases. Interlude had a few good sized hits in the past and it looked like a good move.

Glen was reluctant to give away sixty percent of the record, but I talked him into it, I told him this could put us on the map and make all the other records he had sell.

At this point my band wasn't playing live that much and had evolved into various studio players. Glen and John Aragon convinced me to do the television show alone as "Merrell".

The show went over very well and again I experienced being mobbed by teenagers wanting my autograph at the television studio. I met keyboardist and vocalist Billy Preston who was also on the show, Billy would later go on to play on several *Beatles* songs including the hit *"Get Back"* that was filmed on the roof top of Apple Records in London. My appearance on Ninth Street West led to appearances on other television shows and press and radio interviews. It became obvious that I had to put a permanent band back together to go out and do live shows to promote the record. Jeff

Merrell And The Exiles circa 1965 L-R Jeff Cotton,
Larry Willey, Greg Hampton, Merrell

Cotton came over and said he was interested in rejoining me, and drummer Greg Hampton followed. We convinced Larry Willey to switch from rhythm guitar to bass, and Larry became a fantastic bass player. We now had a great line up for this new version of *Merrell and the Exiles*. We began getting booked at various clubs on the Sunset Strip and San Fernando Valley and played double and triple bills with many well known bands of the day. One day we bumped into singer Sky Saxon of *The Seeds*, he told us he had just cut a song called *Pushin' To Hard* that was sure to knock *The Beatles* and *The Rolling Stones* off the charts ! We laughed, and we were later surprised when we heard the song one night on KRLA and it went on to be a big hit!

We were booked on a television show called *The Bob Howard Dance Time* in San Diego with *The Coasters*. We performed at 2:00 in the afternoon and we had a concert up in Lancaster at the Antelope Valley College at 6:00 that night, how could we ever make it? We finished up the TV show raced out the back door, got the equipment together and headed up the freeway towards L.A. We were driving at speeds anywhere from eighty to one hundred miles per hour!

One guy would watch for police behind us, while the guy in the passenger side tried to keep a look out up ahead, and I concentrated on the driving and passing cars. It was usually about a four hour trip from San Diego to Lancaster and we made it in about three and a half hours, somehow without getting a speeding ticket! We went onstage and knocked the crowd dead! Oh the energy that we had in our youth!

Sometime near the end of the summer of 1965 John Aragon informed us that the *"Sorry For Yourself"* single on Interlude Records had gone as far as it was going to go. He said we needed a quick follow up record to keep up the momentum. He introduced me to two talented singer songwriters, Keith Colley and Larry Mannering, Keith Colley already had a few hit records as a solo artist. They had a song they thought would be perfect for me titled *"Cant We Get Along"*, a nice melodious smooth ballad, John Aragon picked an old standard *"That's All I Want From You"* for the flip side. He booked recording time at Audio Arts studio on Melrose Avenue in Hollywood where songwriter Jim Webb had done a lot of his early demos. It was a good state of the art studio for the day equipped with the latest four track machines and a live echo chamber. We called our old friend John Day to come in and play Hammond B3 organ. The session went very fast and easy compared to spending hot grueling hours in Glen's small studio in the desert. Everyone was very happy with the session and felt we had a hit, Aragon immediately made a deal to have it released on Golden Crown Records.

Large ads came out in *Billboard* and *Cash Box Magazine*, as well as *Variety* and *Music World*. The record was a fairly instant hit on the radio in California and the East Coast, getting to number 3 on a big station in Philadelphia. It looked like it was going to be a big hit and orders were coming in from distributors across the country. We were staying very busy doing live dates in Hollywood and in the Antelope Valley, it was September of 1965 and *Merrell and the Exiles* were on the map, all the years of hard work were paying off. John Aragon said what we needed now was a manager; he introduced us to Gino Belini a fast talking guy from New York who said he was going to take us to the top. We all moved to Hollywood for awhile staying in Gino's swank hilltop house in the hills.

We later found two apartments on Argyle Street in Hollywood, not too far from the Sunset Strip. At first this was a scary situation for the guys in the band and my young wife who all grew up in the small desert town of Lancaster. We played many gigs on the Sunset Strip and we were very busy. Gino decided we needed some sprucing up before we could get gigs in bigger clubs and maybe even Las Vegas. He took us to a special barber in North Hollywood who said he would give us a new more styled look. Jeff Cotton and I both looked at each other with rather stunned looks on our faces. We had long surfer cuts when we went in, when we came out we all looked like Pat Boone! Jeff was just plain pissed off, it took him all summer to grow that hair, and now it was all gone. Gino got us a paid audition up the coast in Oxnard at a classy club called The Carousel, where well known bands played. It had a big marquee with two large palm trees, a large oval shaped bar, a gigantic dance floor, large stage and real nice dressing rooms. The place was definitely decorated very California.

To our amazement we passed the audition and got a six week contract for $900 for four nights a week! We really felt we had made it and we were bringing in some decent money for 1965. The owner of the place was named Steve and he was a very nice agreeable person and was easy to work for. After about two weeks Steve decided we had too much time in between our songs and he either wanted us to go right into the next song like a medley, or have the drummer keep a beat going in between songs. We tried this for one night and Greg the drummer was so tired and sore he could barely walk to the car after the gig. We decided to go into the next song and talk less between songs; this was still tiring as it was like doing a forty five minute long song! We had several other bands come to the club to watch us and the non stop dancing on the big floor was something to see. We had quite a following when the six week contract was up. Gino was getting offers for the band to play out of town and he believed we could make even more money and promote the record by doing this. He had an offer for us to go to Philadelphia where our record had done well, but he said they didn't offer enough money.

He decided to take an offer to play in Portland, Oregon, for twelve hundred dollars a week, six nights a week. We really didn't know a lot about Gino, but he kept us working and talked a good story. We knew he had worked for a private detective agency and he always drove a new car and had a nice house in the Hollywood Hills. We thought he must be doing quite well. One afternoon I noticed something very curious as I came up his driveway in my old 1954 Ford station wagon. He had his new Ford T Bird in the driveway with a long extension chord leading to it with an electric drill hooked up under the dashboard. I said, "Are you having some car trouble?" He said, "No, I'm just taking some miles off the speedometer." He had the drill hooked up to the speedometer cable and was actually rewinding the miles back. He had led us to believe he owned the car, the house and a late model Oldsmobile.

We found out that the new T-Bird was rented and so was the house. Apparently he was late on paying his rent, as I found out when I answered the phone one day and talked to his rather irate landlord. I started thinking that Gino may not be all that he tried to imply that he was. He let us use the house to rehearse in and he would sometimes come home in mid-day in a flurry, telling us that things were just crazy down at the agency where he supposedly worked. He also told us not to answer the phone and to just let it ring.

He turned in the T-Bird and had a trailer hitch put on the back of the Oldsmobile. We went out looking for a U-Haul trailer that would hold all our instruments and clothes for the trip to Portland, Oregon.

We started out on the journey at 2:00 a.m. after playing a gig. Gino figured this would be best because we'd miss all the traffic and get a good start. He was very upset when I told him that my wife was coming along, he told me it would cost extra money for a motel and he just went on and on about it. Finally, he reluctantly agreed when I told him that I would pay for anything extra for her out of my pay. He still didn't like it, but I wasn't going to leave her alone for a month, or more, in the apartment in Hollywood. I was the oldest in the group, but we were all still young, so a lot of questions should have been asked that weren't, such as how much money were we going to make at this gig and exactly how long was our contract for?

We drove all night and all the next day and arrived in Portland around 10:00 at night. We started looking for a motel and Gino again began complaining about my wife being with us and how hard it was going to be to find a motel. I told him to shut up and just pull into the first motel that we come to. He started into one of his lectures about how "you's guys don't know how lucky you are to have this gig!"

We found a little motel that had kitchenettes and we got two rooms, one for me and my wife and one for the other three guys. We got up late the next morning and noticed that the guys were gone and that it was snowing and very, very cold. We walked a few blocks and found a coffee shop and had breakfast, which just about left me broke!

Later Jeff came over and said they were going to dinner at 5:00 and told me they would be back to pick us up. They came back alright, about 8:00 that night, just in time to go to the club. Josie and I were starving! We got to the club called *Town Talk Lounge*. It was complete with sawdust on the floor and big burley lumberjacks who exclaimed, "Looks like school's out", as we walked in. We thought, "Great! We're going to have to put up with being heckled by these guys every night."

Actually, the first night went very well. We had the place jumping and everyone forgot about how young we were. There was a restaurant next to the club, where my wife spent the evening drinking tea while we played and I would visit her on my breaks.

The second night Gino broke it to us that he was going to leave us at the club on a contract for three months and have our checks sent to him first. He would then take his cut out and send the rest back to us, which amounted to one hundred twenty-five dollars each band member per week. He wouldn't tell us how much he was getting paid before his percentage was taken out. He would side track us by giving us one of his slang lectures saying, "Number one, you's guys show up on time every night, number two, you's guys don't take so much time between songs and number three, you's guys don't take too long on breaks."

I talked to the guys the second night and told them, "No way was I going along with Gino's plan, especially being left in Portland freezing our asses off, while he counts our money back in Hollywood." They said they thought he was really going to make us big and that we should stick it out. Things would get better, they said, things looked like they were getting worse from my point of view!

The next morning we woke up to snow everywhere, it was now just a few weeks before Christmas 1965 and Josie and I decided we'd had enough. She would stay in the motel and I would walk the 1/4 mile to the nearest phone booth and call my dad collect, if I called from the motel office, Gino would surely find out. I started out on my walk and it was way below freezing and I didn't exactly have snow gear on! I finally made it to the phone booth, only to find that it was out of order.

By this time my feet were already soaked from walking in two foot snowdrifts along the road. I saw a gas station off in the distance and decided to go for it. Luckily there was another phone booth there and it was working. I got my dad on the phone and told him that our agent was a crook and we needed to get out of here and would he send me bus fare? I didn't have a penny left in my pocket, so Dad called the bus station in Lancaster and found out the rate from Portland to Hollywood and the amount turned out to be sixty-eight dollars for two people. He told me that I was going to need some extra money. I hated to ask him for the money and I told him to just send seventy-five dollars, but he told me that he didn't think that would be enough so he sent eighty-five. I was to pick the money up at the Western Union office in downtown Portland, which would be on the way to the bus station, so it seemed fairly simple.

By the time I made it back to the motel I was soaking wet and freezing, it took quite a while to stop shivering, even after soaking in a hot bath tub. We could only get so much hot water at one time before it would immediately turn ice cold! I wondered how people could live in this cold weather? I remembered my childhood in Kentucky, but I'd always had a warm house back then and plenty of hot water to come home to, and something cooking on the stove. Indeed, California seemed like paradise as I looked at the snow blizzard outside my window in Oregon.

It was evening as Josie and I watched Gino and the guys pile into the Oldsmobile to go to dinner. We decided that this was the time to make our move so I called a cab. We got our two suitcases and my Rickenbacker guitar and told the cab driver to take us to Western Union downtown and then to the bus station. I had no money to pay the cab and luckily the money my dad sent reached the Western Union office. We paid the cab driver and went inside the rather large Greyhound Bus station. We got our tickets but the bus didn't leave until 9:15, so we had about two hours to wait. We went to the cafeteria and got something to eat, we were starved. Just as I was finishing dessert I looked out the window and saw Gino and the guys driving up in front of the bus station. I said, "Let's go out the back and give them the slip." Just as we rounded the corner in back of the bus station we met Gino and the guys head on! Gino told me I couldn't leave because we made an agreement and had a contract. He started shouting and waving his fists in the air, saying that he owned my clothes and instruments and that if I left he would have me arrested for theft. I told him to get fucked and he jumped on me like a monkey, wrapping his legs around me and trying to hit me in the head with his hands! I tossed him in the air and he slid across his back in the snow. Josie and I walked back into the bus station and I told her to wait at the top of the stairs, while I went to the bathroom. I was washing my hands and I looked around the corner in the shoeshine guy's stall and there was Josie. Apparently she had gotten afraid and came down the stairs to the men's restroom. The black shoe-shine guy was looking at her and he said, "Are you a boy, or is you a girl?" Josie told him that she was a girl, he then told her that she couldn't be down there because it was the men's lavatory! We went back upstairs and there was Gino talking to a security guard and then he ran over to me and told the guard that I was the guy he was talking about and to arrest me. He looked so comical and it was obvious that the guard wasn't taking him seriously. The guard asked me a few questions and said that there was no reason to detain me.

Gino followed us all the way to the door of the bus screaming, "I am gonna get you, Man!" We were glad to see Gino and Portland disappear in the distance; we fell asleep on the bus and woke up on the edge of the California border, where we stopped for breakfast.

I definitely had some time to think on the bus ride back to Hollywood and I realized just how tricky the entertainment business was. I was growing up on the road and it was teaching me a lesson that you could never be too careful about anything! Later on in life I would find that it was still very difficult to tell a wolf in sheep's clothing, they came in many different colors, shapes and sizes.

It was about noon when we reached Sacramento, California. Man was I glad to be back in a warmer climate. We bought lunch and had a few dollars and some change left. We stopped again around 6:00pm for dinner. We bought a piece of pie, coffee and milk, which left us with seventy cents. It was about ten o' clock that night when we arrived at the bus station in Hollywood and we were really happy. I remember walking past the crowd on Vine Street, waiting to get into the Merv Griffin show, it was a short walk up Vine to our apartment on Argyle. We slept and got up the next morning, and loaded everything into the 54 Ford station wagon. We had a bag of soft drink bottles that we cashed in at a local store and then we put one dollar and twenty-five cents worth of regular gasoline into the car and headed for Lancaster. The car ran out of gas when I rolled into my parent's driveway at about one o' clock pm. What a trip this record release had taken us on!

Meanwhile, Gino and the guys were still up in Oregon. They played another night without me, but the owner of the club said that they were good but that it wasn't sounding full enough, so the next day they packed up and left to come back to Hollywood. Before reaching Sacramento, California, they were pulled over by the Highway Patrol. The guys in the back seat were woken up with shotguns in their faces!

The boys were put into a juvenile detention center and Gino was booked in jail. What none of us knew was that the guy Gino had worked for at the detective agency had died of a heart attack a few months before and Gino had kept his Oldsmobile and some credit cards, Gino was booked on theft. I hadn't heard the word "Karma" yet, but it would fit him very appropriately! It was determined that the guys had nothing to do with Gino's illegal activities and they were released to their parent's custody. Their parents had to drive up from Lancaster to Sacramento to pick them up. Gino had to call his brother to bring his bail and pick him up, Gino kept my suit and amplifier, which I never got back.

I called the guys and arranged to meet them in Lancaster when they got back. They were all still mad at me for leaving and it seemed that once again the band was breaking up.

Josie and I spent Christmas with our families and the end of 1965 brought to a close another chapter of *Merrell and the Exiles.*

In 1966 I went to work teaching guitar in a Hammond Organ store, then pregnancy and responsibility came along in that order. Later in the year I went to work at a larger guitar oriented store where I had sixty guitar students a week. I later ended up managing another store when the largest music store in town, Lancaster Music, bought the owner out. I played a few casuals around town with various bass players, along with guitar player and keyboardist, Mark Thompson, and John French on drums. I was writing a lot of twelve string guitar songs that had a psychedelic folk rock sound.

I got back together with Glen and I said, "If we are going to record again, let's go down to Hollywood and do it on good modern equipment." He agreed and we made a deal to record in Gary Paxton's studio in Hollywood. Gary had recorded and produced some big hit novelty songs such as, *Alley Oop, The Monster Mash* and *Please Mr. Custer.* Gary had also been part of the duo *Skip and Flip,* who had a hit called *It Was I.* He had a great studio with a state of the art four track machine.

We took along one of my bass guitar students for the session, fourteen year old Jody Cobb. Mark Thompson was on guitar and organ; I was on guitar and lead and harmony vocal, and John Parr on drums, with Don Aldridge and Gary Lotspeich on background vocals. Later we added Bruce Ulch on trumpet.

During this session we recorded *Lila, Mr. Clock, Supermarket, Yes I Love You* and *Glass Chandelier.* It was a terrific session and everyone was astounded at our new sound, Mr. Paxton included!

After listening to the recordings back in Palmdale, Glen decided the songs were a little too far out and could possibly be used for album cuts, but he didn't hear a hit. How many times would I hear that? I helped pay for and produce these songs, yet there was still someone controlling what happened with the music. The songs went on the shelf at Glen's with all the other stuff we recorded with him. After another experience of recording a batch of my new songs, only to have them put on a shelf again, I decided to try taking my music to Hollywood myself. I took some of my songs that I had recorded on my primitive home tape recorder to several companies in Hollywood. My first appointment was with Lou Bedell at Dore Records, they had released some of *Jan and Dean's* first hits. Lou liked the songs but said he had several releases coming out and he couldn't put anything else out for at least six months! I thanked him for his time and left. I was walking past the old Del-Fi Records building and I just decided to drop in. The record company was in back of the Bank of America building off Vine Street. You had to go up two flights of wide marble stairs and then you came to a long hallway with lighted glass display cases that contained all the Ritchie Valens releases and various other groups.

At the end of the hallway was a display that contained the label's latest release by *The Bobby Fuller Four*. I opened the door to the plush office that had an abundance of gold records on the walls and introduced myself to the secretary. I asked if I could see Bob Keene, who was the owner of the company. She asked if I had an appointment and I said no. She said she would ask if he would see me? She came back telling me that the answer was yes and to follow her. Suddenly I was in the office of the man who had discovered Sam Cook, Ritchie Valens, and many well known surf groups. Bob remembered me from *The Impacts*, I told him that I thought I had some hit songs and asked him if he'd like to hear them? He was very interested and put my rough reel to reel demo tape on the machine and we started listening, if a song didn't catch his ear right away he would just fast forward to the next song.

Finally he stopped on a song and said, "That's a hit!" The song was an up tempo English sounding Folk Rocker titled, *Travelin' Light*. I told him that I had a good band up in Lancaster. He told me he could book a session for the following Thursday at three o' clock, we shook hands and I left again with high hopes, as I had done many times before.

I picked what I thought would be the best recording group for the session; Jim Ferguson on bass, John Parr on drums, and Mark Thompson on keyboard and guitar. We arrived at Del-Fi Records and entered the side door that led to the studio. We were really surprised when Mr. Keene showed us inside to a beautiful state of the art, four track studio that you entered at the rear of the main office through a hidden door. He introduced us to the arranger, a big black guy with a great smile named Barry White. Barry was struggling at this point, just getting by as an arranger and song writer. He would later go on to have some big hits in the '70s. Barry and I hit it off right away and he liked my song and thought that I had a very good and original sounding voice.

We went to the piano and I was playing the guitar and singing the song to him and he suggested a key modulation after the instrumental solo that was brilliant! We worked a while on the bass and drum part and he told Mr. Keene that we were ready to try a take. We started recording instrumentally without any vocal and the drummer missed the first change. Recording without the vocal was a new approach that we were just starting to do, all our previous recording was done mostly live with the vocal. It was easy to get lost in a song playing by ear, not hearing the vocal to keep you on track.

We tried it again, take two. This time Barry stopped us and told the drummer to change his accent on the snare drum. Take three we got part way through and the bass player missed the key change. Take four, the drummer missed the intro and he seemed to be getting nervous. We started take five and the drummer blew it again. Barry went in and said, "Let me show you." He sat down at the drums and we cooked! Bob Keene said it was so good we should have recorded it. Then Bob made the suggestion that Barry should play drums on the song. I immediately saw the look on John Parr's face and so did Barry. Barry said that he thought that John could do it, so we tried take six but the pressure was just too much for John and he cracked and lost the beat.

Bob Keene told Barry to get on the drums, John Parr was devastated and he left the studio and went out to the lobby. Take seven, both Barry and Jim made mistakes near the middle of the song. We decided to take a break and have some coffee. John Parr was sitting in a chair with his head in his hands, very depressed. He was a very sensitive person and a few years later he committed suicide while on LSD.

We went back in and did take eight and we finally got it! It had a terrific punchy beat, almost like Motown Folk Rock. We took a break while Bob bounced the four instrumental tracks down to two tracks on another machine and this left two more tracks to add vocals. We never had such luxury before; we were all amazed at this new technology!

I started putting the lead vocal down and Barry had me change a few notes and after about three takes it was done. We all went to the control room and listened to the playback and we were knocked out! This had to be the best recording sound I had ever gotten in a studio!

It was now about one in the morning and Bob said we should quit and resume tomorrow at 3:00pm. We returned to the Del-Fi studio the next day promptly, and Barry introduced me to a mellow little guy named Joe. Joe had the highest natural harmony voice I had ever heard! He and Barry already had their parts worked out and we went in and started singing to the track. We started recording and after about six takes we got it. The sound was tremendous, it had a deep reverb sound on the vocals, like a Phil Spector production, Barry said, "Congratulations, man this could scare *The Beatles!*" We left for Lancaster that night, very happy, Bob Keene said that he would call us in a few days and book some time to record a flip side. Shortly after this we heard the news that Bobby Fuller was found dead in the back seat of his car. *The Bobby Fuller Four* was Bob Keene's only successful group at the time on his Del-Fi subsidiary, Mustang Records. We could never reach Bob Keene after this and not much later the record company went out of business. That was another song that would be forgotten on a shelf somewhere.

My son, Timothy Scott Fankhauser, was born on October 31st, 1966. It was an easy birth. Now more time was spent with domestic matters and taking care of the family. We had moved to a nice two bedroom house on Norberry Street, a quiet neighborhood in Lancaster. I would come home for lunch while working at the music store and watch my son grow strong and healthy.

I was playing part time at a club called *Cloud Nine*, where we backed up *The Isley Brothers* for two nights. Later I ended up playing in a trio on weekends in Rosamond and Tehachapi, near the eastern foothills of the desert valley. I became fairly bored at this time and playing in the middle of nowhere in the desert wasn't what I had originally envisioned. One night in Tehachapi I had a case of boredom while our drummer, a nice Mexican guy named Victor, was singing *Gloria*. He would go into all these descriptions about what he wanted to do with Gloria when he got her alone in her room, and in the end her big brother would walk in with a shotgun! During this part of the song I decided to take a walk, I went next door to the Chevrolet agency and crawled under a truck to take a look at the transmission. I'd had a few beers and this seemed as good a time as any to see how the Chevy transmission and clutch linkage fit together.

By this time my dad had sold the Flight Operation at the airport in Lancaster, he and my mom had moved to Goleta, a small coastal town near Santa Barbara. My dad had a job as the head of maintenance at a company that made electronics. He had kept just one of his airplanes, a single engine Piper Comanche, and he and my mom would fly over to Lancaster and visit us on weekends. They later moved back to our old house in Arroyo Grande and my dad went back to work as a flight instructor at the Santa Maria airport.

The beginning of 1967 saw yet another line up of *Merrell and the Exiles...*

Larry Willey had been playing in a band with Jeff Cotton and two other young Lancaster musicians, Jeff Parker and Randy Wimer. That band folded and Larry and Randy came to play with me, Larry and I had a great vocal sound together and our harmony could really make a song soar! Randy Wimer was a mellow guy who had a strong, but different, style of playing drums, and with Mark Thompson on guitar and keyboard, the band was complete. We did several gigs with this band and held onto our popularity in the Antelope Valley area for a while longer. At this point our record sales and airplay had pretty much diminished.

Meanwhile, *Captain Beefheart's Magic Band* had landed a contract with A&M Records for two singles and they began getting national exposure. They soon topped *The Exiles* in popularity in the Antelope Valley.

We decided that it was again time to record, this time Mark Thompson and I put up the money to record two songs for a single. I booked Audio Arts, the old studio that I had previously worked in with John Aragon. Near the first of February, we recorded two new songs that I had written called, *Tomorrows Girl* and *When I Get Home*. These songs definitely had commercial appeal and were right with the times, rather than ahead. It was at this session that we met a young engineer named Jim Hilton who we thought was really talented. We stopped off in Palmdale and played it for Glen and then left, we figured that if he didn't want it we would just shop it to other labels ourselves. Glen called back and he decided he wanted to release it, so we gave him the tape. Around the end of February 1967, *Tomorrow's Girl* and *When I get Home* were released.

Glen sent the record out through his regular channels and his fifty or so radio stations. We got on the charts on several East coast stations and we got minor airplay on the West coast. We sent the record in to Dick Clark's 'Rate A Record' contest on *American Bandstand*, and again we won! We also received a pick in *Billboard Magazine*.

CHAPTER 7
Return to Central Coast

S ometime during the month of September of 1967, I decided to move back over to the coast, to Arroyo Grande, where my parents were once again living. It was still a mellow small town in 1967, but the population was showing signs of growth. I decided to open a music store and I rented a building in a small shopping center, I knew how to run a store and I had contacts with instrument and record wholesalers. It seemed like a good idea to give my family security and at least I would still be working in some form with music.

It started off slowly, but I soon built up about a dozen guitar students a week. The guitar students were the only real profit at that time and I was just breaking even with the instrument and record sales. I decided after a few boring months to see if I could put a band together. My old friend, Bill Dodd, had two kids by now and worked in a supermarket nearby in the produce department. He was more than ready to start playing music again, and we got in touch with John Oliver, the original bass player from The Impacts. The three of us started practicing in the back of my store after business hours. We began our search for a drummer and we were not having much luck, when one day a young guy came into the store and announced that he played drums. His name was Dan Parrish and he definitely had the look of a drummer, with his short Beatle style haircut.

The Rose Garden Ballroom was in one of its stages of being closed up for remodeling, which it would later go through several times until its demise in the early 19'80s, there were not a lot of choices where we could play. I heard that a new club was opening in Pismo Beach, so I went over to meet the owner, Dave Bianchi, a very nice guy. Dave told me that he would be ready for business the next weekend and if we wanted to come and play as a paid audition, he would give us forty dollars each. So that began a six month stint at the Cove. It was previously called The Cave because the inside walls and ceiling were done up like a cave with a giant aquarium in back of the bar. The place had a good size dance floor and could hold a little over one hundred people.

As soon as the word got out, the place was filled to capacity every night! After approximately a month we met drummer Dick Lee who was much better than Parrish who switched to bass for a while and later moved to northern California and John Oliver came back on bass. Dick

Lee, was working at the Atascadero State Mental Hospital as a psychiatrist technician, Dick previously played drums in a band called *The Brymers* from the San Joaquin Valley. This line up of musicians played for several months, we really didn't have a name for the band; it was just *Merrell and the Boys*. Right before Dan Parrish left the band, we were thinking of names for the group. I wrote down the first initials of each person's last name; FA (Fankhauser), PAR (Parrish), DO (Dodd) and then Dick Lee (KLY) came along. I came up with FAPARDOKLY and everyone looked at me funny and said, "So?" I told them that's the name of our group! Everybody said, "No, it's too weird." Oh yeah, very Psychedelic!

One evening I got a call from Glen MacArthur and he said that he had been giving some thought to releasing an album using some of the material he had on the shelf by *The Exiles*. He went on to say that he was starting a subsidiary label, UIP Records, with his new partner, Roy Boller. I told him great and to go ahead, I didn't think much about it at the time and I didn't think it would actually get released. He asked me what I was calling the group and I told him *Fapardokly*. He answered, "What? How in blazes do you spell it?" I told him and he asked what the name meant and I told him it's the name of an Indian Love Bird. His response was, "Oh!" We said goodbye and he said he would be in touch.

That was right around the first time that Bill and I started experimenting with smoking marijuana, and sometimes things that sounded a little far out at first later on sounded just fine.

One night before we went to the club, Bill and I stopped off at my music store and went into the back room and toked up pretty heavily on a joint. This was Bill's second time he'd tried it and he definitely got a full load! We started driving to the gig and he asked why I was driving so slowly? I tried to convince him that I was going the speed limit, but he wouldn't believe me. He asked me to please speed up, because his wife was going to kill him! I kept telling him to relax and that we would be at the gig soon, but he kept repeating that she was going to kill him.

In the confusion we accidentally turned off the freeway one exit too soon and in a panicked voice Bill asked what I was doing? He told me he was getting out of the car, as I stopped to turn around, before I could stop him, he walked out into a field that was a muddy swamp and immediately had both of his shoes sucked off in the mud! So there he was standing in mud up to his ankles, his clean pants were all muddy and his shoes couldn't be found!

I convinced him to get back in the car and I got some rags out of the trunk, he cleaned up his feet and his pants had mud stains around the bottom that made it look like he had two tone pants with funny cuffs on them.

We arrived at *The Cove* and there was his wife, Rita, waiting for us at the curb. Bill said, "Oh God, this is the end of me." She was always accusing him of running around with some other woman if he was late for any reason. She was a big woman and she always wore heavy red lipstick and loud clothing, this night she was decked out in day glow yellow peddle pushers, with top and plastic shoes to match.

FAPARDOKLY

FEATURING:

SIDE ONE

1. Lila (Funkhouser - Aldrisja)
   1:25 B.M.I. MacArthur Music
2. The Music Scene (Funkhouser)
   1:55 B.M.I. MacArthur Music
3. Sorry For Yourself (Funkhouser)
   1:55 B.M.I. MacArthur Music
4. Glass Chandelier (Funkhouser - Aldrisja)
   2:55 B.M.I. MacArthur Music
5. Tomorrows Girl (Funkhouser)
   2:20 B.M.I. MacArthur Music
6. Indie Cryin (Funkhouser)
   2:22 B.M.I. MacArthur Music

SIDE TWO

1. Mr. Clock (Funkhouser - Aldrisja)
   2:25 B.M.I. MacArthur Music
2. Gone To Pot (Funkhouser)
   2:00 B.M.I. MacArthur Music
3. No Retreat (Funkhouser)
   1:55 B.M.I. MacArthur Music
4. Tiny Mossy Heart Brooks (Funkhouser)
   2:04 B.M.I. MacArthur Music
5. When I Get Home (Funkhouser - Willey)
   2:45 B.M.I. MacArthur Music
6. Super Market (Funkhouser - Aldrisja)
   2:48 B.M.I. MacArthur Music

FAPARDOKLY
Merrell Fankhouser — Bill Dodd
John Oliver — Dick Lee

Love has made possible for some the pursuing of dreams.

The Indian Love Bird has blessed the Fapardokly.

Those who listen will also be blessed.

Many new groups come and go in the music business there are interested in this album is a song dedicated to all the customers of the world "The Music Scene".

For the kindness and support of the following people we dedicate this album to:

Don Aldrige - Gary Lotspeich, Mark Thompson - Lary Willey, Jody Cobb - Jeff Cotton, Ira Furgason - Greg Hampton, Bruce Uhle - John Friesh, Randy Wimer and the late Inez Parr.

The Fapardokly is destined to be the way to reach to the music business.

UIP
••• RECORDS •••

MONO
LP-2250

Produced by
MacArthur and Roller

This is a High Fidelity Recording
Long Play 33⅓ R.P.M.

Rita began chasing Bill around the car; it looked like an act right out of Barnum Baileys Circus. Shouting at him she asked, "Where have you been, where have you been?" The whole time she was trying to hit him with her purse. He said, "Please honey, it was just a little accident."

The crowd that had gathered dispersed and Bill went back to the dressing room and his wife went home to get him a clean pair of pants and some new shoes.

We started playing and Bill would get this funny look on his face and just stop playing, and then he asked us if we all heard that? We told him that we didn't hear anything. Dick Lee and John Oliver had no idea what was going on and they must have thought that Bill was losing it. I was afraid that Dick might want to take him up to the hospital for observation. When we took a break, Bill said that was the greatest horn solo he'd ever heard, but there was no horn player in the band!

It was about this time that I began a very prolific writing spree that lasted for several months and I would sometimes write two songs a day. Some of these tunes would actually later find their way onto the *H.M.S. Bounty* album.

Another night we were playing at The Cove when the club was taken over by a motorcycle gang from Porterville called, "Satan's Slaves." They were some tough customers and most of them were sporting big knives and bayonets. There must have been about seventy of them and they all parked their bikes in front of the club. They came in and started dancing and ordering drinks and literally took over. One of the girls got up on a table and started doing a strip act, with the bikers cheering her on. There was nothing that the owner of the club could do.

We began playing one of my up tempo original tunes called, *"Rich Mans Fable"* and they said they liked it and to keep playing it and not to stop until they told us to. I must have played that song for over a half hour while they just went nuts, shouting and dancing.

The little Pismo Beach Police Department had only two patrol cars at that time and they just stayed across the street at a gas station, afraid to do anything to help the club owner. Finally, a little after midnight, the bikers had their fill of fun and mayhem and decided to leave. All the bikes roared out of town except for one, that backed right up to the entrance of the club, revved up his motor and filled the place full of smoke. We had to open the back door to let all of the fumes out, that was a night I would never forget. We would continue to play at The Cove for several months and we really had some good times there. We frequently tried out my new songs and the ones that worked we kept in the set.

I began to get that old familiar itch to record again, so I phoned Glen and asked if we could come over to his studio in Palmdale and record some of my new songs. He said yes, so we made the drive from the coast over to the desert which was a little less than two hundred miles. We set up our instruments in Glen's studio, this was the first time Dick Lee, Bill Dodd and John Oliver had recorded with Glen.

Glen managed to get a fairly good sound most of the time, but usually we had to do a lot of takes for Glen to get the balance of the instruments and the vocal right. In this session we recorded, *"Gone To Pot"*, *"No Retreat"*, *"The War"*, and *"Be A Good Neighbor"*.

I arranged for a recording session at Gold Star Studio in Hollywood, for the next day and also a photo shoot at a photo studio. We stayed at a motel in Lancaster and the next day after breakfast we got dressed for our photo session. I wanted the guys to look "way out", so I told them, "No holds barred with the costumes!" Bill and I had on Indian robes and Dick Lee and John Oliver came out looking like some "American Indian Hep Cats." The costumes were *really* wild!

As we were getting ready to check out of the motel, Dick discovered he had left his wallet locked in the room, so he went back to the manager's office to get the key to unlock the room. The Manager took one look at Dick and John and said, "No way! I don't know you guys, you didn't stay here last night." Finally after Dick took off some of his garb the manager agreed that he did look familiar, he still thought that it might be a trick and he wanted to call the cops. Dick told him his name, along with other pertinent information and convinced him to go look in the room and that he would find his wallet. The manager made Dick and John stay in the office, with another person who was near the phone and ready to call the cops if any funny business occurred.

Dick finally got his wallet and we left laughing our heads off. We arrived in Hollywood mid morning and went straight to the photographers, who shot a number of poses and we got out of our costumes and left. We ate lunch and arrived at Gold Star Studio and did a quick recording session that produced *"The Music Scene"*.

The guys drove back up the coast, while I stopped off at Glen's studio and dropped off the tape and told him to check with the photographer in a week for the photos. I also told Glen to get in touch with me and let me know what he thought of the song and the photos.

Bill and I decided that we were serious about getting the original music out and eventually moving to Hollywood was the key. We told Dick and John this, but neither one of them wanted to quit their day jobs to run off to Hollywood looking for a pot of gold. So Bill and I began to look around for other players. For a while, a bass player named Gary Windburne, who had played with *John Barbata and The Sentinels*, sat in with our band.

We had a rousing good time at *The Cove* on New Year's Eve, with my dad getting up on stage and playing his country blues song *"Goin' Down The Grade"*. It really brought the house down and I remember my mom and some of my parent's friends being in the audience, cheering my dad on. That was really a night to remember; my dad, the guy who had taught me my first chords on a ukulele, jamming with my rock and roll band!

1968 came in with a bang and Jack Metz, formerly of *The Impacts*, showed up, Jack had become a very proficient bass player, with a good voice. At the same time we met drummer Larry Myers, who had played with local blues bands, Larry played one of the meanest shuffles you would ever hear.

Now we had a new and improved line up and they were interested in taking the plunge into the big time with us. We used the gig at *The Cove* to sharpen up our originals and get our sets tight.

It had been several months since I had heard from Glen and in April 1968 he gave me a call and said that he had put *The Fapardokly Album* out! I replied, "No kidding!" I thought the songs that we'd recorded at Glen's would just end up being a bunch of old songs sitting on a shelf forever. Soon after that he showed up with some copies of the album that was pressed sometime near the end of 1967.

I thought the front cover was terrible; it was a water color of something that resembled a choir of psychedelic monks. The back cover wasn't very good either; we looked like a strange psychedelic tribe from Transylvania! At the time I thought that the choice of songs could have been better, Glen chose a mixture of the very early singles and some of the psychedelic folk rock songs recorded at Gary Paxton's studio, not in chronological order.

The album was released as UIP-lp 2250 *Fapardokly* and contained *Lila, The Music Scene, Sorry For Yourself, Glass Chandelier, Tomorrow's Girl, Suzie Cryin', Mr. Clock, Gone To Pot, No Retreat, Too Many Heartbreaks, When I Get Home,* and *Supermarket*. The exact release date was never really clear; it was sometime between December 1967 and March 1968. Little did I know that years later this album would go on to become one of the most valuable and sought after recordings of the 1960s.

Glen sent the album out to his usual channels, a few to radio, and this time his partner, Mr. Boller, decided they should send a few to college radio. This was something that would not seriously be done by record companies until the 1980s. A few samples were sent to distributors in Europe, but probably no more than five hundred were ever sold. The album made no radio charts and on all accounts was a failure. I forgot about the album as soon as it was released, I did send one to my friend, George Tipton, in Hollywood.

Then one day as I was paddling my kayak in the lagoon, Josie waved to me from the shore, shouting that George Tipton had called, I headed for shore right away and I called George. To my total amazement he said that my song, *Lila,* which was on the album that I sent him, was great! He said that a few of the others were too. He asked me if I had any more originals like that? I said yes and we set an appointment for Monday morning at his office in Hollywood. I really had a lot of respect for George and I thought that if he liked the songs there must be something good there, he had quite a list of hit records to his credit.

I arrived at George's office around eleven o'clock Monday morning and started playing him everything I had. I played him my new songs live on the guitar and he was impressed with how many songs I had that sounded like hits. He said that all I had to do was get these songs around to the right people to hear them, I knew he was right, but how do I get to the right people? He explained the publishing business and how they could get the contacts, he published a few tunes of mine that got other artists interested in doing them and one thing led to another.

Harry Nilsson had now made it up the ladder and had gotten a writing deal with Dunbar Music, RCA Victor's publishing company. George and I went up to Harry's new office to see him and I was impressed, there he was on the sixth floor of the RCA building! Later he had his first album released on RCA titled, *Aerial Ballet*, he wouldn't have to be working in the UCB Bank, or writing in the little office on Cahuenga anymore.

Harry told George and I a story about how late one night his phone rang and a man with an English accent identified himself as Paul McCartney and told him how much he liked his songwriting. Harry told him to "fuck off" and hung up thinking it was a prank! A few minutes later the phone rang again and it was another man with an English accent saying, "This is John Lennon, Harry. Please don't hang up." *The Beatles* invited him to fly over to London to listen to their new album before it was released and it turned out to be 'The White Album'. Harry came back to L.A. with wild stories about having hung out with *The Beatles* in England, he even recounted some of his adventures with *The Beatles* on KRLA radio. Harry went on to have several hit singles and albums.

One evening after a hard day of shopping tunes, I bumped into Norm Malkin and Jack Hoffman, two producer / publishers who had offices down the hall from George Tipton. I had met them a few years earlier on one of my trips to Hollywood with Glen McArthur. They were immediately interested in hearing my new material. We went into their offices and I played them the *Fapardokly* album and my new songs that I had recorded at home on my reel to reel tape recorder. They said they would very much like to publish some of my songs and take me into a studio and make some masters. I said it was a deal, but they would have to contact Glen regarding the publishing on some of the tunes they wanted because I had signed them over to him. They said they would like to hear my band and when we were in town to give them a call. Meanwhile they would contact Glen about making a split publishing deal between him and them on some of the songs.

I flew back up to Arroyo Grande and told the guys in the band the good news, they were very excited. We decided to start saving our money to make our move to Hollywood. Norm Malkin and Jack Hoffman later offered me a job writing for their company, Winston Music, with an advance salary of seventy-five dollars per week for any songs they decided to publish. Plus, I got my own office that was right next to Harry Nilsson's old office.

Dave Bianchi, owner of *The Cove*, was sorry to see us go; it had been a good relationship.

HMS Bounty L-R back row -Jack Metz, Bill Dodd, Larry Meyers, front Merrell

CHAPTER 8
Hollywood Here we Come

I n July of 1968 we all moved to the San Fernando Valley, near Hollywood. I got a house in Van Nuys and Bill, Jack and Larry all got apartments near each other in North Hollywood. We started rehearsing in my garage and made an appointment for Norm Malkin and Jack Hoffman to come and hear us. They liked what they heard and said that they would go to work booking some gigs for us, but the band needed a name. Jack Hoffman came up with the idea of calling us *Merrell Fankhauser and H.M.S. Bounty*, because it sounded British and any band that sounded like it came from England would be a good selling point.

We started playing any gig we could to survive; topless bars, fraternity parties and even a lounge in Watts, in East Los Angeles. One night after one of the gigs at the lounge in Watts, Larry Meyers, the drummer, had a little too much to drink and had some problems getting home. He found his car in the parking lot, but couldn't find the freeway on ramp back to North Hollywood. He pulled into a gas station and the attendant gave him directions, Larry left and drove around for a while and still couldn't find the on ramp. He ended up back at the same gas station and pulled in and again asked the station attendant how to get onto the on ramp. The guy told him that he must have missed the last left turn that he was supposed to take to get onto the ramp. So Larry drove away, only to end up back at that same gas station again! The attendant at the gas station said, "Man, I don't believe it! Is you drunk, or what?" Larry told him he guessed he was because he couldn't find the freeway ramp? The attendant assured him that it was there and if he kept looking he would find it.

Larry said he drove around for another thirty minutes and finally gave up, pulled over and went to sleep. When he woke up it was light and there was the on ramp just up ahead, he got on the freeway and drove home.

We were just making enough money to scrape by, it was harder for Bill, as he had two kids. I only had one child and Jack Metz had one, Larry Meyers was single. I wondered if we would ever get a break. Then Jack Hoffman phoned and told us that they made a publishing deal with Glen MacArthur and that we were booked into Gold Star Studio for Wednesday morning. There we met Jim Hilton, the engineer I had met a few years earlier at Audio Arts Studio. He would go on to produce *The Iron Butterfly*.

The first songs we cut were; *Rich Mans Fable* and *What Does She See In You?* The session was a

breakthrough, we sounded the best we had ever sounded and I was getting to record my new, more experimental, music in a great studio. Norm Malkin took it to several labels. Dot Records was interested and Russ Reagan at UNI Records really liked it, but he said that he didn't hear a hit there. He wanted to hear more and he offered to pay for a session to record two more tunes; if he didn't accept them we could keep the tapes. That seemed fair enough, so Norm and Jack went through my tunes trying to pick what they thought was the most commercial. They decided on *Girl I Am Waiting For You* and *The Big Gray Sky*.

We liked the session before but everybody agreed that it just kept getting better and that these songs really sounded like hits! We took them straight to Russ Reagan at UNI Records and I played and sang him the rest of the songs for the album live on an acoustic guitar. Russ said, "You've got a deal!" Norm Malkin and Jack Hoffman were sure that I had a mountain of what they termed "Commercial Material" in my head and they wanted it. They began by explaining that the other album songs I had were a little "too far out" and we needed more commercial sounding songs with nice love themes and catchy hook lines. I thought this sounds like they want bubble gum songs and I got an uneasy feeling.

I was writing in the office on Cahuenga and Vine in Hollywood, I thought that maybe if I give Norm and Jack their commercial ditty's they will let me include some of my experimental songs on the album, especially the sitar song that I had written - *A Visit With Ashiya.*

We had a meeting set up with Russ Reagan for the following week, I decided to lock myself in my office and write that commercial blockbuster hit that they wanted. Four hours later the song *Things* was finished, I knew it was a hit. I played it for Norm and Jack and they literally jumped up and down! "You're a genius," they shouted. They were sure that we had just the song to knock Tommy Roe's song *Sweet Pea* out of the number one spot on the charts. This had me worried but I thought, oh well, it's just one song.

We had the meeting with Russ Reagan and he told us that he'd have the contracts for the album drawn up, but that it would take a few weeks. Norm and Jack had me step out of the room while they negotiated the front money. I thought it was odd, but they later explained that it wasn't good to have the artist present during this type of discussion.

We decided to celebrate and we went out and had some ice cream and Norm was generous enough to buy me a pint of hand packed Baskin Robbins ice cream to take home.

I was anxious to find out how much front money they had gotten and what kind of record royalty percentage we were getting? As near as I could tell from the front money that they got for the songs we had already recorded, the amount must be somewhere around eighteen thousand dollars. Wow, I thought, this is great! Meanwhile the band was just barely getting by on ninety to a hundred dollars a week each. I told the guys about the album signing, but they could hardly believe it, it wouldn't seem real to them until it started happening. Norm and Jack got us a gig at a big club in San Diego for two weeks, we made over $250.00 each a week and we felt like we were finally doing well.

I had a 1964 Chevrolet station wagon at the time and Jack Metz (now going by Jack Jordan) had a 1965 Dodge four door sedan. Between the two cars we could miraculously get all the equipment and bodies in.

We played the gig in San Diego, which went over very well. Norm called and said that the contracts would be ready to sign Monday morning. We arrived at Malkin and Hoffman's office promptly at ten Monday morning. Upon reading the contracts I realized that the contract was for us to sign with Malkin and Hoffman as producers, they had signed with UNI Records as our producers and we were entirely under their control. They also wanted us to sign exclusive management contracts with them, I had already signed an exclusive songwriting and publishing contract with them. After some debate we signed the contracts, with the understanding that we got a new P.A. system. They also agreed that we'd each receive ninety dollars per week while we recorded, but only if we didn't have a gig for that weekend. They made sure that we had gigs so that they didn't have to pay us the ninety dollars. All of the sessions were filed with the local forty-seven Musicians Union, we would have to go down to the Union to get our checks and cash them and the Union would take out the dues we owed. What a ripp off, we thought. We kept thinking that maybe we just have to do this one time and then we would get our foot in the door. We got our foot in the door all right and a few toes broken when it got slammed!

Much later I would find out that Malkin had all my songwriting royalties for the songs that I wrote for their publishing company, going directly to him. Glen MacArthur never received a penny either. While we were recording the album, the front money from UNI Records couldn't be spent on anything extra to insure that we had enough to finish the album. It seemed like the difficult lessons that I was experiencing in the music business would never stop.

We were sent over to a photography studio at Universal for the *H.M.S. Bounty* cover shots. There were some very nice shots that were taken in these sessions, especially the multilayered psychedelic shot that ended up on the back of the album. I thought it should have been the front cover. Universal City's art department was in charge of the album design and they came up with the idea of putting a close-up of a woman's breast on the front cover. Afterwards, we went to the old trains in Griffith Park for outdoor publicity shots. The *H.M.S. Bounty* album was finished the first of November 1968 and the single, *"Things"*, was quickly released followed by the album a few weeks later. By the end of November, the single had made it into the bubbling under of the hot 100 chart in *Billboard Magazine*. It looked like it was going to be a big hit! We had ads in all the major music magazines and group ads with the rest of the UNI/Shamley recording artists. Russ Reagan, President of UNI Records, really thought my name was different and had bumper stickers printed up for promotion that read, "What Is A Merrell Fankhauser?" There was a phone number on the sticker for people to call in and get information about the band.

The Merrell Fankhauser and the H.M.S. Bounty Album SS701 contained; *Things, Girl I'm Waiting For You, What Does She See In You, Lost In The City, Your Painted Lives, Driving Sideways On A One Way Street, In A Minute Not Too Soon, A Visit With Ashiya, Rich Man's Fable, Ice Cube Island* and *Madame Silky*. The album was really quite good and an innovative breakthrough that showed my maturing as a songwriter and got very good reviews and initial sales and radio play. The album would later find its way into the valued record collectors catalogues.

We started getting a lot of bookings and played everywhere in the state of California. We even played a show near our central coast home turf in San Luis Obispo at the *Madonna Inn*. Our record was number four on the charts at the local KSLY station and we reached the top five position on many other California radio stations. We did an awesome concert at San Fernando Valley College where we opened up for a group called *The Electric Flag*; to our surprise we stole the show and ended up doing a long encore song that drove the place wild! The audience was playing along with us on bottles and cans and anything they could find, this was all complete with a pulsating psychedelic light show. This was the kind of gig we wanted to do, forget the topless bars and little clubs. Norm Malkin would always say, "A gig is a gig, and you have to stay working." We did another great show with *The Blues Image*; we were very impressed with their lead guitarist and experimental rhythm sound, their records didn't sound like manufactured bubblegum music.

One shocking scene was at the Ambassador Hotel a few days after Bobby Kennedy had been shot. We usually loaded our equipment in the freight elevator that opened up in the kitchen. When we stepped out into the hallway that led to the ballroom, there was the blood stained floor and chalk outline where Bobby's body was lying a few days earlier. It was hard to put on that entertaining smile while playing that night in the same room Bobby had given his last speech in!

Our record had achieved a high position on the San Bernardino radio stations chart and we did a big concert in the indoor fair grounds stadium there. *The Buffalo Springfield* and *The Strawberry Alarm Clock* were also on the bill. It started off as a very exciting show, part way through our set something hit me in the back and I noticed that the drums had stopped. I looked back just in time to see Larry Meyers fall over his drums and on to the stage in front of me. He looked up at me and asked, "What the fuck's going on, man?" I knew that he was stoned, but at the time I didn't know what he was on? Jack, the bass player, tried to cover up Larry's fall by saying, "It's all in the act, folks", as though it was a comedy routine. We couldn't believe it when people rushed the stage after the performance, telling us how good we were. The entire concert was broadcast live on KRLA radio. We later found out that Larry was occasionally shooting smack in his heel, none of the other band members were into drugs at the time; an occasional joint was about it. We all knew something else was going on with Larry Meyers.

Larry was having trouble with his increasing use of the various different drugs, one night while he was driving in traffic he got into a wreck with a doctor, and was arrested and thrown into jail. Our road manager at the time tried to cover it up, but we found out that they had pawned Larry's drums for the bail money. We had to raise the money to get his drums back for the gig that night. We got a concert booking at George Air Force Base, which was inland in the desert from where we lived. We were loaded up to go to the gig and Larry didn't show up. We went to his apartment to find that his car wasn't there and there was no sign of him, we left a note with directions, telling him to meet us there. It was quite a long drive and we finally got to the air force base, through the gates to a giant auditorium that already had a few thousand people waiting inside.

We set up our equipment, did a sound check and still there was no sign of Larry. Our roadie, Frenchy, had Larry's drums set up, waiting for his arrival. People were getting anxious waiting for the music to start, by now we were forty-five minutes late! What were we going to do? We waited another ten minutes and then I went on stage and asked the audience if there was a drummer in the house. A few minutes later a rather nervous and reluctant Airman came to the stage. He said that he had played in high school and had jammed with some friends, but that was all the experience he'd had. He managed to make it through the night and he was overwhelmed to have been able to play with us.

After the concert the band started for home. Somewhere on the Cajon Pass we blew a tire on Bill's old Cadillac, my station wagon was in the shop with a blown transmission. We got to the spare tire after unloading the amplifiers and discovered that the tire was flat. Just up the road we managed to wake a guy up who was sleeping in his car and he took us and the flat tire to an all night gas station a few miles further down the road. It was winter and very cold. We asked the gas station attendant if he had a used tire that would fit the rim of the car and he said, " No, but there's a big pile of old tires out back and you can have anything that you can find." I went around the corner and saw this mountain of tires! There I was with my white Captain's coat and white bell bottom pants, climbing in a mountain of tires at 2:30 in the morning. After several tries I found a tire that would fit and the attendant let us use his equipment for free to put the tire on the rim. We hitched a ride back to the car, put the tire on and slowly drove home, arriving at six in the morning.

The next day the band got together and fired Larry and I began calling around for drummers. My old friend, Randy Wimer from Lancaster, was very interested, he drove down and auditioned and we hired him. Randy had gotten very good since I had last heard him and he'd developed quite an original style.

1969 came in with a strong beginning; we did a memorable concert in Bakersfield with *Canned Heat*. I loved "Blind Owl" Wilson, their singer and guitar player, he was great! This was Randy Wimer's first concert with the *H.M.S Bounty* and he did a strong drum solo in our set that really had the crowd rockin!

At about this time UNI Records signed Neil Diamond and as the label began to promote him we watched our record *Things* fall off the charts. Norm Malkin got Russ Reagan to release our second single *Girl I'm Waiting For You*, backed with a new song called, *I'm Flying Home*, which was a psychedelic rocker more in the vein of music that I wanted to do. This was the last song recorded by the *H.M.S. Bounty*.

Girl I'm Waiting For You did fairly well on the charts in California, but failed to make it anywhere else, it was obvious the record company wasn't pushing it. It had looked so promising when we first signed with Russ Reagan and UNI Records.

The first round of promotion for the album was very strong, but now it seemed as though everything was crumbling before our eyes. As the energy with the radio chart action and sales waned, so did the energy of the band.

MU clouds by Marsha Walker

CHAPTER 9
Finding Mu in Woodland Hills

Me and Josie and our son, Tim, were living in a two bedroom apartment on Claybourne Street in North Hollywood. Randy Wimer had moved in with us and was bunking with little Tim in his bedroom.

We had decided that a bigger place was needed and I was ready to get a little further out of the city. Randy suggested Woodland Hills, at the north end of the San Fernando Valley. We drove out on a Sunday and looked the area over. It was very nice and had trees and canyons, with houses dotting the hills, Randy told me that Jeff Cotton was living in Woodland Hills now with Captain Beefheart's Band. We got a local newspaper, found a beautiful three bedroom house on a hill that looked like a mansion to us, rented it and moved in. It was perfect and had a large den with fireplace, where we could practice. The rent was only $275.00 a month. We didn't have any furniture and we felt dwarfed in the large living room, with its eighteen foot ceilings.

We managed to stay working and there was still an abundance of agents who were willing to book us. We started playing for large dances at the big hotels in Los Angeles, such as *The Biltmore, Century City, Beverly Hilton, Ambassador Hotel*, and even the *Playboy Club*. We usually played opposite a big dance band, the money was okay and it was steady.

This seemed like a good time to re-group and work on some new tunes. Bill Dodd and Jack Metz (Jordan) were tiring of the city life and our "pot of gold" had never materialized, so they decided to move back up north to the Central Coast. Bill got his job back at the supermarket and Jack went back to playing small town clubs and lounges.

UNI Records wanted to release a solo single on me as "Merrell Fankhauser", now that *H.M.S. Bounty* had disbanded. Jack Hoffman suggested that I record a song written by folk artist, Fred Neil titled, *Everybody's Talking*, along with *Tampa Run*, that I had written with my old friend, Don Aldridge, who was now going by the name of Shawn Granville. The songs were recorded at Gold Star Studio with a super session band that included; Al Casey, on rhythm guitar, who

MU on Maui L-R Randy Wimer, Merrell, Jeff Cotton

MU KHJ TV LA L-R Randy Wimer. Merrell, Jeff Cotton

had played with Duane Eddy, Jim Gordon on drums, who later went on to play with Eric Clapton, Carol Kay on bass, who had played with Joe Cocker and many others, and Larry Knechtle on piano, who went on to play with David Gates and Bread.

The basic tracks and vocals to both songs were very good, but Malkin and Hoffman both thought they needed some commercial frosting on them so they hired well known arranger, Perry Botkin, to write charts for a horn section for *Everybody's Talking*, I thought it sounded like a Mariachi Band. Then they decided to put the sound of a diesel truck going right through the middle of the slide guitar solo in *Tampa Run*. I went home frustrated, feeling like Malkin and Hoffman ruined two good songs. Never the less, in September of 1969, *Everybody's Talking* backed with *Tampa Run* was released, and to my knowledge, the record didn't make it on any charts. They tried to get the flip side played, but still nothing happened and it quickly disappeared.

Harry Nilsson recorded *Everybody's Talking* at the same time and his version was a hit and was used in the movie Midnight Cowboy.

Malkin and Hoffman's plan to make me do manufactured music had caught up with them and I got out of my contract with them and the label.

We had several different bass players come and go and we had a young guitar player who was a double for George Harrison, named Steve Deluna. Randy and I bumped into Don Van Vilet one day at the local Safeway store and he invited us over to his house. He didn't live far from us, but his house was further up in the canyon and was set back from the road. The yard had a lot of sleepy looking trees and bushes. When we got to his house, our old friends were there which included, Jeff Cotton, John French, Mark Boston, and Bill Harkelroad. Jeff looked like a scarecrow with a straw mop of long hair and he was so thin and nervous he looked like he was ready to fold up. Everyone was very pale because they didn't go out much in the daytime; they were up most nights playing music.

Randy and I would go back several times to join in the all night jam sessions with Don and his *Magic Band*; it was a strange scene to drive up to the rather spooky looking place that had weird music leaking out of the house. I heard that the nearby neighbors were frightened and pretty much avoided any contact with the band members, and Don's girlfriend, Laurie, who did the shopping and cooking. It was later discovered that Laurie would dose the band with LSD in their food and this way Don could get them into his way out level of musical endeavors.

We went over one day and John French had a splint on his finger and Mark Boston had a cut on his lip. Don explained that Mark was fucking the band up. The next time we went over another guy was blamed for fucking the band up. Each time it was a different band member who was blamed for not playing his part right. Jeff Cotton had been with *The Magic Band* for nearly two years and had recorded some great slide guitar licks on some of the albums, but life as a "Beefheart" musician was starting to wear thin. Several times he ran away from the house and came to our house for sanctuary. One evening Bill Harkelroad came around in his old

Cadillac Hearse to get Jeff, and Jeff nervously left with him.

Apparently there was a skirmish one night at the "Beefheart" house and it turned out that Jeff was the guy who was being blamed for fucking up the band this time. Jeff got roughed up and was taken away to Olive View Hospital in the San Fernando Valley. After a few days in the hospital, his parents took him home and tried to rehabilitate their son.

A month later Jeff called me and said he would like to come down and play with me, but that he was afraid of "The Beefheart Clan!" I assured him that Randy and I would protect him and that he would have nothing to worry about. Randy and I drove up to Lancaster to pick Jeff up and his parents asked us to please make sure that the Beefheart guys didn't get him. We told them not to worry.

Jeff and I immediately started writing songs together and tried to keep his presence low key at my house in Woodland Hills. I made sure that he took two hot baths a day and ate right, his nervous system was a wreck. After a few months he began to mellow out and regain his confidence.

We started playing the hotel gigs, with me on guitar and vocal, Randy Wimer on drums, Steve Deluna on guitar and Jeff on bass. Steve felt awkward in the band after awhile, as he knew that Jeff was a much better guitar player than he was and that Jeff should be playing guitar instead of bass. One night we all had a flash to call Larry Willey, who was still in the desert playing bass in a blues band. We called Larry up and he said, "What took you guys so long to call?" We drove straight up to Lancaster that night and picked him up.

Randy had rented a small house across the valley in Chatsworth, in a rural area, and Larry moved in with him. We began to rehearse every chance we got and we were all very dedicated and it was paying off. We developed an incredible timeless style of music that would hold its own for many years into the future.

The songwriting collaboration that Jeff and I had during this period was very prolific, he had a tape recorder in his room and I had one in the living room. He would write instrumental parts in his room and I would put lyrics and melody to them. Sometimes I would come up with an instrumental idea, or lyric, that I couldn't finish and Jeff would take it in his room and finish it. We would do late night jams with Randy and Larry, and sometimes a song would just evolve, we were churning this stuff out like pancakes! We always made sure that we had the old reel to reel tape recorders rolling; in less than a few months time we had nearly fifty songs.

One day Randy came over and told Jeff and I about some strange girls that he met up the creek while he was hiking near his house. He said that they asked him for some food and wanted to know if he had any kind of drugs? He told them that he could go and round them up some food and they told him they'd wait there. He returned with food and a joint, they got stoned together and the girls asked him if he'd like to have sex with them? He told them he didn't think so. They told him they were camped about a mile up the creek and invited him to come and visit them sometime, but not to come at night because Charlie would kill him! He said, "Okay, anything you say." They disappeared up the canyon. We thought how strange that was, and later we realized that they were some of the Manson gang members who later committed the horrific murders of Sharon Tate and her friends. The Spahn Movie Ranch, where they all hung out, was just a few miles away from Randy's house!

We were playing the L.A. club and hotel circuit, biding our time and working on our original material, and when the time was right we would record it and take it to labels ourselves. Randy had bought an older Chevy van and somehow we could get ourselves and all our instruments crammed into it, every weekend we were off to our gigs. There were so many memorable nights playing; the band was really hot and we had quite a following of fans that

MU rehearsing L-R Larry Willey, Merrell, Jeff Cotton

would come to all of our shows. We were playing in the large lavish ballrooms on giant stages where well known big bands like Neil Hefty and Nelson Riddle would play.

We looked a little out of place at these elite gigs with our long hair and wild clothes. Jeff wore a 1928 ringmaster's suit, complete with tails and I had a 17th century green velvet coat that I had bought at a MGM movie lot auction. Randy wore his special white karate style suit and Larry was all in blue velvet. Some of the audiences would shudder when we walked onstage and they'd be wondering what "these hippies" were going to sound like. We'd tear into a *Rolling Stones* number and they would go crazy! We did a mixture of up tempo blues with just enough of the current day songs, plus our own material, to satisfy the audience.

We were getting rave reports from our agents who booked us in these rather straight gigs. They tried to get us to cut our hair and wear matching suits, but we told them, "No way, we'd quit before we'd do that!" They let us have our way, and we kept the hotel circuit for three years, along with doing concerts and clubs.

We had a friend who'd brought over some real strong hashish from India and he gave us   a big brick of it, we started getting into smoking this stuff, and Larry especially really liked it. We were playing monthly at *The Coconut Grove*, in *The Ambassador Hotel*, we usually went on after the big band, or we'd just alternate sets with them. We found a spot at the end of a hall in an alcove on the sixth floor, where we would go to smoke. We took a break and Larry told us that he was ready for the sixth floor, so we got in the elevator and pressed the number six. Larry was in a hurry and told Randy to "load the pipe now". Larry lit the pipe and took an enormous hit, the door opened at the sixth floor and to our total astonishment there was a cop sitting in a chair in front of the elevator door! Larry could no longer hold back the smoke and he promptly blew it in the face of the policeman, who shouted "stop!"

Randy hit the down button on the elevator door and when we reached the basement we scurried into a freight elevator that would let us out behind the stage. The big band was still playing and I went around to the stage door and asked the security guard what was going on up on the sixth floor. He looked at me and said with a grin, "You guys didn't go up there?" That's where they're holding the jurors for the Manson trial." I thought, my God, they might have thought that we were part of the Manson gang when we'd appeared in the elevator!

All through our last set we were worried that they were going to come on stage any minute and take us all away. On the drive home, Larry promised that he would never do that again. We all laughed and said, "Boy, that was a close one."

One day Jeff Cotton decided to walk down to the local music store to get some picks and strings. We were all sitting around having lunch and we realized that Jeff had been gone for quite sometime and we wondered what had happened to him? Randy needed to go out to run some errands and he went down to the music store to look for Jeff. When Randy inquired about him at the music store they told him that the guys from Beefheart's band had taken him away. When I found this out I got in the old Chevy convertible that I had at the time and headed up the canyon to the Magic Band's house.

I arrived and knocked on the door; Don Vilet answered and said, "You're just in time. Follow me," we went into the rather large bathroom and he locked the door behind us. There was Jeff sitting in the bathtub whimpering like a puppy dog. I asked, "What's going on?" Don said, "We were just having a little talk, weren't we Jeff?" Jeff could hardly raise his head to talk. Don told him to tell me what was going on and he could hardly look me in the eye as he said, "I am going to play with Don's band again." I asked Jeff if that was really what he wanted to do? Jeff couldn't talk and I figured that he was either drugged or hypnotized.

Don said," Look at this, Merrell," as he handed me a wire mesh cage of poisonous spiders. "What would you say if I made one of those spiders smoke a cigarette?"

"That would be a good trick," I answered.

At this point I knew it was going to be a battle of wills and that it wasn't going to be easy to get Jeff out of there, unless I did it by force. I knew that none of them were strong enough to stop me, but I was curious at this point and decided to play Don's mind game. I felt the air get heavy in the room and it took a great deal of concentration to stay alert. He tried to belittle me in front of Jeff and I would ask him pointed questions back. Jeff kept sobbing and repeating that he was nothing and telling Don that he was sorry for messing up the band. I told Jeff that he didn't have to be sorry about anything and I kept repeating to him to be himself. That infuriated Don and his eyes would glow with anger, Don and I were both Capricorns and it was like two stubborn goats locking horns.

This went on for hours, from about four in the afternoon until eight at night. Jeff would sway back and forth; one instant he was going home with me and the next Don had him again and he would say he was staying with Don.

Finally I said, "Okay, stay here and rot, you wimp."

Don laughed and said, "He's a great guitar player, but he will never amount to anything because he won't stick with it. Do you think he will stay with you?" No way, something else will come along and he will be off on another tangent, he's a loser."

At this point Don had me convinced and I was so tired that I just wanted to leave. Then I thought, "Wait a minute, Jeff was once my best friend, I taught him some of his first chords and lead guitar licks, I am not going to leave him".

We battled on for what seemed like an eternity and we were all exhausted. I told Jeff to get on his feet, and that we were going home, it took several tries and finally he got up and we walked out. I took Jeff home and ran a hot bath for him and made him stay in it for an hour. He would later thank me countless numbers of times for getting him out of Don's control, I loved Jeff like a brother.

From that point on Jeff seemed to be obsessed with religion, and good and evil. He began studying the Bible and then he went to the Rosicrucian philosophy and the study of Egyptology, which I got into also.

We really didn't have a name for the band at this time and our agents were on us to come up with a name for the group. I made up something different every time they called. Finally, we all sat down and started thinking of names. Everything sounded ridiculous, nothing fit. One day we found a book titled, *The Lost Continent of Mu*, an original 1932 edition by Colonel James Churchward. I really didn't think too much about it at first, but later Jeff started reading it and really became fascinated.

I was walking up the canyon in Woodland Hills one morning, when I looked into the sky and there was a cloud that formed a perfect M U. I thought, 'That's it. *MU!*' I ran back to the house and told Jeff and he agreed that *MU* was the perfect name for the group. Jeff started studying the book, *The Lost Continent of Mu* and decided it was destiny that we call ourselves *MU* and that we were somehow related to the lost race of Mu! I laughed and told him that was interesting. The more he read the more he decided that everything that was unexplainable had its origin in the Land of Mu!

The four forms of MU, originating from the seal tradition of Lemuria, symbolizing creation.

MU – Merrell Fankhauser, Jeff Cotton, Randy Wimer, Larry Willey

Side One		Side Two		
1. Ain't No Blues (Cotton)	(4:03)	1. Eternal Thirst (Cotton, Fankhauser)	(5:34)	Produced by MU in association with Herb Newman.
2. Ballad of Brother Lew (Fankhauser)	(4:30)	2. Too Naked For Demension (Cotton)	(5:30)	Studio: Wally Heider, L.A. Engineer: John Golden
3. Blue Form (Cotton, Fankhauser)	(4:03)	3. Mumbella Boss To La (Cotton, Fankhauser)	(2:19)	Photography: Chan Bush Jack Duganne
4. Interlude (Cotton)	(2:18)	4. The Clouds Went That Way (Fankhauser)	(3:16)	Graphic Engineer: Ernie Taylor
5. Nobody Wants To Shine (Fankhauser, Cotton)	(4:09)			Special thanks to: Marty Gabler, Bob Weiss, Jack Mallman, Charles Axton, Phil Moldineri, Audrey P. Franklin, Norm Malkin, George Hilts, and Warner.

Then I started reading the book and I too became fascinated with the theories put forth by Colonel Churchward. Supposedly, the lost continent of Mu was a large body of land that submerged some eleven thousand five hundred years ago, all of the South American, and some North American Indians were said to have come from there. Many remnants of the lost civilization could be found in several places in North America, as well as the Pacific Islands, including Hawaii. Some modern day archeologists and scientists now believe that there could be some truth to this; maybe all the people didn't arrive in what is now America, via the Bering Land Bridge. The thought of all this definitely took Jeff and I to a different level of perception and soon Randy would follow. Larry was not as interested in this as the rest of us; he came from a more earthly plane. I felt that there was nothing wrong with that and that it was good to have a down to Earth bass player. He was more interested in how much money we were getting for the next gig and getting a record deal, which wasn't a bad place to have his focus.

Songs about Mu starting materializing, sometimes Jeff and I would stay up all night writing songs and we really began to believe that the knowledge of Mu was being sent to us. One night Jeff and I heard the words to a chant that we quickly wrote down and made into a song titled, *"Mumbella Baye Tu La"*. "We later found out that this was an ancient Swahili chant about the sinking of a distant land. We went to the library and got books on African folk translations and couldn't believe what we had written. I thought it was just "mumbo jumbo" at first, but the words actually meant something! It must be a coincidence, I thought. Interestingly enough, later I would find out that the spiritual community of Halcyon, which was practically in my backyard in Arroyo Grande where I grew up, believed in the Lost Continent of MU.

We gave Randy all the new song demo tapes to take home to his cabin in Chatsworth so that he could practice the drum parts and Larry could practice his bass parts at the same time.

I remember that the summer of 1970 was hot and dry, one afternoon we heard fire engines further up the canyon, but we didn't pay much attention to them. Then we noticed that we kept hearing the sirens and decided to check out what was happening, we walked up the street and found the entire hillside engulfed in flames. The fire had spread to Malibu and was spreading north and south at the same time. The wind kept changing direction and no one was sure which way the fire was heading. We had a gig to do that night and I told Josie to keep a watch out and if the fire got too close to load up important papers and valuables, grab Tim and drive down to the big Safeway parking lot.

We did the gig and as we were driving on the Ventura freeway toward Woodland Hills, the entire valley was engulfed in flames all the way to Chatsworth. The fire had jumped the freeway, gas stations were blowing up and houses were on fire! We got off the freeway, and everything around Ventura Blvd. and Topanga Canyon seemed okay, so I knew that my house was all right. We later found out that the entire area where Randy had lived was burned to the ground. All of Randy and Larry's belongings were gone, along with an extra set of drums and the tapes of over fifty of our original songs! Due to the complete destruction of Randy and Larry's house, they had to move in with us. There was a guest room in the garage where Jeff was living and we converted the rest of the garage into a room for Randy and Larry. Our plan was to stay there until we found an even bigger house that would accommodate all of us more comfortably.

Another tragedy struck that year of 1970, with the death of my father. He had died of a heart attack while driving home from work at the airport, after he'd spent the day in the air giving flight instruction to students. He was only fifty-five years old, needless to say, it was a horrible loss to our family and things were never the same. My mom sold our house on Palm Court in Arroyo Grande and went on to buy and sell a new house every year after that, it was obvious how restless she became with my dad gone. She finally found what she was looking for when she opened The Vault Boutique in Arroyo Grande. By this time my sister Linda, had graduated from beauty school and was married and had a daughter named Kirstie. Mom financed the Grand Street Parlor Beauty Salon for Linda, that was the happiest that I saw my mom and sister in a long time.

After the death of my father, I was feeling very alone, so I started looking for my own spiritual path. I began to meditate more, took LSD, Peyote, Cyliciban, and Mescaline. Basically I did everything I could to widen the doors of perception. I wanted to believe that there was a better place after life, but no one could prove that there was. I got further into the Mu philosophy and Zen Buddhism. I studied Yogananda, Gurdijeff, and the *Tibetan Book of the Dead*, Mayan Indian Legends, and *The Bible*. Nobody really had any answers, they told nice stories but it was all from the lips of man and interpreted by man's small mind. The only truth that I could see was for all beings to live in peace and love, while they are here on Earth. Man may never know what waits on the other side, until he takes that trip.

We met an agent who heard us playing in the house one day as he was driving by, he was very interested in the different style of music that he heard. He told us that he was working on a documentary film and asked if we would do some background music for it. We said yes and he took us into the private home studio of country star, Jimmy Wakely. We got along well with Jimmy and his wife, Inez. We recorded our part for the agent's film and during the session we warmed up on two of our originals titled, *Swiney Eyelow* and *L.A. In The Woods*. Jimmy loved both of the songs and said he would let us record them if we gave him the publishing on them, and possibly his son Johnny, who was now recording for Decca Records, might like to cut them. We went home very happy and felt like we were starting to get somewhere in regards to recording our own original music the way we wanted to.

Jimmy Wakely phoned us and we set up a recording date, we got our friend, Glen, who played piano with a band called *Carp*, to play on the session. The lead singer for *Carp* was soon to be actor Gary Busey. Gary was playing drums and he and Randy would sometimes get together and jam. The session went very smoothly and everyone, including Jimmy, was happy. *Swiney Eyelow* was a kind of up tempo Delta blues style song about a guy named Swiney that gets lost in the swamps in the South, but would creep around and scare people at night. *L.A. In The Woods* was Jeff's lament about how nice L.A. would be if it was still woods before all the high rise buildings, traffic and smog came along. Jeff played some outstanding slide guitar on both of these songs. We took the songs around to a few record companies and they liked the sound of the band, but 'they didn't hear a hit'.

During this period, Don Vliet would send the guys from his band over to check up on us to find out what we were up to, they would usually appear late at night. Bill Harkelroad or Mark Boston would come over either singularly or together and just say they wanted to visit. Jeff usually stayed in his room during their visits. One night Harkelroad came over about 2:00am and asked to see Jeff. I told him that everyone was asleep, he kept insisting and I told him if he didn't leave I was going to make a neat pile of toothpicks out of him. He left!

The very next night we got a knock on the door around ten pm. This time it was a little guy in a tweed suit, with a little hat and elf shoes with turned up toes. He introduced himself as Ernest Toppington the third and I thought that Don had sent him over. He had a strong Irish accent and he said he was a friend of our old manager, Al. I let him in and I recall that we had all just smoked a bowl of hash and the odor was still lingering in the room. Ernest picked up the pipe and put something in it and told us to try it. We all took a hit, then Ernest walked over to the fireplace and threw some colored dust in it that billowed out into the room with bright yellow and blue colors. The last thing I remembered as I passed out was seeing him standing in front of the fireplace and smiling. When I woke up I was sitting on a bench on Ventura Boulevard, quite a ways from my home! I couldn't remember how I had gotten there? I started running back to the house and I could feel a sensation of undulating waves of air pushing against my body.

When I arrived at the house, the front door was open and the wind was whipping through the house. Everyone was gone, Josie was asleep in bed and Tim came out of the back bedroom and asked where I had gone? I told him that I'd just gone for a walk and we went to sleep, it was definitely a strange time. Jeff, Josie and I all experienced something else in the house one other time; it was the sensation of having something flow over our bodies at night, which held us down. Larry didn't like hearing about such things and he would leave the room. We were all getting a little far out and we expected that anything could happen at any time.

Finally, we found a nice two story house with four bedrooms, on a street with no house in back of it. It was perfect for us to play our music in, we felt that a change was needed and there was a lot of energy that we had to let go of at the old house on Tendilla Street. By this time I had bought a used 1969 Cadillac and we hired a couple of our old friends from the desert, Charlie and Woody, as roadies. We had met an agent named Marty Gabler, who had heard us at the Beverly Hilton and had started booking us at different clubs and concerts. Marty introduced us to an attorney who was very into our music named, Phil Meldman, and he told us that he would put up some money for us to record an album. We agreed on a 50-50 split on everything that we might make off the album with Phil. He had the contracts drawn up and we were close to signing them when another disaster struck.

On February ninth 1971, at six am, everything began to shake violently, our bed was sliding across the floor and my first thought was that I had to get to Tim. I got up and tried to walk and it was like walking on wobbly concrete. We were on the second floor and I watched the stairwell bend in about three feet as the wall cracked. The windows in Tim's room were the individual louvered type and I watched several fly out of the open door of his room and break against the wall. I went into Tim's room and the shaking stopped. Tim peeped out from under his covers and asked, "What happened, daddy?" I told him we had an earthquake but that it was over now. The aftershocks went on for weeks and everyone was sure that this was it; California was going to drop in the sea and the ocean would again return to the desert! Jeff Cotton was sure that the lost Continent of Mu would rise in the Pacific Ocean any day.

The band played a large concert at The Beverly Hilton during this time and we decided to play all original music. We had a split audience; on one side the more conservative older crowd and on the other side, the rebels and hippies! We started into the set and we got complaints from the straight side of the audience saying that we were too loud and to play something they could dance to. Then a fight broke out in the middle of the room and on the last note of *Nobody Wants To Shine* there was a strong after shock. Everyone stopped and a hush fell over the room as the huge chandeliers in the grand ballroom swayed back and forth. I said, "Let that be a lesson to you" and then we left the stage. There was no applause, just bewilderment on everyone's faces. We thought that we had better get this album done soon or there won't be a studio to record it in, we were booked for two weeks in Wally Heider's studio in Hollywood. It was a joyous two weeks as we flew through our well rehearsed originals, most of the recording was done live, no overdubs, straight to sixteen track tape. We got along well with our new engineer, John Golden. Recording that album was one of the most inspiring times that I'd had in the studio to that point. The album was done on July first of 1971 and Marty Gabler, our agent, started shopping it. He was met with a lot of red tape and problems getting in at record labels, so we decided to release a single on our own label to get something out.

Mantra m-101 *Nobody Wants To Shine* and *Ballad Of Brother Lew* was released September of 1971. We mailed it out to mostly California radio stations and we got some minor airplay in small markets and placed copies with a few distributors. Only a thousand copies were pressed and we probably sold four hundred and gave three hundred away. A few months later we met with Herb Newman of ERA / RTV Records and in December of 1971 the first *MU* album was released. RTV 300 by *MU* contained the following songs; *Ain't No Blues, Ballad Of Brother Lew, Blue Form, Interlude, Nobody Wants To Shine, Eternal Thirst, Too Naked For Demetrius, Mumbella Baye Tu La* and *The Clouds Went That Way.*

The album became an instant hit on late night FM radio stations across the United States. The record was distributed fairly well and sold on both the East and West coasts. Wallichs Music City, on the corner of Sunset and Vine in Hollywood, did a special window display with the album cover and statues of the members of *MU*, which were sculptured by famed Hungarian sculptor, Frank Borzai. *MU* was immediately booked on six shows of local DJ Elliot Mintz's TV show, *Head Shop*, Elliot would later work for John and Yoko Lennon.

Enter promoter Audrey P. Franklyn. Audrey had previously worked for Gene Norman's, Crescendo Records, and was presently working for Ella Fitzgerald. She thought *MU* was the greatest thing since apple pie! We were the *avant garde* rock group that she was ready to tell the world about. The first thing Audrey did was to have David Sheehan, from CBS Channel 2 news in L.A., come out with a camera crew and do an interview and tape the group live. It was on the evening news at 6:00pm and 11:00pm and made quite a stir.

At this time, Marty found us a nice house in the valley that had a swimming pool and it was cheaper than the house we had in Woodland Hills. The new house on Desoto Street, in Canoga Park, was previously home to *The Flying Burrito Brothers* and The Blues Image, it was dubbed "The Rock Ranch". It had a half acre with a big yard and trees and plenty of room for Tim to play. The first thing I would do in the morning after playing a gig the night before was to dive in and swim some laps, it was great!

Our album had helped us to get more and better gigs. We bought a large enclosed truck for the equipment and later we traded in our old Fender amps for these huge Acoustic amplifiers. We were advancing up the ladder of the music business; we did over a hundred radio, TV and press interviews in less than eight months. I heard from Jimmy Wakely that his son, Johnny Wakely, had recorded my song, *Swiney Eyelow*, with James Burton, who had played with Ricky Nelson and Elvis Presley. I never heard if the record came out or not? I was so carried away with the ride *MU* had taken me on that nothing else mattered, nothing! I became very obsessed with my career at this point; if I wasn't out doing interviews or playing at night, the band was rehearsing. It didn't leave much time for Josie and Tim, I didn't see what was happening with our marriage at the time. We started doing bigger and better gigs and the money that we were bringing in was making us a decent living and we even had a savings account. We got a regular once a month spot playing on *The Queen Mary*, which was moored in the harbor at Long Beach, California. We were also playing at The Coconut Grove once a month and we did a few memorable large concerts at Antelope Valley College, proving that our old fans were still rooting for us in the desert.

One Saturday afternoon, Larry Willey was sitting in the backyard sunning him self and he looked up and noticed a toy helicopter landing in front of him. He was sitting there looking at the helicopter and picked it up and noticed that it had a long thin wire underneath it. Larry decided to pick his teeth with it and somehow it slipped around one of his molars. He came running in the house and with slurred words said, "Hey guys, I got a helicopter stuck in my mouth." We said, "What?" and we all busted up laughing.

Larry said, "Come on you guys, it's not funny. It's stuck in my tooth!" We thought, 'Oh God, leave it to Larry to get a model helicopter stuck in his mouth'. It was blue and yellow and the rotor was at least a foot in diameter. It was the funniest sight, seeing that wire attached to Larry's mouth.

We all began pacing and trying to figure out what to do? We called a few dentists, but being a Saturday they were all closed. We only had a few hours until we had to leave for the gig. I said," Well Larry, looks like you're going to have to sing like that tonight and maybe you will start a new fad!" The rotor was quite large and it covered most of his face. It was hilarious. I said that we may be able to go in there and clip the wire to get the helicopter off his face, but that he'd still have the wire stuck in his mouth. He told me to do it and I said, "This is a job for Dr. Fankhauser", and I got my wire cutters.

We had him lean back in the light and I detached the helicopter, but we still had a big piece of wire coming out of his mouth. He started to bleed a little and we got some cotton and stuck it around both sides of the wire and then Jeff and Randy helped to keep his mouth open. I could see where it wrapped around his tooth and was cutting into his gums. I went in and cut it as close to his gums as I could and it slid around the corner of the tooth, just enough for me to grab hold of it with the needle nose pliers, and it came out. Larry was so relieved; we changed our clothes and left for the gig.

Randy came home one afternoon with two new friends that he had met at the local music store. He said that we all shared a common interest in our search for truth through spirituality. It seemed that his new found friends had studied some of the same things as we had; the Rosicrucian Philosophy, Buddhism and *The Bible*. Randy introduced Jeff and me to Keith Green and Todd Fishkind. Keith seemed like an alright young guy, very talkative and kind of hyper. Todd was quiet and very mellow, and they both had long hair like ours.

Keith immediately grabbed a guitar and started playing his songs for me, with Todd playing along. He sounded like he was somewhere between Bob Dylan and *Crosby, Stills, and Nash* in his style, with a mixture of love ballads and antiestablishment, angry young man type of songs. He had a cool voice and a lot of enthusiasm, but I told him that he needed to develop his own style a little more. Little did I know that he would later go on to be one of the most popular Christian musicians of the late 1970s and 1980s.

Randy and Keith became good friends and spent a lot of time talking philosophy and religion. Randy was studying *The Bible* quite a bit at this time, and some nights we would have some of our friends and fans over for a night of scriptures, music and meditation in that order. The *MU* house started becoming a sanctuary for troubled teenagers, and lost musicians and songwriters, trying to find their way.

Randy met a young folksinger named, Connie Butler, who he started going out with for awhile, we gave her an opening spot on a few of our concerts. We were doing our best to evolve out of worldly things and embrace true spiritual brotherhood. Larry Willey just wanted to be what he thought was normal; go out with girls, have a few beers, smoke some dope and eat steak. Jeff and Randy would get on Larry's case about this quite a bit and they would try to influence him to become a vegetarian like the rest of us. Larry started leaving every Sunday for Lancaster to party with his friends and didn't return until he was needed for an interview or upcoming gigs. He didn't like doing interviews and would rather not have to say anything.

One time we did a radio interview at KPFK in Los Angeles, it was a long interview that lasted an hour. We were all sitting at a long conference table with individual microphones. Larry nodded off and fell asleep. When the D.J. asked Larry a question, Randy nudged him and he woke up and let out a real loud fart and fell over in his chair. We all started laughing hilariously! Larry got the biggest kick out of this; that he had farted over the radio!

We had our good times and some great sessions and amazing gigs, but Larry began to drift away more and more from the philosophy, and the things that *MU* wanted to do as a band. We mutually agreed and in the summer of 1972, Larry left the band and moved back to Lancaster. Keith Green was coming over to our house more often and was warning us to beware of false prophets. He said that those of us who held the truth had to stick together, each time, he would play us his latest song that he had written. He was concentrating on developing his own style and we always encouraged him. I had written a spiritual ballad titled, *You've Been Here Before*. Keith really liked the song and when he heard that we were going to record it, he volunteered to sing harmony on it with us.

The session was done at Wally Heider's Studio B, in Hollywood, where we had cut the *MU* album. The song sounded even more enchanting when it was recorded and had an almost ancient quality about it. I sang lead, and Randy, Jeff and Keith sang harmony.

At the time, what I didn't realize was that my wife, Josie, and Keith had gotten close, so close that they had an affair. I was first told about this by our newspaper delivery boy who saw them necking on our couch. It was hard to believe at first that either one of them would do that, especially when Keith came on with such a brotherly love vibe. I confronted Keith about it and he was truly sorry and still wanted to be my friend. I told him that he was lucky I didn't punch his lights out! That was the last time I saw Keith, I found out years later that he died in a plane crash in Texas. I realized that I hadn't been home with Josie on a weekend in over five years. I had been spending so much time on my career that I had neglected my marriage.

That was just the tip of the iceberg. *MU* was scheduled to play a big concert at Antelope Valley College the next weekend. We drove up early in my mint green Cadillac and the roadies followed later with the equipment. The concert was packed full to capacity. The opening band was a group of different musicians led by drummer, John French, and a few other former *Captain Beefheart* members. They opened the show with a good strong set and I wondered how we would go over without Larry. The crowd roared as we went on and we gave one of our best performances yet as a trio, with Jeff and me both trading off on guitar and bass. Jeff was especially magnificent that night on bass and slide guitar, he totally captivated the audience. I sang my butt off that night like it was my last time live on stage; we ended with a twenty minute encore song and left the stage with a standing ovation.

I went around to the dressing room to get Josie and she said she wanted to stay at her parents' house for a few days. I said okay and left. I phoned her a few days later and she told me that she didn't want to come back yet. I later found out from friends, and her mother, that she had spent the night with her old boyfriend, Doug Moon, a former *Captain Beefheart* guitar player. She finally came home after a few weeks and I was so angry when she told me about her affair that I slapped her and threw her across the room to the couch. I tried a few times to patch it up but every attempt was more futile than the last. It was a blow to my ego, and I felt the rage of jealousy flowing through my veins. Her seeing girls flirting with me at concerts might have had something to do with her infidelity even though I had never been unfaithful to her. I came home from a gig one night to find her and Tim gone, she had moved to her sister's house in Newhall.

I went on with my career in the band and tried to accept my life without Josie and Tim. A few months went by and one Monday morning about eight am, in August of 1972, I awoke to a knock at the door, it was the Marshal serving me with divorce papers.

The band had been communicating with our old friend, Jeff Parker, who had now moved to Hawaii. He told us that we should come over and check out Maui, as he had purchased some acreage and it was really the "Land of MU". We were all intrigued about rumors of strange ruins near the ocean, not too far from his land. We decided to take a few weeks off and we flew over to check things out, I was so inspired on this visit, that I wrote a song called, *On Our Way To Hana*. Hana is a little town that lies forty-five miles out in the jungle from the airport on Maui, and the two largest towns Kahului and Wailuku. The drive to Hana is one of the most beautiful in the world, with one cascading waterfall after another on the right side and a panoramic view of the blue Pacific to the left. I wrote the song in the small village of Huelo on the road to Hana, Maui was truly paradise in 1972!

We returned to California and continued to play our gigs as a trio and save our money for the move to Maui. The thought of moving to an island in the Pacific gave me something positive to focus on and I began to study about the lost land of Mu even more. I felt a sense of destiny and as my father and his father before him did, I too was moving west.

We recorded a new song that I had written titled, *One More Day*, an up-tempo rocker complete with Jeff Cotton's searing slide guitar. Everyone agreed that this was the commercial hit that *MU* needed to put them on the charts. Audrey Franklyn and well known radio promoter, Barney Fields, signed on to promote the single. *One More Day*, backed with *You've been Here Before*, was released November 1st, 1972. The record landed on several charts across the country and a trickle of sales started coming in.

Near the end of the year we got a spot on the most popular TV music show in L.A. at the time called "Boss City" and was hosted by D.J. "Real Don Steele", *MU* was a big hit on the show. *MU* then recorded *On Our Way To Hana* in February 1973 and it would be set for release in the next three months as a follow up to *One More Day*. It looked like 1973 was coming in on a positive note. At the beginning of the year we did a great interview with our old friend, Lew Irwin, at Earth News Radio, he had a show that broadcast all over the U.S.A. and parts of Europe. We also did a memorable concert at El Camino College in Torrance, with Country Joe McDonald, that was MU's last concert in California.

Jeff Parker rented us a house in Haiku, on Maui. He flew over to California to help organize our move and to help us decide what we should take with us, or what to get rid of. Parker said that he would help finance our move, and in return we would help build his cabin and put in a water system and tank on his land. Parker would take over playing bass in the band, making us a four man group again.

There were a lot of last minute details to take care of. I sold my mint green Caddy, the equipment truck and two of the extra acoustic amps that we had. I was sending copies of our single and album to radio stations and stores in Hawaii, along with a stock of records to

Parker's P.O. box. It was going to cost five hundred dollars just to send our amplifiers and P.A. system to Maui. We made a late night run to the cargo company at LAX the night before we left and everything was crated up and on its way. We said goodbye to our house took our guitars and suitcases and headed to the airport, with a parade of fans and friends following us.

We arrived at LAX, checked in our baggage, said goodbye to our friends, and some weeping groupies, and away we flew into the friendly skies to Maui.

CHAPTER 10
All good Hippies go to Maui

It was February 28, 1973. We landed on Maui and the most wonderful feeling swept over me as I stepped off the airplane, I really felt like I was home! Jeff Parker's girlfriend, Kathy, was there with a truck to pick us all up. Our instruments would arrive in the next few days on a cargo plane. Parker took us to the house that he had rented for us and we picked our rooms and settled in.

Parker had his cabin on the edge of the rain forest in a somewhat half completed stage, but there was no door or closed in walls. He said he liked it that way, but Kathy didn't. He was a real dyed in the wool hippie type, eating all the right organic foods and smoking the best Maui Wowie, but he panicked if he didn't have at least ten thousand buried in a jar somewhere on his land. He could also get very angry at Kathy, or any of us, if he didn't get his way. Right off, I saw that this might not work out with Parker joining the band. We had to teach him all of the bass parts to our songs and this was going to take several months.

Parker had a schedule planned for us to work on his land every morning till after noon when the tropical sun got too hot and then clean up and go back to our house and rehearse. It seemed like we were all in Parkers chain gang following his orders. He wanted us to keep to ourselves, be careful of who we talked to, and don't get involved with any chicks. The mornings on Maui were beautiful waking up to the smell of Plumerias and Gardenias in the air, birds chirping and that wonderful clear blue sky and ocean. It was a dream come true except for living under Jeff Parkers dictatorship. My mom and Sister Linda and my young son Tim flew over to Maui for a ten day visit. It was good to see Tim and he got right into the swing of things and was soon running around naked in the jungle diving off of waterfalls with the rest of the Hippies in rainbow land. One afternoon *MU* was rehearsing in our house and our roadie Spider came over with some real strong Maui Wowie he had grown and my mom decided to try some. After a few tokes she said, "I don't get it, this stuff doesn't do anything". So Spider rolled another one and told her to smoke it, pretty soon she was outside playing ball with Tim laughing her head off at anything and everything! She still swore she didn't feel a thing. Everybody was impressed by my sister and nicknamed her, "Merrell's movie star sister". It was a good visit and they flew back to the mainland full of the Aloha spirit.

After about two months the money we had saved in California ran out, I wanted to go out and get a gig somewhere, but Parker said he wasn't ready. There weren't really a lot of places to play on Maui at that time. There were only a couple clubs and the hotels had mostly Hawaiian music. We decided to finance our own concert at the new Lahaina auditorium.

The band *Crazy Horse*, without Neil Young, was the first band to play there. We booked the auditorium for June and started a promotion campaign; we had big posters printed up in L.A. with the help of promoter Audrey Franklyn. We had a Maui artist do special artwork for the poster with a saucer flying over the crater with a full moon; we billed the show as a full moon concert.

We got the only rock band on the island at the time, *The Space Patrol*, to open up for us. The bands lead singer was Leslie Potts who had appeared in the movie "Rainbow Bridge" a few years earlier with Jimi Hendrix. Leslie was in a scene where some hashish had been smuggled to the island in a surf board, Leslie was seen ripping open the surf board and taking a healthy toke and coughing his lungs out! Jeff parker had previously put up $5000 to help with our move and rent, and we were now dipping into it for the concert promotion. There was really no record kept of how much money was being spent, Parker would just pull out one hundred dollar bills from his wallet when it was needed. A lot of promotion and preparation was going into the concert; we had radio ads set to run three weeks in advance on Oahu and Maui.

Our single *One More Day* was on the local radio charts and there was quite a buzz in the islands about this new band from California called *MU*. As we got near the concert deadline of June 15, 1973, Jeff Parker got more nervous. He said we needed more radio ads and more newspaper ads, and out of his wallet came more one hundred dollar bills. I told him this was not needed as we had articles in both Oahu and Maui newspapers, but he wouldn't listen. When I inquired as to how much we had spent he just said, "A Lot".

We had special stage lights flown in from Honolulu, as there were none available on Maui. We had to rent a truck to get the equipment across the island to Lahaina. Our friends Spider and Richard had immediately volunteered to be our roadies for all our gigs on Maui. Everyone was full of beautiful love and light and they did indeed seem like our people, the children of the rainbow. One couple in particular had an abundance of love and knowledge of living off the land; their names were Matt and Carmen. They were more than willing to help any searching hippie find a home in the jungle and teach them how to grow food and make use of things that most people in city's would throw away. They knew a lot about the old Hawaiian ways and the names of different plants and their medicinal values. Matt was a blonde wiry medium built guy who spent a lot of time exploring the jungle. We spent many hours talking about the ruins he found in the jungle and lost civilizations, we became very good friends.

His wife Carmen was a very beautiful and gracious lady of Yaqui Indian decent, and was skilled in many things including stone work. She helped many a young hippie girl learn how to live off of the land in the jungles of Maui. Most of the people living in this area were either originally from California or Oregon. I found that we all had very similar beliefs, and many looked as though they could be blood brothers and sisters. It was almost as if you knew them before and they knew you.

Everyone was doing what ever they could to make sure MU's first concert on Maui was a success. Finally the big day of the concert in Lahaina arrived, Saturday June 15, 1973. We arrived in Lahaina in the afternoon and went to the auditorium to oversee the setting up of the equipment and lights. We did a short sound check and went to a house on the beach that had been arranged previously where we had dinner, got ready and returned to the auditorium to find the parking lot full and the place was packed! There were over 2000 people inside, at that time it was probably one of the biggest rock concerts ever on Maui! *The Space Patrol* band opened the concert with an amusing intro; they carried their lead singer Leslie Potts on stage in a coffin. *The Space Patrol's* set went over very well with the enthusiastic crowd.

Jeff Cotton ambled on stage with his bass clarinet tantalizing the audience with some wild sounds. Then the rest of *MU* joined in on stage for two hours with some of the most exciting music the island had ever heard, tribal jazz rock at its best! At one point I asked everyone to reach up and feel the energy and all hands were in the air as we finished the concert with our song *End Of An Era*. The concert was a big success and we cleared over three thousand dollars after expenses, which was pretty good for our first self produced concert on Maui in 1973. We went back to our house in Haiku on the edge of the rainforest feeling pretty good that night with the concert behind us and a stash of cash to keep us going.

It was time to get back to work helping Jeff Parker get his jungle retreat together. There was a lot of work to do, building walls in his house, building a green house and most important putting in a water system. It was my job to help design the trestle that would hold the three thousand gallon water tank, we had it finished in about three weeks with the water tank in place. Parker had ordered a special ram water pump, a perpetual motion pump, that once started, it would keep going as long as it had water pressure going into it from the stream. It had a spring and chamber design that was very innovative. A special concrete sluice box was built and installed in the stream with a filter system to feed the water into the pump. We were all amazed when we started the pump and watched it push the water up the hill to the tank a good hundred feet. Parkers land had two small valleys, one with a beautiful stream running through it with little waterfalls flowing down the valley. The idea at first was to have us build two more small cabins in the valley on the other side of Parkers cabin and a recording studio. Parker introduced us to the process of growing Maui Wowie, the strong psychedelic herb.

We planted one hundred and fifty Plants in very large holes with plenty of fertilizer that we hauled down by hand in the dense jungle to the spot just off Parkers land he had carved out with a chain saw.

I thought at the time it was a little too large and could easily be seen by air. We had a special watering hose that was hidden in the lush foliage that went from his water tank to the patch and could be pulled back up across his property line after watering. It was quite a job that took a month to set up and get planted with the special *indica* seeds.

Our days were usually spent working on Parkers land from early till afternoon, then a quick swim in a nearby pool, have lunch and go to our house in Haiku to rehearse. Parker's only form of electricity was a gas generator he would only start up to run power tools. He used kerosene lanterns for light and propane for his stove and refrigerator. Musically the band was sounding very good, Parker wasn't as good on bass as Larry Willey, but he did a good job after months of Jeff Cotton teaching him runs to our rather unorthodox music.

I was finally getting over my divorce but still missing my son Tim, the hard work and tropical island life eased the pain. It was hard to believe I had spent over five years playing in L.A., I was glad to be away from the noise and pollution in the city. I started spending a lot of time exploring the jungle and asking the older Hawaiian locals what they knew of the pre Hawaiian culture and who had built some of the ruins and water tributaries that could still be found in the forest. Most replied with a smile, "It was the Menehune's, the little people". No one could actually say where the Menehune's came from, almost like it was a secret, could they be the ancestors of the people of the Lost Continent of Mu I wondered?

Then I found several Hawaiian books about the lost tribe of Mu, and one in particular that was very interesting titled, *Children Of The Rainbow*. The book was written by an old Hawaiian and contained information that was passed down from family to family by a Kahuna and described in detail the religion, legends and gods of pre Christian Hawaii, the teachings of the people of MU. The deeper I probed the more the myth seemed to be real. I spent many days and hours exploring ruins and digging into the layers of earth surrounding various sites

There was a place not far from Parker's land near the ocean in an overgrown valley where three tall pillars stood on a terrace of finely cut stones that resembled Mayan Indian ruins.

There was a fourth pillar that had broken off and was lying in a pile and partially under water in a pool with a small waterfall flowing over it, this was right out of a scene from an Indiana Jones movie that hadn't been produced yet. I managed to crawl under the hau bush on what appeared to be an ancient stone sidewalk that led from the pillars down to the ocean and ended abruptly underwater with a hill of lava on it. Could this be a lost temple of MU? I spent many hours meditating there which was hard to do with hordes of giant mosquitoes biting you. I did manage to take some pictures of the pillars that were approximately twenty five feet tall arranged in a half circle. The pillars seemed to be made of interlocking hex shaped rods of stone with no mortar or cement holding them together. They were so perfect that they appeared to have been milled or machined to a fine degree of exactness. Nothing like old Hawaiian structures that were clearly just lava rock boulders piled up with logs and a thatch roof.

Meanwhile we were still farming with Parker or El Jefe as he liked to be called. He would get upset easily if we didn't arrive early every morning precisely on time for work on his land. He was the same with his girlfriend Kathy, always making sure she was kept busy. She was a beautiful soul very attractive with blond hair and always ready to help with any task. She took care of all of the guys in the band as brothers, making great vegetarian dinners and fantastic mango and berry pies. Kathy would always do more than her share and worked very hard and had an abundance of knowledge in ways of living off the land.

We planted a large crop of papayas and bananas and started construction on an orchid nursery that Parker hoped would bring in more money for his little empire. The pot crop was going to be sold when ready and help support the band and build the other cabins and a recording studio. It seemed like a long shot to me but Parker said that the pot crop could bring in around one hundred thousand dollars and plenty of the sweet Maui Wowie to smoke when harvested. It would take almost six months to mature for harvest, it seemed like a long time but as they were watered and fed they reached an incredible height of twenty feet!

Tension started to grow between the band and Parker as the wait for the harvest continued. The music at this time seemed to be taking a back seat to our duties working on Parker's farm. Jeff Cotton and I were concerned about this as we had two gigs coming up to play. The first one was a big party at a large octagon shaped house in the jungle called "Wood Rose" where *Crosby Stills and Nash* would sometimes party with the owners Jim and Jenny Dow. We were on our way to the party and as we rounded a curve on the country road we saw a beautiful girl with long brown hair holding a violin. I opened the door to the van and said, "Going to Wood Rose"? She said yes and got in, it seemed very natural and almost pre destined, we were immediately attracted to each other. We asked her to join us on our acoustic set, it was amazing how she played so perfectly, almost like she already knew our original songs without ever hearing them before! The entire party of one hundred people fell in love that day; it was an incredible high that I will never forget. Mary Fiddle as she was known and I exchanged phone numbers as we left the party. She explained she was visiting from Northern California and was staying with a friend named Erna Woo who lived near us in Haiku. We had an offer to play a wedding for some friends we had met through Matt and Carmen, it was in an old plantation house in Haiku, a joyous gathering of brothers and sisters. There we met Jim Murray who was once a member of the '60s psychedelic band *Quicksilver Messenger Service*. Murray was now retired on Maui and scarcely played; we did encourage him to come on stage for a rousing jam. We also met Barry Mayo who was a recording engineer on "Quicksilver's" *Just For Love* album recorded a few years earlier on the island of Oahu. We also met ex members of Ken Keasey's merry pranksters and some popular Gurus along with an assortment of dope growers and outlaws.

That evening really brought the Maui family together and everyone present was sure the band *MU* was going to be as big as *The Beatles*! It all seemed like a beautiful dream where everyone had known each other in another life and we were all destined to help each other. By now both of our singles, *One More Day* and *On Our Way To Hana* were on the Hawaiian radio charts, at that time you could say we were the most popular band on the island of Maui.

Barry Mayo made us an offer to record some of our new songs with a four track tape recorder and some microphones and a mixer he had used on the last Quicksilver project.

We definitely had some of L.A.'s harshness washed off of us by the tranquility and beauty of Maui, and our new songs were taking on a new air of space age folk rock with an indefinable ancient quality. There was a feeling of mystical enchantment about everything we were doing at this time, and the music was coming out of me like the water in the jungle streams flowing down the face of Haleakala crater and into the ocean. I felt I was truly part of the nature spirit of the forest, swimming in the streams, diving off of waterfalls and swinging in the trees like Tarzan. It was like re living your childhood and truly finding yourself at the same time. Everyone needed to experience this I thought, living your entire life in cities was so unnatural. Every being on the planet needs to stay in tune with nature to keep this special gem in the universe alive, I felt this was my goal to share this message with everyone through music. Everyone has a different dharma or path to get to this point, and I thanked all the gods' everyday for helping me to finally arrive. I was achieving a sense of peace that I hadn't felt since I was a boy playing in the woods in Kentucky.

We received a letter from our old producer Phil Meldman back in California that United Artist Records in London was interested in releasing our first album in Europe. We were very happy about this as we previously had interest from promoters there to play in Britain.

British disc jockey John Peel had been playing our U.S. album on the radio in England.

This was good news indeed to me, Jeff Cotton and Randy Wimer, but Jeff Parker was putting out negative vibes regarding the deal with United Artist and Meldman. Parker felt that giving Meldman fifty percent of the album was unfair. This just seemed to create more tension in the group, Randy, Jeff Cotton and I decided it was a done deal and we were glad to have a major record label releasing the album. We tried to tell Parker we will do better on the next deal with the songs engineer Barry Mayo was going to help us record. This seemed to satisfy Parker for the time being, but he said, "We won't make that mistake again as long as he was in the band!" Meanwhile Audrey Franklyn was promoting our records in L.A. to the press and radio, this was also a sore spot with Parker as Audrey had exhausted our mainland bank account of two thousand dollars. Money did go a lot further in 1973 but we would tell Parker it can only be stretched so far, and she was keeping our name alive on the mainland.

One day while we were practicing in the house in Haiku an old army truck with a *MU* symbol pulled up in the driveway. It was a fan of the band named Gary from Hana who had been sent there by Red Shepard who was one of the Broadway stars of the musical "Hair'. Red wanted us to do a concert in Hana that would include other artists and bands. It seemed like a good offer and we made the forty five mile drive through the jungle to Red's house for a meeting. We arrived around noon and had an interesting time talking to Red Shepard, he was full of ideas and exuberance. He explained the lay out of the concert and showed us the hill he was having a large teak wood stage built on. It had a view of a forty foot waterfall, and the ocean in the background.

It was equally as good as the back drop for the movie South Pacific. Ramblin Jack Elliot, a folk musician in the style of Bob Dylan, would open the show, followed by Bonnie Bramlett and her band, David Carradine, who had the hit TV series *Kung Fu* at the time, and *MU* would headline. The entire concert would be filmed with two 35 millimeter movie cameras and sound mixer. He was planning to release it as a film titled *Maui 74* with a soundtrack album. He said contracts would be drawn up and sent to everyone in the next few weeks. The concert was set for the week end after Christmas, quite an exciting event we thought!

The weeks passed by and Red Shepard came to our house to confirm the concert was set and it was just taking a bit longer to get the contracts from his attorney on the mainland.. He said everything was in order and all the percentages and rights would clearly be outlined in the contract. Parker was again suspicious and he and Red Shepard didn't seem to get along to well either. I said all we can do is just wait and see what happens and how the contract reads.

Our crop of Maui Wowie we had planted was getting close to harvest and we cut a small sample and it was very good, sweet and power full with a juicy fruit taste. Parkers land bordered a Portuguese rancher and one day some cows got through a hole in the fence and went into the valley where the pot garden was. The rancher discovered the pot while rounding up the cows and called the police. Parker found himself in custody and all our beautiful Maui Wowie was cut down and hauled away in trucks. The narcotics officers stopped in Paia for lunch and bought Parker a salad before booking him in jail. Parker called a prominent attorney by the name of Brooke Hart who had gotten many a hippie out of a similar jam, by afternoon Parker was out on bail and stopped by the band house in Haiku very angry. I said, "Well I guess it just wasn't meant to be", this made him all the angrier. His lawyer made a good case in court that there was really no proof that Parker planted the pot and it wasn't on his property. Parker got off and released with nothing on his record, but we never heard the end of his complaining about the $2,500 he had to pay the lawyer.

The day of the big Hana concert was almost on us and still no contract. Red Shepeard's Messenger Gary showed up and assured us everything was on and the contracts would be there at the concert. He gave us some money to help rent the truck needed for our equipment and PA system. Our roadies Spider and Richard went in town to pick up the truck, and we got everything packed up and ready to go. The timing of the trip to Hana came at a bad time as we were in the middle of a gas shortage and fuel was scarce. As we traveled the long and winding road to Hana there were hippies everywhere abandoning their cars that had run out of gas on the way to the concert. Jeff and I remarked at how many bearded long haired hippies wearing robes we saw, looked like Jesus. We arrived and just as we finished setting up the equipment David Carradine and his wife actress Barbara Hershey came up the driveway, we struck up a conversation and a number of us were invited to his cabin. David and I took turns playing our latest original songs on acoustic guitar, a pre concert warm up. I did *On Our Way To Hana* and David ended the session with his *A great Big Cosmic Joke.* David was at the height of his popularity at the time with his TV show Kung Fu and was looked at as somewhat of a Guru by many.

Everyone was waiting for Ramblin' Jack Elliot to arrive to open the show, he was now about twenty minutes late. A car had been left at the little Hana airport with instructions for him to drive to the concert only three miles away on the Hana highway. Little did we know that Ramblin' Jack had hit the bottle on the flight out to the jungle strip and he veered of the road and hit a power pole that coincided with a fast approaching storm. All the power at the concert suddenly went out. Ramblin' Jack came staggering up the driveway with a little cut on his forehead and was taken to a cabin to get ready for the show. The storm approached with a fury and all the equipment was hauled inside the large living room and re set up. There was now close to four hundred people and they couldn't all possibly fit inside. There was a covered lanai just outside the large doors from the living room. Red Shepard had his carpenters quickly construct a makeshift plastic wall to accommodate the crowd. There were still many people stranded on the Hana highway trying to get to the concert taking cover from the storm in the jungle under trees and tents. It was now raining pretty good and a portable generator was set up to power everything. All the performers started doing acoustic sets to an enthusiastic audience. Ramblin' Jack had passed out and didn't open the show as planned. Near sunset the electricity came back on and *MU* took the stage with a scorching electric set that really got the crowd going, miraculously the rain stopped and the clouds receded to a gloriously beautiful tropical sunset. Red Shepard was carried away with the enthusiasm of the crowd and encouraged everyone to tear down the plastic walls that surrounded the lanai that he had so painstakingly had the carpenters erect. We ended our last song with an OM chant , the crowd kept the OM chant going for twenty minutes with everyone looking out to sea, as if a space ship were going to come down and pick us all up! It was quite a sight to behold. Red Shepard exclaimed "This was a success no matter what else followed".

That night I had a few drinks with Bonnie Bramlett and we talked about what a happening this was and how she would love to live on Maui and write beautiful songs. Then David Carradine and his wife Barbara magically appeared playing flutes serenading the back stage party, it was really a scene out of a '60s movie. We left and drove back home to spend the night and planned to return the next day to do the second part of the show. We were all hoping the weather would co operate and the camera crew could get the filming done. Our roadies Spider and Richard stayed behind to watch the equipment.

We returned the next day that was a perfect sunny Maui day. Bonnie Bramlett and her band opened with some gutsy blues but it just didn't fit the surroundings and the crowd wasn't very into it. David Carradine followed with his band that featured his wife Barbara on flute. Dewey Martin of Buffalo Springfield was supposed to be playing drums but he had fallen down and broke his arm so Randy Wimer took his place in David's set.

David's set was a little erratic and he improvised a lot, and might have been a little to high and ended up getting sick on stage and had to quit. *MU* took the stage with a two hour set of supercharged space rock that took the audience to a euphoric state that was helped by the sweet smell of Maui Wowie in the air. It was the high point of the two day event and at one point I felt as though the entire band was levitating. It was all filmed with the best 35 millimeter movie cameras and professional sound. It was getting near dusk and Ramblin' Jack Elliot went on to close the show as everything was winding down. He was quite high on various substances and didn't realize he forgot to put his pants on when he left the dressing room. There he was standing on stage with a cowboy hat and an aloha shirt, naked from the waist down! I told one of the stage hands I hoped he didn't lean into the mic, I got a good shock earlier from that same microphone. Ramblin' Jack got the audience's attention and they too decide to take their clothes off, soon there were a lot of stoned hippies wandering around naked. In all the excitement we forgot about the contracts, Red Shepard said he would mail them to us. He had quite a large clean up on the grounds to deal with after this two day mini love in. On the way home we wondered if we would ever see a contract, we decided it was a good experience no matter what came of it.

We eventually received the contract a few weeks later, on first reading it didn't look to good as we were only going to receive two percent of the movie and proposed soundtrack album after expenses. We also had to sign away our rights to the publishing on our original songs, our attorney advised us not to sign the contract. The rest of the performers did the the same. Red Shepard tried to convince us to sign, but we told him only if the percentage was raised and we kept our publishing rights. He said Megus Films in Hollywood who had the footage wouldn't start editing the film till all contracts were signed. Our promoter Audrey Franklyn saw the film at a private screening in Hollywood and said unedited footage was stunningly excellent! We never got to see the film and it disappeared along with Red Shepard.

After resting up for a few days we decided it was a good time to take a break and go explore Haleakala Crater . We went up to the crater one afternoon to the ranger's station to get permits and make reservations for two cabins. The trip would take two days to walk across the crater floor and out the Kaupo gap. We decided to drive up to the rim of the crater and take in the sunset, it was almost dusk when we got to the top of crater, all four band members and Parkers girlfriend Kathy were there. We rolled a big joint and gazed into the clear sky and watched the sun sink and the moon come up. As it got dark the display of stars was incredible at ten thousand feet, it was like being suspended in the universe looking up from the top of Haleakala crater. All of a sudden a streak of light came from out of nowhere and seemed to be suspended over the crater floor. Then two more pulsating lights joined from opposite sides forming a triangle. This went on for several minutes and then they came together and shot straight up and disappeared as fast as they appeared. There was also a group of tourists watching this display of lights and none of us could figure out what they were. We knew they were not helicopters as there was no sound.

As we left I was reminded of the story one of the film crew of the Jimi Hendrix movie *Rainbow Bridge* had told about encountering a hovering disc in broad daylight on the floor of the crater. It was said that Hendrix walked out in to the lava field and said, "Welcome space brothers". Unfortunately they couldn't get a camera set up in time to film the incident. Some people even believed there was a hidden saucer base in one of the lava tubes below the crater floor, as UFO's had been seen coming and going from the floor of the crater and even diving into the ocean throughout history. The ancient Hawaiians even had a name for them, "The flying pearly shells". Journalist and UFO researcher Steve Omar wrote many stories in the local Maui newspaper about these sightings. I was inspired to write the song *Calling From A Star* after our crater sighting and *MU* would later record a slow version of the song.

We got packed up for our crater expedition the next day and Jeff Parker decided not to go, it would just be me, Jeff Cotton, Randy and Parkers girlfriend Kathy. Jeff Parker would take us to the top of the crater where we would walk in and pick us up two days later on the other side of the island at the bottom of the Kaupo gap. We started down the sliding sands trail walking on crushed cinder that made you feel like you were on the moon, it was in this area that a scene from the movie *Rainbow Bridge* was filmed with two dancers doing *Tai Chi*. As we progressed down the trail it looked as though we were entering an animated landscape with cinder cones of pink, green and blue perfectly positioned on a floor of black and gray cinder. It was then I noticed my compass was spinning wildly with no north, south, east or west in the prehistoric valley known as "Haleakala" the house of the sun. It was very inspiring and I was hoping we would see a UFO. We did take a trek through a lava tube before reaching Holua cabin where we would spend the night.

The clear night sky in the crater was incredible, looking up really gave you the feeling that you were out in space among the stars.

The next morning we got up early at Holua cabin and had breakfast, I was looking out at the vast expanse of the dried lava flow when I spotted what appeared to be a pyramid sticking out on the horizon. It could only be seen when the sun was at a perfect angle, if it was to low it would be lost in the shadow of the rim of the crater. I decided to hike over to it by myself and get a closer look, the distance was deceiving and it turned out to be much further than I thought. I had to jump large chasms and navigate hills with razor sharp rocks. When I finally got to it I was amazed at the sight of a perfect pyramid that stood about thirty eight feet tall with smooth polished sides. I got the feeling that it was just the top of a large structure that continued down under the lava. I climbed up on the side of it and began to feel dizzy and tingly so I got down and started walking back to the cabin. I came back a few years later and took a picture of it that got in the local newspaper. Apparently nobody had ever noticed it before, and I suggested it might be a remnant of The Lost Continent of MU.

I was so tired I could barely make it to the next cabin. By the end of the second day we were all groaning with exhaustion as we walked out the Kaupo gap with our legs feeling like jelly. It's not an easy hike for even an experienced hiker, we were all glad to see Jeff Parker waiting for us in his Land Rover. It took a few days to rest up from this latest Maui adventure. The crater trip was a good way to end our first year on Maui, and I wondered what other adventures await us in the future.

CHAPTER 11
The Rise and Fall of MU

It was now 1974 and our next project was to start recording the new *MU* songs with engineer Barry Mayo. We had easily two albums of new songs written by now and we were busy going through the songs to decide which ones should be recorded first..

One night as we were finishing dinner there was a knock on the door and there stood a very beautiful Chinese Hawaiian girl named Erna Woo and Mary Lee Fiddle with a big plate of cookies. Come in we said to these two beauties bearing gifts. I asked if Mary had brought her fiddle and she said yes. After tea and cookies we started playing and singing for what seemed like hours as if all time had stopped. Jeff and Erna naturally gravitated to each other and went off to Jeff's room. Mary and I sat in the living room talking about music, life on other planets and my quest for the Lost Continent of MU. Around dawn the girls left and Randy got up and was ready for rehearsal.

Barry Mayo arrived with all his recording equipment and began turning the house into a recording studio. The house had a large enclosed porch that led into the living room complete with a window between the two rooms that made an instant control room. Barry made a drum booth out of our anvil instrument cases and blankets in the corner of the living room to isolate the drums from the rest of the instruments, my bedroom would be used as the vocal and acoustic guitar booth. Since we only had four tracks most of the recording would be done live except for certain songs we saved a track for background vocals, horn parts or extra percussion. Erna and Mary were visiting more frequent now and it was obvious that Jeff and Erna were becoming an item. Jeff Parker didn't like this and he told Jeff Cotton he didn't want them around when we were recording. Both Erna and Mary were very self assured and head strong and this bothered Parker. Around this same time Kathy introduced Randy Wimer to her girlfriend Cindy, another cute blond hippie girl with a glowing smile. Parker said Cindy needed a place to stay and she would be a good person to run the house and cook and clean. Cindy was a great vegetarian cook and hard worker and helped sew and keep our clothing together. Cindy soon moved in to Randy's room, and they looked like the perfect pair. Randy had Cindy make us pies and tropical smoothies from all the indigenous fruits including wild mountain berries. We became quite a family and Jeff Parker and Kathy would even stay over some nights after rehearsal for fantastic vegetarian feasts.

For awhile we got on a homemade ice cream trip, and we tried several different flavor recipes from a book called Ten Talents Cook Book. One night two of our friends, a couple named Greg and Masako came over with some fresh coconuts and we decided to make a new flavor of ice cream, "Coconut Carob" with cashew milk, honey and an ingredient called slippery elm. We all took our turn churning this mixture in the ice cream maker till we decided it was done. We began to dish it out and noticed it had an odd kind of gray color, I thought, "Wow I have never seen gray ice cream before"? It was very rich and we all had these giant bowls of this stuff and proceeded to gobble it down. Greg and Randy even went back for seconds, I couldn't finish mine and I sat my bowl in the sink. Later when Greg and Masako had left and we were cleaning up I noticed my bowl of ice cream hadn't melted in over two hours! I said, "Look guys this stuff doesn't melt, maybe we've invented a new kind of ice cream!" We all laughed and went to bed for a good nights rest as Barry Mayo was coming over in the morning to install more recording equipment.

Around 2:00am I woke up to the sound of people vomiting in the backyard. I thought, "Yeah I don't feel too good either". I went out the back door and found Jeff Cotton leaning over the fence and Randy holding on to a tree and I joined them in a good puking session. We all looked very green in the Maui moonlight, after it was all over I said, "It must have been that non melting ice cream", we started roaring with laughter. That stopped our experimenting with homemade ice cream flavors for a long time.

The next morning engineer Barry Mayo was there bright and early and a friend Eric Brown came by with more microphones. All the recording equipment and mixers were hooked up and an oscilloscope was brought in to check everything out. Barry really did a professional job of building a four track studio on an island with limited equipment, at that time there wasn't a studio on the island. The first day of recording went very well and by six in the evening we had three songs down, *Children Of The Rainbow, Calling From A Star* and *Haleakala*. We were amazed at the quality of sound Barry got on the modest reel to reel four track tape recorder with no reverb or compressors. We all had a hard time sleeping that night with the anticipation of the next day's recording session.

Erna and Mary came over in the morning of the second day of recording and listened to the music we recorded with great enthusiasm, and both offered to play or sing background on any of the songs. Parker arrived and Erna and Mary left, it was obvious there were bad vibes between them. Erna and Mary didn't hit it off with Cindy at first either, Cindy didn't like anyone entering her domain in the house of *MU* and especially her kitchen. We resumed recording and did *Blue Jay Blue* and *Who Will Write This Song*. We had a problem with the mixer and background vocal microphone, so we shut down for a few days for repair. Barry scouted around and found another musician to borrow a few more microphones from. Jeff Cotton and I were both getting a little annoyed with Parker at this point with his lecturing us that we shouldn't have girlfriends. He had a girlfriend and now Randy had one. It seemed Parker was obsessed with his control over everything about the band. Jeff Cotton and I were starting to think of mutiny, but Randy didn't go along with us as he had a good setup with

Cindy and her vegetarian dinners and delights.

Me, Jeff Cotton and Randy decided to take a few days off and explore the jungle towards Hana and look for magic mushrooms. We were off bright and early the next morning on the road to Hana., and it felt good to have some breathing space from all the energy in the house. We looked all day and couldn't find any mushrooms, a friend we met who lived in Nahiku said there were plenty psychedelic mushrooms at the cross in Hana, so off we went! As soon as we pulled up on the top of the hill overlooking the bay and little town of Hana, we could see the mushrooms, they were everywhere. A big cross had been erected years ago by the wife of a minister in honor of her husband because he loved the place so much. After I had eaten a few "Sacred Mushrooms", I thought I knew why the minister loved this place. Jeff Cotton and I ran laughing and stumbling through the fields collecting and eating mushrooms, we must have each eaten close to sixty, we didn't know at the time that this could be a near lethal dose. In my euphoria I decided I had found the key to the universe, and I quickly grabbed bags and bottles to put them in to share with others who might also want to have the key to the universe. Soon we found ourselves in another dimension unable to speak and having difficulty walking. We made it back to our truck where we collapsed near Randy who had been crying after only eating around fifteen mushrooms.

I felt myself melting into the earth and becoming one with the island, I could feel the waves lapping at all my shores and the trade winds blowing through my trees and the streams and waterfalls flowing down my face and in to the ocean. I was truly one with nature and the planet and now I was leaving my body. I felt as though I had turned in to an electric vapor and I could perceive things never before imaginable. There were no great secrets, everything was perfect and I could communicate with Jeff and Randy without any speech. We had all let go of our earthly ties and stepped beyond the doors of perception!

We were lying on the ground unable to move for hours as our spirits soared through the cosmos. After some time a group of tourists drove up and noticed these long haired hippies lying in the grass with their eyes glowing and transfixed, Randy was in his underwear and Jeff Cotton and I only had shorts on. We were very sunburned from lying in the intense tropical sun all day. One older gentleman came over to Jeff and tried to talk to him and took his pulse exclaiming, "This ones still alive". He said, "They must be on something". I managed to make myself talk and told him we were meditating and we were alright. My voice sounded like it was in a tunnel and my words echoed on forever. The man looked at me kind of scared, and they all got in their car and drove off. This shocked me out of my trip and I slammed back into my body, I managed to get back to my feet but it was like walking on clouds. I went over to the truck and sat down and drank some water, and began communicating by telepathy to Jeff and Randy and told them we should leave. After a bit we got in the truck and I drove down the hill to the little village of Hana, I was driving but it felt like flying. I did realize that we needed gas and I stopped at a gas station where some tourists and locals were milling around. It seemed like everyone's eyes were on us as I got out of the truck and asked for ten dollars worth of regular. Our eyes were glowing and every object, cars and people looked funny. Jeff Cotton just started cracking up laughing real loud, I was sure everyone knew we were on mushrooms. I went around the truck to get Randy and he was standing there crying about how beautiful some plastic flowers looked in an advertisement. He didn't want to leave them all alone and I convinced him they were alright and that this is where they lived, Randy got in the truck and we left. We decided to spend the night at our friend's cabin in Nahiku as it wouldn't be a good idea to drive the forty five miles of winding road through the jungle back to our house at night.

It was almost sunset as we arrived at the cabin in Nahiku. As we got out of the truck I noticed I could see Jeff Cotton's heart beating rapidly through the skin on his chest. We all had rapid heart beats and felt we might be going to die any minute. Our friend told us there was a small amount of poison in each mushroom and we drank some tea to try to flush it out of our systems. We settled in for the night and tried to get some sleep, the jungle sounds seemed to intensify with the bugs and mosquitoes so did the effects of the magic mushrooms. Jeff Cotton and I were sure we were both going to die and we were once again out of our bodies and looking at the cross on the hill in Hana, only this time the cross was spinning and pulling us to it. I asked Jeff if he was seeing the same thing and he said, yes.

All at once we were both mounted on the cross and looking at each other, I asked Jeff again to tell me what he saw, and we both saw the same thing! Then we both heard a voice asking a question, "Do you want to stay, or do you want to leave"? We both said, "Stay" and we were slammed back in our bodies with aching pain. We were both sick to our stomachs and Randy was just lying on his back moaning.

The next morning I knew we were all damn lucky to be alive, especially Jeff and I as we had eaten so many mushrooms. When we arrived back at our house everything was just as we had left it, but we were totally changed. Nothing would be the same from then on.

Erna and Mary came over and we told them of our experience and they agreed that we were lucky to be alive. Jeff, Randy and I were all having stomach and kidney pain along with aching muscles. Erna made us some miso soup and tea and her and Mary spent the night.

Mary and I were falling in love and it was at that time that I met her two children, Molly who was nine and Phillip who was ten. They were nice kids and a bit head strong like their mom, but I enjoyed having kids around again as I missed my son Tim. All of a sudden we had a full family house and as the recording sessions continued it became a little difficult. Mary decided it was time for her kids to visit their dad in Oregon who she had been divorced from for a few years. Mary was a trained classical violinist from when she was young and then went in to Bluegrass, Country and Rock and Roll. She planned to fly the kids back to their father in Oregon who now had a new wife and child, and return for the next round of recording sessions. Mary and I had some great violin parts worked out for some of mine and Jeff Cotton's songs. All we had to do was convince Parker that this was a good idea.

It was now February of 1974 and the recording sessions at the *MU* house were in full swing. We put the finishing touches on *Blue Jay Blue* and *Who Will Write This Song* and went on to work on *In MU , You're Not The Only One* and *The Love We Bare*. The last three songs had been inspired by the magic mushroom trip. Jeff and Erna were spending more time reading the bible and she was telling him about her Christian Seventh Day Adventist upbringing. Erna also told Jeff she felt the devil was present in the *MU* house and he should leave, Randy started feeling the same way and had decided Jesus had saved us all and we should follow him. I said fine I'm sick of Parkers trip also, lets finish the recording and then split.

I guess I overlooked how serious Jeff and Randy were taking the devil in the house bit and I soon realized that anyone who didn't completely go along with their belief was in cahoots with the devil! Cindy was of the same mind as Randy and this was starting to make a separation among the members of the band. Luckily we got *Waiting For The Sun, End Of An Era, Daybreak Sunshine, The Awakening, Drink From The Fountain* and *Make A Joyful Noise* recorded before to much dissension set in. Mary flew back from Oregon and I was very excited to try her violin on mine and Jeff Cotton's song *You And I.* A session was set up for the next day and part way through the recording Jeff Parker arrived and said it sounded awful. Mary was having a hard time hearing the mix in her headphones, but after a few takes we got a good one. Jeff Cotton and I thought it sounded great and was a nice change to our guitar sound. Parker just sneered. Next we started on my song *The Land Of MU,* that was recorded much faster and came out very good.

During the sessions the following week we recorded *I Saw Your Photograph, It's Love That Sings The Song* and *Showering Rain.* They were all nice mellow songs and Jeff Cotton's songs in particular were all showing signs of his bible studies and orthodox religion. This was very much to the dismay of Jeff Parker who would rather stay in a kick ass Rock and Roll format. Mary and I were now very much in love and were writing arrangements for her violin to all the new songs I was writing. Mary and I sang together on my song *I saw Your Photograph* that was recorded live, the other band members saw how good Mary and I sounded together without them. We were trying to do some overdubs with Erna Woo singing on Jeff Cotton's song *Drink From The Fountain,* this was making Parker furious. Erna had a pitch problem and it was sounding pretty bad, it took Jeff Cotton awhile to admit that it wasn't working. Erna was very beautiful and could dance, play piano and auto harp but she didn't have a professional talent like Mary Lee.

We had planned a big party and jam session for the last day of recording. Cindy and Kathy were busy preparing food and pies and had bought some wine and beer. There was quite a bit of tension in the air as everyone started arriving at the *MU* house in Haiku. We started off with what I would call some jungle space blues with Jim Murray former "Quicksilver" member sitting in on guitar. Everybody was trading guitar licks and parts of it were sounding quite good. Erna and Mary seemed a little upset that they were not included in the jam. Apparently Mary and Cindy started drinking some wine and Mary proceeded to drink everything alcoholic in sight. Cindy reported that Mary was drunk and had driven off with our truck, Randy being the trusting soul that he was had left the keys in the ignition. Jeff Parker and I jumped in his Land Rover and took pursuit up the winding road that leads to the little town of Makawao. As we rounded a turn coming into town we saw the truck in the middle of an old Catholic cemetery. I got out and found Mary staggering around in the tombstones, I asked her, "what do you think you're doing"? She screamed and said, "Get away from me, who are you"? I didn't see how she could be this out of it on beer and wine, a girl on horseback shouted out that the police were on their way. I put Mary over my shoulder and carried her to Parker's Land Rover and told him to drive her home. I got the truck out of the cemetery before the cops arrived and drove home. Parker was flipped over this spectacle and apparently Mary tried to exit his vehicle while they were driving which really made a nervous wreck out of him by the time he got back to the house. The party broke up and Cindy was sure Mary had only drunk alcohol and there were no drugs in the house. I would later find out that alcohol was like poison in Mary's system and she had a problem with it. Everyone went to sleep, and the next morning Mary said she couldn't remember much but she wouldn't do it again. We never heard the tapes of our last jam and Barry put them somewhere but they were never found. Jeff Cotton soon moved out of the house and into a tent beneath Erna Woo's bedroom window and announced they were getting married.

Parker wanted to kidnap Cotton and dose him with acid to bring him back to his senses. Parker was ranting, "How could he do this, he's going to ruin the band!" Hmm I thought this reminds me of what Don Vliet had told me about Jeff Cotton years ago, that he would go off on a tangent and wouldn't stick with anything. The more Parker made a big deal about Cotton getting married the more Cotton would stay away. We were not playing, no plans were being made for recording or touring, I was watching the band *MU* falling apart right before my eyes. After nearly six years of hard work we came up from nowhere to becoming a popular band with an album getting radio play and worldwide sales, and now we were sinking just like the Lost Continent of Lemuria.

Randy and Cindy and I and Mary were still living in the house in Haiku trying to decide what to do. One day when Mary and Cindy were gone Jeff Cotton and Erna came by the house and told me they thought Mary Lee was a disciple of the devil and that I should leave her and the house. I said, "gee don't you think you're going a little to far with this"? She was such a beautiful lady and I thought anyone that can play a violin like that has got to be a good soul. Jeff Cotton tried to convince me she was evil and was leading me down a path of darkness. I later talked to Randy and Cindy and they both had sensed some deception from Mary and didn't trust her. Mary had bought an old Chevy station wagon and would 'take some space' as she called it from the house and go to Lahaina by herself and play music. I found out she would do some heavy drinking and sometimes get in fights on her 'space taking sessions'. The next time she came back from one of these wild weekends in Lahaina I had her things packed and moved out of my room on to the front porch. Mary said, "What is this"? I said, "I didn't think it was working out and we should split up", she started to cry and said she loved me and fell into my arms, and I just melted.

It was just Randy, Cindy, Mary and I in the house now, and we didn't talk much. Days were spent in confusion trying to decide what the next step should be to get all the band members talking again. Randy and I went to talk to Parker and he just started ranting and raving about the five thousand dollars he had put into the band and how he wanted to stop Cotton from marrying this Erna Woo, the Yoko Ono of *MU*! I really didn't think this was fair to Erna or Yoko. We all received wedding invitations from Jeff and Erna, the ceremony was to take place at Wood Rose in front of the big waterfall in the valley.

Parker kept saying, "There's still time, lets get Spider and kidnap Cotton". Randy said, "If its what Jeff Cotton wants, we shouldn't stand in his way". I agreed, Parker was very angry with our attitude and would no longer talk to me and Randy. Randy and I decided we no longer needed the big house and we should find smaller separate places to live. Randy got a job doing gardening at the Wood Rose estate in exchange for a rent free guest cabin on the grounds. Matt and Carmen asked me to come live with them on their rambling jungle commune in Huelo. And we said good bye to the house of *MU* in Haiku.

Matt and Carmen were a little surprised when I showed up at their house with Mary Lee but they accepted her and gave us a nice room on the second story above their living room. It was quite a large house that they had built from left over lumber from construction sites and windows from old plantation camps. It had a nice kitchen, several bedrooms and a large meditation room with a piano. Matt was an expert at building interesting structures out of very little material. There was a big twenty by forty foot building with a sleeping loft on the property with a tree growing through it in back of the main house, that they called "the tree house", it was used as a guest room and art studio. There was also a building on the lower area of the property that was like a garage with a cottage that they called "Car Parts". A big strong mechanic named Bud Lindsay lived there and he kept the vehicles and a tractor in running order. There were lots of papayas and bananas and a vegetable herb garden growing in abundance, watered by the cool tropical rain every night. Mary started giving Matt and Carmen's two lovely daughters Fiama and Saroon violin lessons in the tree house, it was amazing how quickly they caught on to this difficult instrument. We would sit around at night after dinner singing and playing, the sound of three violins and acoustic guitar was very enchanting echoing in the jungle.

One night after hearing Mary and I playing and singing Carmen said, "The two of you are great, you don't need those guys in the band, you could make it on your own". The seed for the duo of "Merrell and Mary" was planted that night, I believed Carmen was right Mary and I were making some of the highest inspirational music I had ever heard, and we sounded like four people. Matt began telling us of his plan to bring some of the Tibetan lamas and Rimpoches to the island for a meditation retreat and he wanted us to be part of the ceremony and play music. We were overjoyed and thought this would be a wonderful high event.

The day of Jeff and Erna's wedding had arrived, Randy had decided he couldn't make a lasting commitment to Cindy and they split up and he flew his old girlfriend Connie Butler over for the wedding. It was a beautiful day for a wedding, the sky was a beautiful blue and all of Erna's Hawaiian family from Oahu was there. Jeff Cotton's dad and mom, Ralph and Marge Cotton had flown in from California. Jeff and Erna had asked me to play my song *The Source* with Mary on violin at the ceremony in front of the waterfall. It was just gorgeous beyond explanation as I played my acoustic guitar and the caravan of guests walked down the path into the valley to the waterfall. Large bundles of flowers were being dropped over the waterfall and were floating in a rainbow of colors in the pool below. It was as spectacular as any scene from the movie *South Pacific*. After the ceremony a large reception was held on the grounds of Wood Rose and Jeff Cotton, Randy, Mary and I played a few mellow songs. I played a Rock and Roll song on the end and Jeff Cotton seemed a little irritated and quit. That was the last time Myself, Jeff Cotton and Randy Wimer played together. I glanced up to the top of the hill overlooking the valley and off in the distance I could see Jeff Parker sitting in his Land Rover watching the scene below.

One of our fans at the ceremony told us that there were rumors that something was wrong and that *MU* may be breaking up. I was asked why Jeff Parker hadn't shown up for Jeff Cotton's wedding? Did that mean Parker was no longer in the band? Parker definitely made a statement by not showing up and Cotton took it to heart. A meeting was finally set for us all to get together at Jeff Parkers house to discuss the fate of *MU* as a band. The air was so thick that night you could cut it with a knife, I knew it was over as we all walked into the room. Jeff Cotton announced that he was quitting the band, that the lord had told him to stop playing, and he was becoming a Seventh Day Adventist and couldn't play for money on weekends. We were all a bit astonished by this statement to say the least, Jeff Parker really was at a loss for words and just started yelling about the five thousand dollars he had put into the band. Jeff Cotton said he would pay his part back in payments, whatever Parker said, Jeff and Erna had an answer. I addressed the point about the lord telling him to quit playing, I said,"The lord gave you this talent and it's a sin not to use it". Then Jeff and Erna started quoting scriptures, and Parker is threatening to sue. That was it, the final demise of the band *MU*.

All of our equipment and master tapes from the recording sessions at the <u>MU</u> house in Haiku were now in storage in a room behind Randy's cabin at Wood Rose. Randy had the key to the room and made a deal with Parker that he would let him take the equipment if he got to keep his drums and he would work for Parker to pay back his part of the debt. I managed to get the PA system in pieces but before I could get a truck to get any of the amplifiers, Parker took them into an unknown storage facility in town. The room looked completely empty, but little did I know that in the corner of the room under a cardboard box full of assorted electrical parts and wires lay the last recordings of *MU*! Trying to negotiate with Parker to get one amplifier back was futile, he was holding everything until he got his Five Thousand dollars back, he later sold the amplifiers to somebody in California. The original value of the acoustic amplifiers was way more than five thousand dollars. We had worked hard for years in L.A. to buy those amplifiers, and now along with a great band, it was all gone. This was truly a shitty day in paradise for me. What happened to our musical dreams, the creative recording sessions, the great concerts, and most of all the brotherhood?

CHAPTER 12
Living In The Jungle

I tried to enjoy the rest of the summer in the jungle at Matt and Carmen's living a Tarzan life style swimming in the pools and playing with the kids. I was still having a hard time accepting that the band was gone; I soon became restless and began formulating plans to return to the mainland and record the new music I was writing. I had met John Severson who had started *Surfer Magazine*; he was now living in the cooler upcountry area known as Olinda. John invited Mary and I to come up to his house and have dinner with him and his wife Louise and their two daughters Anna and Jenna. Mary immediately hit it off with the two Severson girls and she had two more violin students. Before long I had an all girl violin quartet backing me up at parties. John invited Mary and I to live in his guest house for awhile, so we said good bye for now to Matt and Carmen and moved in with the Severson's. I helped John in the garden and we built a garden shed to keep his roto-tiller and various garden tools in. I loved nature and growing things but I was really yearning to Rock and Roll again.

A friend named Jim Loomis who was a free thinker and retired school teacher from California, invited us to build a cabin on his land further out in the jungle that we could live in for a few years rent free. I went out and looked over the land that was in an area known as Kailua in the valley of Hanawana. It was about two miles from the Hana highway down a steep dirt road in thick jungle, not a neighbor for miles. We took Jims offer and I cleared an area by the stream and went to work. I had enough money to buy enough wood and corrugated roofing to build a twenty by twelve foot cabin. I only had enough money to build a floor and roof, so for awhile we had no walls. We had to huddle together on a mattress covered with a mosquito net in the middle of the floor to stay dry in the rain storms at night with Mary's violin and my Martin guitar in bed with us. I met an older Hawaiian man named Bob Wilhelm who owned the land across the stream, and he nearly cried when he saw me reconstructing some of the ancient Hawaiian rock walls and replanting a sweet potato patch.

He explained that his children all moved to the mainland and got jobs in the city; they had no interest in working the land. He noticed I had no walls for my cabin and said they were tearing down some old redwood water troughs up in the forest and would I like some of the boards? I immediately said, "yes!"

He used to work for the East Maui Irrigation and got a dump truck and took Mary and I up into the beautiful rain forest. There was a little miniature railroad with a hand car on it that they used to inspect the water system. We road the hand cart into the forest where we found stacks of redwood planks perfect for the walls of our cabin. We worked all day and unloaded the lumber next to our cabin. I thanked Bob repeatedly for his help, we would see him often and he always had a twinkle in his eyes and a great smile. I had no power tools and I went through at least three Japanese hand saws cutting the wood and constructing the walls. I even made a door out of the redwood that reminded me of something I saw as a child in an old western movie. I made a small porch complete with a bamboo railing that looked like an exotic cover of a Martin Denny album. One night a magical feeling came over me as I heard the water trickling over the rocks in the stream and the soothing sound of the waterfall in the distance.

I picked up my guitar and a rhythm and chords came out in perfect beat with the flowing water in the stream. Mary picked up a paper sack and a pencil and started writing down notes and lyrics, and in about five minutes one of my favorite original songs *Waterfall* was born. I was so afraid I would forget it that I stayed up singing it all night till dawn and went in town and recorded it on a friend's tape recorder. Many of the songs I wrote in the little cabin in Hanawana would be on the 1976 *Maui* album. We had a little dinner party when the cabin was complete with Jim Loomis and friends. Jim had a talented son named Gannon who was about thirteen years old at the time; he had blond hair and blue eyes and reminded me of my son Tim who I hadn't seen in almost two years.

Gannon was a beginning guitar player and I taught him some chords, it was great to see a young person excited playing music. We had quite a few sing alongs with the Loomis family in the little valley of Hanawana. Sadly Gannon would drown in one of the jungle pools a few years later.

Mary and I decided it was time to go in town and audition at restaurants and clubs. We were hired at the first place we auditioned, a large restaurant in Kahului called *The Pizza Factory* we ended up playing there every weekend for over a year. We were making $80 each plus tips a night, which wasn't bad for the time. We were drawing good crowds and developed quite a following as *Merrell and Mary*. The owner put a big ad in the newspaper and later gave us a $20 raise. We saved up a good amount of money and I decided it was time to go to the mainland and get a record deal. I had more than enough new songs for an album that were inspired living in the Maui jungle.

All our friends and fans were bummed to see us leaving, we had become an inspiration for couples, and our romantic folk rock ballads had become "Their music". Everyone tried to convince us to stay on Maui, "Why do you want to go back to that noise and pollution", they would say. I assured them we would be back after we recorded our songs and got a record deal.

Mary Lee And Merrell

Merrell At The Waterfall

CHAPTER 13
Recording on the Mainland

February of 1975 we flew to California and landed at LAX where we were picked up by Mary's father and mother who lived in nearby Redondo Beach. We bought a car and started making appointments with record labels and producers. To my surprise most of the people I had known had changed company's or no longer were in the business or had passed away. I did manage to make an appointment with producer Phil Meldman and told him the sad tale of the break up of MU. Phil was very impressed with my new songs and the full sound Mary and I were making as a duo. Phil was working with actor Patrick Wayne, who was John Wayne's son, and wanted us to play live for Patrick in his office on Sunset boulevard. Patrick was very impressed with the originality of the music and how we sounded like four people. He immediately called Dino Airelli at Shelter Records and made an appointment for us to see him. Dino was overwhelmed with our sound and booked a recording session at MCA studios for the following night. The session was meant to be a demo to play for Denny Cordell the owner of Shelter Records. We went through about nine songs very rapidly and everyone thought the songs were exceptional. It was going to be a few days before Dino could play our demo for Denny Cordell so Mary and I decided to drive up the coast to introduce her to my mother Evelyn and my sister Linda. Mary got along with the family right away and they loved the new music we were making together. My sister Linda was getting married for the second time and asked us to play music at the reception, our music was perfect for the low keyed reception and everyone had a good time dancing to Mary's bluegrass fiddle tunes.

Dino Airelli hadn't faired to well with Denny Cordell at Shelter Records, he turned us down! Mary was upset with this news saying, "I thought you said we were going to get a record deal and make lots of money!" After years in the business and knocking on doors I was used to the rejection, I tried to convince Mary that this wasn't our only shot and Dino was still going to try to get us a deal. She was depressed and also missed her kids. I missed my son Tim and made arrangements with his mom Josie, who was now living in Palmdale and on her third marriage, to pick him up. I took Mary down to her parents in Redondo Beach and made the drive up to Palmdale and picked Tim up, we were glad to see each other. I took him down to Mary's parent's house for the weekend and took him to Marine land, it was a nice reunion. Mary was getting more depressed and was drinking and arguing with her parents. I learned from her mom that Mary had a drinking problem since she was a teenager and had been arrested once. I realized there was more to this beautiful lady that played the violin than I knew, I loved her and felt like she just needed a break in life and everything would be alright.

Our spirits were lifted when Dino Airelli called and said he wanted us to go to a studio in San Francisco and add more instruments to the songs we recorded at MCA. I took Tim back to Palmdale and Mary and I drove to San Francisco and met engineer John Nowland. John was a very nice guy and he also worked for Neil Young at his studio on his ranch in Woodside. We had Maui bass player Ollie Ignacio, who was now living in northern California come in and record some parts along with Jimmy Dillon on guitar. It was a long night session and John invited us to spend the night at his house. The next morning we got up and left to visit some of Mary's friends in Santa Rosa and my cousin Joyce and her husband Bill in Novato. We had a great time visiting everyone in Northern California and I enjoyed meeting my cousins husband Bill who was really a talented artist and he offered to do a background painting for our album cover. We headed back to L.A. and returned the tapes to Dino Airelli, who was now working for George Harrison at Dark Horse Records.

Dino said he was going to arrange a meeting with George and play our songs for him. We waited at Mary's parent's house for a few weeks with no call from Dino. Around this time our friend from Maui, guitarist Jimmy Dillon was working on an album at *The Moody Blues* keyboard player Mike Pinder's studio in Malibu and invited us to come to a session. Pinder had a beautiful state of the art 24 track studio high in the hills of Malibu with a spectacular ocean view. Pinder and I got along well right away and I sat down at the board with him as co engineer. I ended up being translator for Mike to the musicians and Mary as he put them through the paces trying to get the musical arrangement he wanted on tape. The session lasted into the wee hours, and we woke up late and said Aloha and drove back to Redonodo Beach. . Mary began drinking again and was telling me what a jerk I was for bringing her to the mainland and putting her in this position. I said I was sorry and left to visit my friends David and Barbara Jungclaus and their family in Westlake. David and Barbara both worked in the movie business as film developers and editors. David had done a lot of study about the Lost Continent of Mu or Lemuria and was also interested in UFO research. We always had a great time together and he was like an older brother to me. Finally I received a call from Dino Airelli who said George Harrison liked my song *On Our Way To Hana* and expressed interest in maybe playing slide guitar on it. George thought the rest of the songs were just too slow and dreamy and lacked sentiment. I thought, "What the hell is he talking about"?

Shortly after talking to Dino I got a call from Rick Heiman on Maui who had produced *The Cyrkle* who had a hit titled "Red Rubber Ball". Rick said that he and his backer Jay Bass would like to come over and finance the finishing and release of our album. They wouldn't be able to do this till they harvested a crop of Maui Wowie. I thought I'd seen this movie before and wasn't sure how this story would end? Mary called me at the Jungclaus house in Westlake and said she was leaving her parents house and going to stay with friends in northern California, I lost track of her for awhile until she would call up from wherever she happened to be at the moment. She was playing for a while with her old friends in the Tommy Tutone band in Willits, and she got a job teaching music at a school in Ukiah and was saving money to get her kids back and make a new start. At this point she was hostile and blaming me for not making enough money to get them a new start. I explained to her that I had some backers to finish the album and we would pay her studio time if she wanted to play on it. She said she would, and I told her I would be in touch. Jimmy Dillion and I started working on the rest of the songs to finish the album and played a few gigs. We hooked up with drummer Bill Berg who had played on Bob Dylan's album *Blood On The Tracks,* Bill agreed to play drums on the album.

Rick Heiman flew over from Maui with a large stash of Maui Wowie and cash to finish the recording of the album. We booked time at His Masters Wheels, a studio owned by Elliot Mazer who had produced Linda Rondstat and other artist's. The studio was located in downtown San Francisco and many well known bands had recorded there including *The Grateful Dead"*. The engineer was a great Scottish guy named 'Smiggy', who had played in a band called "Blue". We became fast friends and had a great time recording together, we would have a toke of that sweet Hawaiian weed and get down to recording that real mellow Maui music. I had previously sent Heiman some master slide photos of Mary and I to show Jay Bass as possible cover shots for the album. Jay called us and said he would be bringing four hundred dollars to us for Mary's studio pay along with some fine Maui buds and the photos. He arrived at my cousin Joyce's house in Navato where we were staying, and when I went out to greet him he had a strange bewildered look on his face. I said, "Jay what's wrong"? He said, "Oh my god, I left the satchel with the photos, money and pot on top of the car when I left Sausalito!" A few weeks later Jay got a call from the Sausalito post office saying they found a satchel with his name and phone number on it in a drop box. At first Jay was afraid to pick it up but finally went and got it, he found a note inside that read, "The pot was really great and the money came in handy, and the pictures were cool also, thanks", at least we got the photos back! Meanwhile back in the studio the sessions where going great with myself on guitar, Bill Berg on drums, Jimmy Dillon on guitar, Ollie Ignacio on bass and Steve Meese on piano. We were flying Mary down from Ukiah every Friday to put her violin parts on the songs over the weekend.

Smiggy and I had a little ritual we would do every time we would lay down a part that we thought was extra wonderful, we would yell in unison, "Tweezers in the sky" and rub our hands together real fast and light up a joint! Everyone in the studio would roar laughing and shake hands. During one session we did a splendid mix on my song *The Source* and we set the tape down on a pile of tapes sitting next to the console and went on to the next song to be mixed. Later when we were ready to join the two songs together on the master tape reel, the song on top of the pile was an unreleased *Grateful Dead* song? No matter how we searched through the pile of twenty or so tapes we couldn't find the master mix of *The Source.* We had to remix the song and I made sure we refrained from smoking until after the mixes were done and assembled each day. The album was finished the night before Christmas eve of 1975 and it was snowing on the Golden Gate Bridge as Mary and I drove north to Navato. Mary had saved all her session money and what she had made at the school, she quit her job and retuned to L.A. with me. In a three day whirlwind we managed to get the art work for the cover done and the tapes turned in to the pressing plant for Heiman and Bass's Maui Music label..

Mary got a plane ticket and flew to Oregon to get her kids, we said good bye and didn't know when we would see each other again. Mary realized how long and hard the music business was and there was no guarantee of a pot of gold waiting at the end. I went to my mother's house in Arroyo Grande and waited for the release of the album. February of 1976 Merrell Fankhauser's Maui Album was finally released and I went to L.A. and delivered albums to distributors and had a

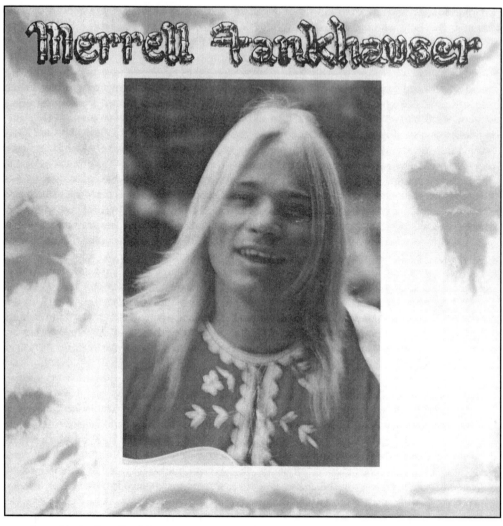

meeting with Audrey Franklyn to promote it. Heiman and Bass didn't want to come up with any money for Audrey to promote it, but she went ahead and set up some radio interviews and magazine articles. The album was much more laid back then the *MU* band recordings and had a symphonic spiritual Maui folk rock sound. Some review's said it was one of the most pure recording's ever made and it might even be a new kind of music. The front cover of the album had me in a red Indian shirt with a blue sky with white puffy clouds in the background, a red white and blue theme that made it perfect for the nations two hundredth anniversary! I drove all over California doing radio and press interviews and distributing records to stores. Rick Heiman went back to the islands to promote and distribute the album there. It received great radio play and press on all the islands and several interviews were booked for my return. It was now summer of 1976 and Mary and her children were now living in the little northern California town of Cotati with one of her old girlfriends. One of my promotional trips took me to the area and I stopped by for a visit. Mary was acting stand offish at first, and told me she was playing with a bluegrass group and Tommy Tutone's band. I gave her an album and went back to my cousin's house in Navato. I managed to save some money from my gigs and started planning my return to Maui. My friends from the island had been calling me and writing me saying how Maui needed mine and Mary's music. Jimmy Dillon and Ollie Ignacio had moved back to Maui and had formed a band and were playing gigs there.

Mary had been listening to the album and had decided it really was something special. She invited me to come up to Cotati and I told her I was going back to Maui. She said her and her kids Molly and Phillip would like to go with me. It was a beautiful summer in northern California, wild flowers were blooming and love was once again in the air. We spent a few weeks playing music, swimming and exploring Mary's old haunts. The day finally came for us to return to Maui. My cousin Joyce's husband Bill Navas would drive us to the San Francisco airport and keep our car for our future visits. The car was a big Chrysler station wagon that we had nicknamed Nigel, it had been so loyal on this long mainland trip. Driving to the airport Mary said,"Lets see if we can get one of our songs on the radio". As soon as we turned on the radio we heard *On Our Way To Hana !* We flew into the friendly skies for Maui with our music filling the airwaves in California.

CHAPTER 14
Return to Maui

We landed on Maui and decided the cabin we built on Jim Loomis's land in the jungle would not work for the kids, as it was so far from the nearest school. We spent a few weeks staying with friends and ran into Jeff Cotton and Erna who said they were renting an apartment in town in Kahului at a place called Harbor Lights. We applied and got a two bedroom apartment on the third floor for only $350 a month, which was very reasonable for 1976 on Maui. We bought a car and got the kids enrolled in school and settled back into island life. I soon found out this was quite a different life than we had experienced living with our friends in the jungle. I had several altercations with young Hawaiian ruffians and thieves in the parking lot trying to steal parts off of my car. We were now living in a hard core local area and they didn't like Haoles very much. I decide rather than fight these guys I would get them stoned and sing to them, I became brudda Merrell to them forever. We were invited to all the luaus and I became friends with both the honest and dishonest. I thought my Indian blood helped me in some way to understand the plight of the Hawaiians and the spirit of Aloha. I learned much of the old ways from the elders I would meet. I was doing anything I could to keep the family secure, playing gigs and even selling pot. It was brought to the attention of the manager of the complex that I had thrown in with some rather undesirable locals and it became a cat and mouse game for him to try to catch us at something.

The manager was an ex Marine and we had a confrontation after he had beaten up one of the locals. I told him, "He should lighten up on these people and show them some respect". He didn't like me saying this in front of his fellow workers and began a plan to have us evicted. Matt and Carmen once again came to our aid and said they would rent us the tree house in Huelo. The last night in Harbor Lights we had a party with all our local friends, drinking, smoking and playing music. We got a warning to quiet down around nine and our Hawaiian friends sort of took over and said, "No way!" Next there was a knock on the door and it was the police. The room was full of marijuana smoke and everyone was ditching their joints out the windows. Two of our rather large friends Joe Namahoi and Dennis Hosino answered the door and wouldn't let the cops in. The two Hawaiian cops were small compared to our friends and couldn't budge the door. Dennis Hosino had gone to high school with one of the cops and started putting him down in fast rapid fire pigeon English. The police left and the party disbanded and everything was cleaned up. Soon six very large Maui cops came to the door and I let them in and watched them search the place and come up with nothing.

We got up early the next morning and moved into Matt and Carmen's tree house in Huelo. Molly and Phillip returned to Oregon for another visit with their father while Mary and I looked for a suitable place to bring them back to. After only a few days Mary and I were not getting along very well as she didn't like the indoor outdoor style living area and the tree growing through the middle of the house. Mary began giving Matt and Carmen's girls Fiama and Saroon violin lesson's again and that distracted her from the primitive jungle living conditions for awhile. Some land with a partially built house by the stream in the valley nearby came up for sale and Matt and Carmen bought it, and Matt offered to rent it to us for two hundred dollars a month. It had no water system or electricity but it was a deal for two acres in paradise by a stream. Matt and I built a bedroom on to the existing structure for Molly and we made a cozy bedroom on the second story for Mary and I. There was a small living room next to the kitchen that we made a corner into a sleeping area for Phillip, the place turned out very nice for a jungle pad. I made a gravity water system to the kitchen sink and got a stove and propane tank. We even hooked a blender up to the chain of an old bike, and you could sit and peddle and make a smoothie at the same time. I held on to the tree house at Matt and Carmen's that gave me some space when Mary's moods would change like a jungle barometer in a tropical storm.

My sister Linda, her husband Rick and daughter Kirstie were coming over from California for a ten day visit. Matt and Carmen didn't exactly like my moving a family in the tree house for ten days but they were nice about it. During my sisters visit we planned a trip to Hana to see the beautiful waterfalls and swim in the pools. I had the old 1971 Ford truck that we had in the band *MU* and Mary was driving the 1969 Oldsmobile we had bought when we returned from the mainland. We loaded up the truck and headed for Hansawa's store to get food and drinks for the trip. We had to go up several large hills and the truck was overheating, we pulled up to the gas pumps at the general store and I checked the oil and put my hand on the radiator cap and it blew off and severely scalded my arm, chest and face! Apparently the radiator cap was loose and all it needed was a little nudge to explode. My skin immediately started to melt and peel from my face, chest and arm, I was in excruciating pain. Someone from the store tried to spray Bactine on it which only made the pain worse, you could see the meat on my arm and bicep that looked like a pink cooked hamburger. Onlookers were shocked, Mary said, "Oh just put a long sleeve shirt on him and give him a beer and he will be alright". My sister Linda wanted to take me to a hospital, but I said, "No take me back to Matt and Carmen's". Mary just kept complaining how I messed up the trip to Hana. Matt and Carmen were gone when we got there so I went down to the stream and submerged myself which helped with the pain. I walked back to the house delirious with pain and Carmen was there and I told her how I got burned. She told the girls to go out in the yard and start chopping big pieces of Aloe, which she sliced into long filet's and laid them on all my burns. It was amazing how it took the pain down to a tolerable level. Mary and the kids went home and my sister and her husband and daughter went to get something to eat.

I went up to the tree house and laid down in my bed and looked up at the beautiful blue sky and tried to erase the pain, yes there could be both pleasure and pain in paradise. A few days later I was feeling well enough to try to take Linda, Rick and Kirstie into the jungle to have a picnic and swim in a pool by a waterfall. It was painful to do anything and I had to keep my burns coated with Aloe and a light cloth rapping. I tried to show them a good time until the day they flew back to California. On the way to the airport we stopped at an old Hawaiian temple called a Heau overlooking the harbor in town. It was a very inspiring view, and little did we know young Kirstie had picked up an interesting rock from the temple. As we were checking in the baggage at the airport she showed us the neat rock she had found. I said, "Where did you get that"? Kirstie said, "From that old place we were at". I looked at my sister and we both said, "Let's get in the truck". We went back to the Heau and had her put the rock back exactly where she found it. We had just enough time to get back to the airport before their flight left. We all knew the stories of tourists taking rocks back to the mainland to have accidents, bad luck and even death. The state of Hawaii gets hundreds of packages of rocks mailed back to the islands every year, with letters telling what happened to them and where they took the rocks from. It is strictly Taboo to take any rocks from Heaus or sacred structures.

I drove back to the tree house in Huelo very weary and in pain and fell asleep. The next morning I awoke feeling very weak and dizzy, and Matt and Carmen invited me down to their house for coffee and Carmen changed my Aloe and bandages I was trying to drink my coffee when all of a sudden I told Matt, "I'm going to pass out". He grabbed me and laid me down on a bench and I woke up as he was pressing on my temples and asked, "Merrell are you still in there"? I said yes, and he gave me some homeopathic pills to swallow, and told me I should stay with them for awhile. They helped me to one of the back bedrooms next to the meditation room that would later be the Tibetan Lama Karmapa's room on his visit. I drifted off into a deep sleep and woke up to what I thought was the next day, But Carmen informed me it was now the morning of the second day. I had been asleep for two nights and a day! I thanked them for taking care of me and they gave me a stash of Aloe and I walked home to the tree house.

It took nearly three months to heal and I had several water blisters nearly four inches long on my arm and chest. As a thin layer of skin grew back I started putting marigold oil on and the itching was pretty bad as I watched dead skin falling off. To this day I have only a small red area near my bicep and no scaring anywhere due to the miracle plant *Aloe vera*.

Merrell And Mary

CHAPTER 15
Enlightenment from Another Land

Matt Westcott announced that the Tibetan Lama Karmapa and other Rimpoche's were coming to Maui from Tibet and would be doing a three day meditation retreat at Matt and Carmen's jungle estate. It was a perfect tranquil setting for the retreat with lotus ponds, meandering peacocks, and waterfalls and pools. There was a large ceremony planned for the first day on the spacious lawn at the estate where a tent and pedestal was erected on a special carpet for Karmapa and the Tibetan horn and drum players to stand. Mary and I and about three hundred hippies attended the famous Black Hat ceremony. It started off with a prayer and meditation for peace and harmony for all beings on planet earth. At the culmination of the ceremony the valuable jeweled black hat was placed on the lama's head with a drum roll and resounding bellow from the Tibetan horn section. Everyone felt so elated and talked about how the high reminded them of a certain drug they had taken. Wow, did this mean we could get high without taking drugs? Everyone had a good buzz going for quite awhile from this experience. The group meditations went on for two more days, one interesting encounter came when a Sioux Indian medicine man showed up and sat by one of the Rimpoche's that was leading the meditation that day. In a question and answer section, someone asked the Rimpoche and Indian medicine man if there were beings from outer space? Even though the Tibetan Rimpoche didn't speak English and had an interpreter, he and the Indian looked at each other and said, "Yes!" I asked about the existence of the Lost Continent of MU, and the Rimpoche said it was written in their tablets. The Indian said all of the north and South American tribes came from a now submerged land in the South Pacific.

Mary and I took refuge with the lama and we were asked to play music for him, it was the first time the lama would hear modern music from the west. I made sure we played him our highest cosmic music, *The Source*, *Garden in The Rain* and a few others from our Maui album. When we stopped there was a silence and the lama asked, "Where does the music come from"? I answered, "Everywhere", he smiled and said, "Very good". Later in a private ceremony lama Saiwan Jeme gave me the Tibetan name Lodru Jantso which means "Oceans of Intelligence". Some years later in the eighties I would write a song with this title.

This event seemed to unite Mary and I very strongly again and I moved into the house in the jungle valley with her and the kids and we became a family. Days were spent working on the house and I built a nice covered porch to spend the warm evenings on. We even bought a TV and hooked it up to a gas generator I had bought to run power tools. Most of our jungle neighbors were against the establishment and viewing any negative news that was broadcast on television was considered strictly Taboo. However when word got out that we had a TV in the valley they started dropping by in the morning with the TV guide section from the Maui newspaper asking if we were planning to watch a certain movie that they just happened to notice was playing that night? Soon we found our porch full of hippies watching TV at night, smoking pot and eating pop corn! There was no hot water or shower at the house, only an area in the stream where we cleared some large stones and made a small pool to bathe. I built an outdoor shower stall and gravity fed another line to it from the stream and bought a Paloma hot water heater that was really a neat invention. It resembled a scuba tank and had a copper coil inside that heated the water as it ran through it without having to heat a big tank like a regular water heater. We would only light the heater when we were taking showers to save on propane. There were now two five gallon propane tanks to hall back and forth into the valley, along with food, laundry and garbage. We used candles and kerosene lanterns for light at night, and an ice chest to keep perishables in, which meant hauling in ice. A neighbor down the valley purchased a submarine battery and put a paddle wheel in the stream hooked to an old Plymouth alternator to charge the battery and power the lights and appliances in his house.

This was a time when everyone was naming their kids some cosmic or Hindu name like, Rainbow, Morning Star or Sananda. We had to park our car at the top of the hill and walk down a trail about an eighth of a mile across two foot bridges to the house. At times it was pure paradise and other times it was extreme hardship. Getting the kids to school when it had been raining for two weeks was very difficult. A typical winter morning we would meet neighbors trying to drive up the two miles of dirt road that had turned into a slippery mud slide to the Hana highway. Cars and light weight pick up trucks would slide off the road and get stuck. I had the 1969 Olds Cutlass with a big V8 engine that had big tires and jacked up suspension and it would sort of leap frog up the muddy road. It was like a Baja run where everybody would stand on the side of the road and see who could make it out.

One night after playing a gig in town Mary and I came home and parked the car in our spot above the valley and proceeded to walk down the trail to our house. Because it had been raining so hard the few days previous the stream was running full force and nearly submerging the first foot bridge. It was a clear moonlit night and we were still in our clean clothes, I was carrying my Martin guitar and Mary was carrying her expensive violin. She had a few drinks at the gig and was a little wobbly. I was holding her hand and leading her down the trail, when we reached the bridge she stumbled and pulled us both into the fast moving stream. Both of our hands went up in the air to protect our instruments that saved us from being swept under the bridge. I pulled myself up on the bridge and then helped Mary up. I was angry at first and started telling her how stupid she was and then we both looked up at the moon in the beautiful Maui sky and started laughing hilariously.

In the '70s and '80s Maui seemed to be the destination for every Guru, healer and cosmic spiritual leader on the planet. The island had visits from Timothy Leary, Baba Ram Dass, Rajneesh, and a long list of characters from every religion known to man. Everyone had their particular brand of salvation to sell including enlightenment. Along with them came many seekers and posers from all parts of the country and Europe. Some were real hippies that believed in peace and love and a healthy diet void of tobacco and alcohol, but it was alright to drop a little acid or smoke as much sacred herb as you wanted. On one occasion a young Baptist minister and his wife came to the island selling their kind of spiritual elevation.

A well to do couple who had a nice house in Haiku notified me that this new enlightened one was giving a talk at their house and if I knew anyone that would like to hear him speak to bring them over for a potluck on Friday night. Mary and I had met an old Hippie from San Francisco named Scary Larry at one of our concerts. He had worked for Bill Graham as a stagehand at the Fillmore auditorium and was helping us as a roadie with our equipment in exchange for a place to sleep and food. We took Scary Larry to the event and arrived around six o'clock with a nice salad Mary had made. Larry had long wild brown hair and a beard that stuck out in every direction and was wearing a tie dyed t-shirt and old ripped up jeans with no shoes. Most of the people we met there were from Beverly Hills or New York and were dressed in fine silk and cotton shirts and blouses with the popular yoga style pajama pants and expensive jewelry. Scary Larry dug right in to the long pot luck table of food and went back for seconds several times. We were already getting some hard looks from the host and hostess concerning Larry's appetite.

Everyone finished eating and it was time to hear the minister turned cosmic leader speak. He started off with a history of how he became a minister and how through his studies and visions he had shed his worldly cloak and achieved a high level of enlightenment. His wife passed out some pamphlets that included an invoice sign up sheet for the particular level of enlightenment you wanted to achieve. Mary giggled a little after reading this. The minister explained if you wanted to take level one, the one week retreat it would cost two thousand dollars. If you wanted to go to an even higher realm and take the two week course, that would cost only four thousand dollars! He spoke in a mesmerizing voice with all the fervor of a southern minister. Some of the people actually signed up for the two week course hoping to view the gates of heaven and leave their earthly problems behind. Mary squeezed my hand and giggled again. Then our leader asked each individual what they hoped to get out of the course? When he asked Scary Larry he said," I'm mainly here for the food". Larry went on to say that he had lived on the streets of San Francisco and had eaten pumpkin pie out of a Dempsey dumpster and, "he really couldn't tell what the hell he was trying to sell"? Oooh, everyone was astonished, the host and hostess told us to leave and take Scary Larry with us! We left and were followed by over half of the audience.

Mary and I continued doing gigs in town and had a very large following. We formed a band with guitarist Jimmy Dillion and Ollie Ignacio on bass and a conga player. We got an offer to open up for Reggae band *Toots and the Maytals* at the Lahaina outdoor Amphitheatre The concert was a big success and helped sell more copies of our album and gained us even more loyal fans. The version of my song *On Our Way To Hana* that we recorded in San Francisco was getting a lot of play on Island radio and was even used as background music on a tour bus going to Hana.

In January of 1977 Rick Heiman informed me that a record producer in L.A. named Artie

Wayne had heard my Maui album and thought the song *Sail It Over The Ocean* could be a hit if it had a more commercial arrangement. Artie flew over to Maui and I re wrote some of the song following his instruction. I also played him my new song *Dharmic Connection* that contained subject matter from my Tibetan studies; Artie liked the song and thought it would make a good flip side for my single. He booked time in a studio in L.A. and I was to fly over to record in two weeks.

CHAPTER 16
Back To L.A.

I flew once again to the city of the angels to begin another recording project. Artie Wayne picked me up at the L.A. airport and took me immediately to guitarist Art Munson's house to work on the arrangements for the songs and to write the charts for the rest of the musician's. Art had played with surf guitarist Dick Dale in the good old days, so we both felt a kinship right away. Art had become a well known studio musician and had played on many hit records. We had Gary Malabar of Steve Miller's band on drums, Colin Cameron on Bass, and Bill Cuomo on piano, all veteran studio players. My song *Dharmic Connection* was recorded at Clover Studio in Hollywood and the session went very well and everyone liked the song and said we should do more.

Artie Wayne introduced me to engineer and producer Joe Klein who had his own studio called L.A. Trax., I noticed right away that Joe was a real recording genius and he had a great sort of Jerry Lewis meets Don Rickles sense of humor. We got along well.

We decided that Mary needed to fly over to put her violin on *Dharmic Connection* and add a few parts on *Sail It Over The Ocean.* We picked her up at the airport and went to dinner and straight into the studio. Mary was a little jet lagged and tired so we didn't get much done and decided to start fresh the next morning. The next morning Artie was in his exuberant producer mode and started coaching Mary on her violin parts that really came out quite extraordinary. That night we put the violin parts down to *Dharmic Connection* and *Sail It Over The Ocean,* she did a fantastic job, a demonstration of what a great violinist she was. The next day Mary flew back to Maui and her kids who had been staying with friends.

I had brought a considerable stash of Maui Wowie with me and Joe Klein and Artie Wayne's eyes lit up when they saw this, they both said, "Can you get more of this"? Joe started making a side deal with me to trade pot for recording time, I had no idea how much money Rick Heiman had given Artie Wayne to produce the recording sessions. I thought Artie was supposed to be paying Klein for the sessions; the entire deal was a mystery. I later found out that Artie Wayne had used the money that was supposed to pay for my sessions to finance his own album that he later sold to Casablanca Records. Joe Klein invited me to stay at his house in Hollywood and we made plans for me to come back and record more of my songs. I was working on a faster version of *Calling From A Star* that I had wrote previous on Maui. Joe seemed to think *Sail It Over The Ocean* needed a guitar solo and called in studio guitarist Ben Benay who had played on records by *The Association, Steely Dan*, Dolly Parton and many others. Artie Wayne had Joe Klein's studio booked to record his own songs, and no money was left to finish my two songs so I flew back to Maui.

When I came back to Maui I found my Oldsmobile Cutlass stripped on the Hana highway where Mary had left it when it ran out of gas. I heard she was hitting the bottle again and was just staying drunk, it was very sad and I tried to overlook it. I bought a 1971 Plymouth with a 318 V8 engine, the hot rodder in me just wouldn't die and a powerful heavy car would make it up the muddy jungle roads in winter. I played gigs on Maui for a few months and saved some money and got some pot from several growers and went back to L.A. in January 1978. Joe Klein picked me up at the airport and I stayed at his house and went to the studio everyday helping him with whatever project he was working on.

It was at this point that I met Doug Feiger, later to be lead singer in *The Knack*. I helped him and the band *The Sunset Bombers* work on an album for Ariola Records. They had this wild and crazy lead singer named Nick who was in and out of drug rehab for speed and various other substances. *The Sunset Bombers* had a Friday night gig at a big club on the Sunset strip and they let Nick out of rehab for the weekend to do the gig. Joe picked Nick up and dropped him off at the house with me while he did some errands and said, "Watch him and don't let him take anything!" Oh, great,, I'm supposed to restrain this muscular drug addict. The first thing Nick said when Joe left was "do you have the combination to Joes safe, I know he's got lots of drugs in there"? I said no, and Nick began to search the house including all of Joe's dresser drawers! He said he was going to leave and find some drugs, so instead of fighting with him I rolled a big Maui Wowie and said "Here Nick try this" ! After taking about six heavy tokes he mellowed out and I started telling him he needed to get ready for the show tonight and I got him into some old World War Two flight style attire with a bombers aviation cap. He really liked it.

Joe finally arrived and we ate and Joe drove him to the gig, we had to hold Nick in the car as every time he saw a hot chick he would lunge out the window and yell "nice ass bitch, nice tits!" After being locked up in rehab for a week he was going wild! Once he got on stage and started performing he was fine.

Joe and I would work on my songs in between the other projects, and it was slow going.

One night while we were getting high at Joe's house he started playing the piano and I picked up my guitar and in an hour or so *The Mothership* was written. We now had another space rock song to go along with the new version of *Calling From A Star*. We booked a session to record these two new songs with myself and Ben Benay on guitars, Colin Cameron on bass, Bill Cuomo on piano and Gary Malabar on drums. Peter Noone of *Herman's Hermits* later came in and sang background vocals with me on *Calling From A Star*. The session went as smooth as silk and in a few hours we had both songs recorded. Gary Malabar told Joe he got the best sound on his drums ever recorded, everyone was very pleased. One day during a break in recording Linda Carter who had the hit TV show "Wonder Woman" stopped by the studio with the bass player's girlfriend to meet me. She was very beautiful and really a nice genuine person. She loved my music, especially my song *The Mothership,* she related it to the story of Genesis in the bible. She was singing in Las Vegas and expressed interest in doing the song in her show. We had a nice private talk in the studio office and she gave me a kiss and left. All the guys in the band wanted to know what happened? Artie Wayne said I can see it now, "Merrell and Wonder Woman together!" I found out later that Linda Carter had called the studio a few times asking for me but we never got together again.

Joe kept the big bag of Maui Wowie I brought over locked in his safe and everybody that dropped by Joe's was getting high. I never really knew if it was being tabulated, and when I asked Joe for an accounting he said, "Don't worry about it Mer, you're the Maui man". I wanted to get the songs finished and released, but the sessions kept dragging on between holidays and trips to desert hot springs and Joes other projects.

During this period a lot of labels both foreign and domestic were reissuing my older albums. I managed to make enough money to buy a new 1978 Firebird, now I was driving in style! I got to visit my son Tim again who had been living in Moab Utah with his mom and her third husband. Tim and I went up to my moms house in Arroyo Grande and we had fun for a couple weeks. He had started playing guitar and I could tell he was serious about it; being left handed it was hard for him to find a guitar. I got him a right handed Gibson SG copy and had it changed to a left handed model. I wrote out some left handed chord charts for him and taught him some leads. From that point on he improved rapidly and it was obvious he had a talent for playing and singing. The vacation with Tim was over and I went back down to Joe Klein's studio in L.A. and we finally got all the parts for my songs recorded. We needed to rent some equipment for Joe to do what he called his, "Maximum Impact" style of mixing. Joe did have a unique technique of mixing before automation was invented for mixing boards. He would mix as far into the song as possible before a big change in instrument levels was needed, then stop the tape and make changes in the levels, mix that section and splice the tape. I was skeptical at first but I immediately saw how skilled Joe was at splicing the tape on a drum beat, you couldn't tell, it was spliced! Nowadays with automation and computers things like that are done quite often. We got great mixes on *Calling From A Star,* and *Sail It Over The Ocean,* and we took a break.

We got keyboardist Marty Davitch who was on a TV soap serial "The Days Of Our Lives" at the time, to add some synthesizer to our space rock song *The Mothership.* All that was left to do was mix *The Mothership* and *Dharmic connection* and we would be finished. It had been nearly a year of recording at Joe's studio just to get these four songs finished.   Around this time I got back in touch with Harry Nilsson and he invited me to a party he was having at his house and asked me to bring my acoustic guitar. I was surprised when I walked in to see John Lennon sitting in the corner of the living room full of guests. Harry said "this is my friend Merrell from Maui and he's going to play a few songs for us".

I had a joint rolled behind my ear hidden by my long hair that I pulled out and lit, I took a big toke and passed it around. I clobbered about 15 people with that one joint of fine Maui

Wowie. I have to admit it was the only time in my life I got a little stage fright, but I made it through *On Our Way To Hana*. When the song ended everybody went, "Wow", and John asked, "What inspired that song"? We started talking and got into a little cognac and coke and the rest of the evening was spent enjoying the comedy of Lennon and Nillson! They would later go on to some wild adventures in the clubs in Hollywood.

A few days later Joe Klein and I attempted to mix *Dharmic Connection* after having some drinks and coke following dinner, and the mix was definitely not up to par. We tried it another evening sober and got a great mix. Joe and I were having a good time together but things were just moving to slowly for me, one evening at his Malibu pad he suggested I sign a contract making him my exclusive producer, manager and a percentage of the publishing. I felt pressured by this offer and Artie Wayne was trying to do the same thing plus Artie had spent money on his project that was supposed to be spent on mine. This situation left me owing Klein for studio pay but I never received an accounting for all the pot I had given them. The next day Joe Klein and I got into an argument at his Hollywood house when I said I wanted my tapes and an accounting. Joe went to the closet and got the tapes and I left and took the tapes to The Hit Factory studio in L.A. and finished the mix on *The Mothership*.

Merrell atop Haleakala

I later made a deal for *Calling From A Star* and *Sail It Over The Ocean* to come out as a single on a small L.A. label. Audrey Franklyn and another record promoter were able to get some substantial radio play, but without financial backing it soon disappeared. Meanwhile film maker Charlie Booth from Detroit was interested in making a film of me singing *Calling From A Star* on top of Haleakala crater on Maui. I flew back to Maui and set up lodging for Charlie and the crew in Kula on the slopes of Haleakala which is on the main road leading to the top of the crater. Joe Klein came over and he and Charlie's cousin Phil who was part of the crew, took some psychedelic Maui mushrooms and laughed their heads off for hours the night before we went to the top of the crater.

We got up and left at 4:00am to be set up on the overlook at 10,500 feet precisely as the sun came up. We started shooting on 16 millimeter film with Charlie's brother Woody running the big camera, several takes were done with me singing along to a tape just as the sun came up. We were just about ready to leave when a blank faced man with short hair in a blue blazer approached us and flashed a badge. He was curious as to the purpose of our filming and what areas of the crater we shot and did we film the science dome on the rim? The dome was rumored to have a laser weapon in it and several people had reported seeing strange beams of blue light in the night sky.

He took us into the office in the observatory and questioned us together and separately and took down our driver's license info. He said he wanted to have a copy of the film and that we needed a permit to film there and pay a fee. We said the film had already gone down the mountain and it was to dark and nothing was useable, and he let us go. The tourists and onlookers wondered what was going on when they saw me in a white robe being escorted out to our vehicle in the parking lot. I wished I would have had the entire scenario on film!

The long trip of almost a year working in Hollywood took a toll on mine and Mary's relationship, she said, "You love music more than you do me". Her drinking had again escalated and I decided to rent a room in a beach house near town in the village of Kuau.

An artist friend named Gopal and his girlfriend Orana lived there and we had fun hanging out and I started learning to windsurf. One day I got a letter from Appaloosa Records, a label in Italy that they would like to put out the second unreleased album by *MU* that had been recorded in the house in Haiku. I found out the tapes were still in the old jungle shack were we had stored the PA and other equipment. I had to practically chop away the jungle growth to get to the door of the shack that fell off its hinges when I opened it. There to my amazement under the box of old wires and a rusted Vox wah wah pedal was the two reels of *MU* master tapes! There was a puddle of water right next to the tapes and I looked up and noticed I could see daylight coming through the roof; but luckily the tapes were not damaged. I went back to California and mixed the four track tapes in a new studio near my mother's house called Emerald City in Grover Beach. There I met Bruce 'Lumpy' Sahroian who was a good engineer and bass player, he freaked when a Hawaiian cockroach ran out of the box and he chased after it with a can of Raid. I sent the mixed tapes to Italy and it eventually came out in 1982 as *MU The Last Album.* There was still over a half of an albums worth of songs left as it all wouldn't fit on one vinyl album I later made a deal for the remaining songs to come out on

Artie Wayne, Merrell , Joe Klein

Source Records a small East Coast label as *MU Children Of The Rainbow*. Source Records also later released the *Calling From A Star* sessions on vinyl LP as *A Day In Paradise,* It was a hit with the collectors but again without large financial backing there was no commercial success.

I got a call from film maker Charlie Booth and he said he needed some close-ups of me to finish the *Calling From A Star* Film and he was working at his dad's studio in Marin California. He was having trouble editing the sound to the film, so I contacted my old friend David Jungclaus who had worked in the film industry for years and he said he would go along with me. I picked David up at his home in Westlake and we hopped in my Firebird on a sunny summer day and left L.A. and headed for Marin. We arrived at Charlie's studio in the evening and he said it was to late to work so we went to dinner. Then we followed Charlie back to his rented house in a woodsy area where it was rumored actor Jack Nicholson lived. We found out quick that Charlie and his crew were heavily into pot, hash and coke and everyone was over indulging which made David and I wonder how anything was going to get done on the film? The next day everyone finally got up around 11:00am and we went to breakfast. We went to the studio to work but first some heavy tokes of pot and hash were ingested by the three man crew and the hash dealer that had eyes as dark as a raccoon.

Around 3:00pm the 16mm film camera being operated by Charlie's brother Woody was set up and the lights were adjusted for the first take of my close-up for *Calling From A Star.*

Sometime around 8:00pm we had a few takes in the can and it was time to break for dinner. After dinner it was time for more drugs and around 1:30am Charlie said we had enough takes. We got up around 11:00am again the next morning, had breakfast and headed down to San Mateo where Charlie wanted to introduce us to a producer who was making a movie about smuggling marijuana out of Mexico. We arrived and were greeted by a smiling jovial guy with a beard named Gordy, who immediately dumped a big pile of cocaine on a plate and offered it to everyone. David Jungclaus had never done coke before and it wasn't my drug of choice either, but we both had a few snorts. The hash dealer had his face buried in it for quite awhile and he looked like he had a milk mustache. We listened to everyone talking all at once rambling on at the speed of sound about how this movie called Grifa was going to be the biggest thing ever released!

It was getting dark and we decided it was time to get back up to Marin. Our host instructed Charlie how to get back on the freeway and back to San Francisco. Charlie was driving his Ford van with me and David and part of the crew and the hash dealer who was now curled up in a ball behind the back seat. Somehow in Charlie's cocaine hazed fog he missed the freeway on ramp and we ended up in the downtown financial district. We were driving around for what seemed like forever trying to find the onramp when we noticed a cop car next to us and one on the other side of the intersection. We went around the block and there were two more cop cars at the intersection. The hash dealer said, "Oh no this is it were all going to jail!" Charlie wanted to drive down an alley and jump out and leave the van. All I could think about was that David Jungclaus's wife would never speak to me again if I got him in trouble on this wild trip! We knew the hash dealer had a lot of drugs on him but we didn't know exactly what they were? I told Charlie not to panic and just take the first left towards the ocean and stay in the speed limit, all of a sudden a sign appeared that we were now entering the Golden Gate Bridge. Everybody let out a big sigh of relief as we crossed the bridge and made it back to Marin. David and I got up early the next morning and said goodbye and headed back to his house in the L.A. suburb of Westlake.

It took months for Charlie to edit the *Calling From A Star* film and I finally got a copy and had it transferred in L.A. to three quarter inch video. With the help of Audrey Franklyn we started getting it aired on television in California and Hawaii. That ended another mainland adventure and I flew back to Maui and the quiet life in my jungle cabin.

Maui Joe

CHAPTER 17
Light At The End Of The Tunnel

I was in deep shock with the death of John Lennon in 1980, it was a very sad time. A group of us went to the top of Haleakala crater for a moment of silence along with the rest of the world. I felt a kinship with his spirit and his belief in peace, love and brotherhood, it was a very tragic loss for everyone. I started thinking about my influences in music, Elvis Presley, Buddy Holly and John Lennon. I had a dream that I had died and I saw them all in heaven and when I awoke I picked up my guitar and the song *Buddy Elvis and John* popped out! I had some other new songs written and Mary and I flew over to California and booked some time in Emerald City Recording, a studio near my mom's house on the central coast. The musicians on the session where myself on vocals and guitar, Mary Lee on vocals and Violin, Lumpy Sahroian on bass, Darrel Thatcher on Steel guitar and Art Dougall on drums. We recorded *Buddy Elvis and John, Maybe You Can Call Me Honey, Thought I heard A Melody* and *Some Of Them Escaped It All.* Mary flew back to Maui and I went down to L.A. to shop the tunes. I bumped into my old friend Kenny Smith who was now working for Mo Town. I then went to see ex *MU* producer Phil Meldman. Phil was working for famed film maker John Frankenhimer and had met movie and record producer William E. McEuen who had produced *The Nitty Gritty Dirt Band* and Steve Martin. Phil set up a meeting with Bill McEuen and he liked my songs and said he would finance some acetate LP demos to shop to labels. We went into Artisan Sound in Hollywood and cut some demos and I sent them to Bill McEuen who was very busy at the time producing and managing the Dirt Band and Steve Martin. I did some gigs and interviews and flew back to Maui. I still had a room at the beach house near Paia and I would visit Mary who was still living in our jungle house in Huelo. On one of these visits she informed me she was pregnant with my child and she intended to keep the baby. We decided it would be best if she moved out of the rainforest and closer to town and the hospital. We found a house in Haiku and moved about five months later to a cabin in a valley closer to the town of Makawao.

Film maker Charlie Booth called and said he would like to make a half hour video to go along with the *Calling From A Star* film he had made. Video was now becoming the new format for music and Charlie saw a great sales opportunity . We had a rough script to shoot a video compilation of my songs that told a story of what a day on Maui with Merrell was like titled *A Day In Paradise.* We had a fun day filming on the beach at Kuau with the full band that included myself on vocal and guitar, Mary Lee on vocal and fiddle, Steve Meese on bass, Jim

Murray on guitar and Ray Purcell on drums. We managed to get a great take of *On Our Way To Hana, That's Alright* and a *Blues Medley*. Charlie was perched on a tall ladder with a large new video camera with a long cable going to a deck with audio coming in from a PA mixer. The atmosphere was enhanced with dancing girls and curious onlookers. We were very happy with what we captured that day for history on this new technology called video.

I started organizing an expedition to go to the desolate south side of the island to examine ruins of a village that had been destroyed by lava over eight hundred years ago. We had a meeting and artist Gopal, his girlfriend Orana and a young French girl named Elena who I had met during the filming all said they would like to go. Hawaiian historian Epps Sargent and his friend Satch said they would go along to help carry supplies and camera equipment. Charlie Booth and his girlfriend Laurie reserved a suite at a hotel in Wailea to return to after our 3 day trek into the old lava field, known as the King's Burial Ground. We drove to the end of the gravel road at McKenna beach and started walking on a trail that eventually turned into a stone road with three foot walls on each side. I had been told that around eleven miles out the king's road there were many ruins and a large temple like building on a hillside. We hiked about five miles and took a break; someone brought some LSD and decided it would be fun to take. The girls and Epps Sargeant all dropped but Gopal and I where at the head of the trail and decided

Merrell And The Maui Band

not to take the acid.

What we were seeing was awesome enough without the aid of a hallucinogen. We were walking on a stone road that went on as far as the eye could see with ruins of ancient buildings half covered in lava going up the desolate mountain side. It looked like the aftermath of an atomic bomb and it was hard to judge distance in this wild landscape. It was said that there was once a mysterious white race that lived in the area when the Tahitians first landed, and a stone axe head was found there believed to be of Viking origin.

The entire region was steeped in mystery and it was said that many people of Hawaiian royalty were buried there and the locals were afraid to be there at night. They said you could hear human voices whisper and the crying of babies in the dark night.

The going got tough when we suddenly ran into a small hill of lava that covered the road and we had to climb over the sharp jagged lava rocks to the road that continued on the other side. I noticed everyone was getting further behind us and a few were staggering and had fallen down, the LSD had really kicked in. Charlie managed to film some of this with the big video camera that was very cumbersome to carry in this rugged terrain. I found some ruined stone houses by the beach and decided to make camp for the night, we managed to start a fire and had some soup and sandwiches and turned in for the night. Elena was getting freaked out and I had to hold her through the night and guide her through her trip. Everyone was hearing strange sounds as the wind whipped across the barren stone wasteland howling like banshees, it was scary enough without LSD. In the morning everyone was wasted and it was obvious we were not going much farther. Charlie and I explored over the next ridge and managed to get a few more shots but carrying the camera, tripod and deck was just to much. We went back to camp and got everyone ready to slowly walk back. Water was running short and it was slow going as the hot tropical sun beat down on these would be explorers. We made it back to civilization and the very comfortable hotel at Wailaea and some hot showers and cool water. Myself, Charlie, Laurie and Elena had a nice dinner while listening to Martin Denny playing live on the piano, he even did his hit, *Quiet Village.* A few months later I would make a trip with Matt Westcott all the way to the ancient building on the hillside. It was an impressive structure that seemed to be built on an even older foundation that had an Egyptian style cellar beneath it. Nobody knows the origin of this large structure; Matt called it, "Lost City Hall".

I flew to L.A. with Charlie Booth to edit our new half hour video in a editing studio in Hollywood. Charlie said he only had enough money for ten hours of editing; it was obvious we were not going to have enough time to finish. Charlie was staying in the Hollywood Hills with an eccentric young 'know it all' guy named "Dana the Boy Wonder". One night after an editing session Charlie flew back to Detroit and left the tapes with Dana the boy wonder. I called Dana and asked if I could come up and get the tapes, and he said he was holding them until Charlie paid a $150 phone bill he owed him. After a few days Charlie sent him a check and I got the tapes. My mom lent me enough money to finish the editing with Barry Schwortz in Santa Barbara. Barry was the head of photography at Brooks Institute and had photographed the shroud of Turin for Look magazine.

I paid a duplicating studio in Hollywood to make one hundred copies on VHS tape of the half hour video *A Day In Paradise*. I sold a few video tapes with an ad I put in *Goldmine* magazine and got it aired on television in California and Hawaii. Source Records on the East Coast put out a nice vinyl album of the *A Day In Paradise* soundtrack. I went back to Maui just in time to meet up with *Quicksilver Messenger Service* guitarist John Cipolinna who was visiting the island, we met at Baldwin beach and decided to do some recording together. Jim Murray talked to Harry Davis who just put together the only multi track studio on the island called "The Winery". Jim assured me he would give us a good deal and we booked time for the next day at twelve noon. I figured it might cost $500 tops, Harry was not clear how much he would charge us and just said, "I'll give you a good deal".

It took almost two hours to get all the equipment functioning properly and time was going by. We had myself and Cipolinna on guitar's, Steve Meese on bass, pregnant Mary Lee on violin, and Ray Purcell on drums. Jim Murray said he had a back ache and spent most of the time lying on his back, he did get up and play some guitar on the *Blues Medley*. It was an exciting event with quite a few onlookers and people listening outside the door. I did my best at directing everybody as we would launch into one of my songs that I was singing live in the room. We did an interesting jam on *Calling From A Star* and *On Our Way To Hana* and Cipolinna did a nice slide solo on *Waterfall*. We took a break and ate some pizza and went back in and did rousing versions of *That's Alright Mama* and the *Blues Medley (Got Me Runnin / Spider and The Fly)*. The session ended about midnight and Cipolinna's friends wanted to know where there were some nice waterfalls and pools they could swim in. I gave them directions to twin falls in Huelo and they said they would be there around noon the next day.

The next day I drove to twin falls and there was John Cipolinna sitting in the rent a car on the Hana highway reading a guitar magazine. I said, "Hey John didn't you want to go to the waterfall"? John said, "Nah I was trippin' out on these new Gibson guitars". He asked if I had any weed and we smoked a joint and I said Id give him a call next time I was in California , that was the last time I saw John Cipolinna. I noticed a few months later he gave a great review of the fun session he did with me on Maui in an article in Goldmine magazine.

Trying to deal with Harry Davis to pay the bill was another story; I gave him $300 and was making payments. Every time I'd ask for an accounting of the total, his hourly rates would go up. I guess he figured the importance of the session made it valuable and he just kept upping the ante. I never got mixes of the versions of *Calling From A Star* and *On Our Way To Hana* that we did. I was lucky to get mixes of *That's Alright Mama, Waterfall* and the *Blues Medley*. Around this time I bumped into Sky Saxon of *The Seeds* who was now living on Maui with his two wives, Wings and Lamed. Sky would pop up and sing with me on a few gigs and we even did an impromptu recording session in a house on Maui.

Mary was getting far along in her pregnancy but we were still playing gigs. We got an offer to do a big concert in an upcountry auditorium near Makawao for an organization called "Peace Moves". We had myself on vocal and guitar, Mary on vocal and violin, Steve Meese on bass and Ray Purcell on drums but no second guitar. We were discussing what the set should be when a young guy with long brown hair walked up and said, "I 'm a guitarist and I'd love to play with you". I said, OK we will try you on a few songs and see how it goes". The young guitarist was Donnie "Divino" Smith who would become one of my best friends and play on many recordings and gigs with me. The concert was a hot fiery explosion with me, Donnie and Mary taking some great solos, Donnie and I made plans to get together at his rehearsal studio in Haiku and work on more songs. We later did another concert together in Wailuku that would be the first benefit concert for the newly established Tibetan Dharma Center. The resident Lama Ten Sing was there applauding our efforts.

February 22, 1983 was a wonderful day as our son Maui Joe was born, and what a cute little blond ball of energy he was, every month he was rapidly growing and becoming very active. By the time he was a year old he was swimming in the pool with me and helping me plant papayas and bananas. For awhile all was perfect in paradise, but soon Mary's drinking returned with the excuse that beer made good mothers milk! I would come home and find her passed out on the couch with empty beer cans everywhere and Maui Joe playing by himself on the floor. I started playing gigs with Donnie Smith and the band without Mary. She did play on my songs *Stone Indians Prayer, Time Of The Day* and *Daddy's Song* that we recorded in a makeshift four track studio in a Quonset hut in Haiku. Maui Joe could be heard giggling on the end of *Daddy's Song*. With these songs, and the songs I did with Cipolinna and the songs recorded earlier at Emerald City, I now had enough for a new album, once again it was time to do the mainland shuffle.

I was afraid to leave Mary and the baby, and Mary's kids Molly and Phillip were now teenagers and doing their own thing. From all indications it seemed Phillip might be going down an alcoholic path the same as his mother. We decided to move again back to Huelo, this time to a little house with electricity on higher ground more near the Hana highway.

January of 1986 I went back to California and got in touch with Kenny Smith who now had his own studio and was running the old R&B label D Town Records. Kenny liked all the new songs I had an offered to put out an album. . All we needed was three more songs, so we went into his studio with me on vocal and guitar, Bobby Omsby on vocal and bass, Debbie McKay on vocal and Bruce Hively on drums. We recorded *Who Can You Call* and *Don't give up the*

Ray Purcell, Mary Lee, Merrell,
Jim Murray, John Cipolinna, Tim Carr

133

Rock and added *Cocaine And Aeroplanes* to the line up and the album was finished. We christened it *Doctor Fankhauser* and Kenny rush released it to good reviews and substantial radio play; he also licensed it to a French and German label.

At the same time I got an offer from Lumpy Sahroian to produce and album in his Emerald City studio on the central coast and I began writing some interesting space rock style songs. In less than two months we knocked out an entire album titled *Message To The Universe* with myself on vocal and guitar, Lumpy on bass, Billy Fapiano on guitar and Art Dougall on drums. I made a deal with the U.K. label One Big Guitar; it came out with a great cover painting of me playing with an alien band on Maui by artist Gopal. It didn't get very good reviews or sales and soon disappeared. Meanwhile the *Doctor Fankhauser* album continued to sell and get more radio play. I was gaining legions of fans during this period with several labels reissuing the *H.M.S. Bounty* album and sealed mint condition copies of the *Fapardokly* album were now going for $1000 a copy!

I returned to Maui to find we were being evicted from our house as Mary had failed to pay the landlord the money I had sent. So I rented a room in a house in Makawao as we needed something fast. I single handedly moved all our furniture and refrigerator by myself. The rainy season was on and it was getting close to the end of 1986, Mary found some drinking buddies nearby and spent most of her time drunk somewhere. She left Maui, Joe and I on New Years Eve and didn't come back for nearly two weeks. A week or so later we went to a friend's birthday party and she got drunk, when we came home and I wouldn't give Mary the keys to the car she hit me in the mouth with a beer bottle and knocked out one of my teeth and ran out of the house. I walked to a nearby pay phone and called Donnie Smith and he came and got me. I was bleeding with the nerve hanging out of my gum in excruciating pain. I had to endure the pain for three days before a dentist could see me and do a root canal and patch me up.

Mary and I were over. I stayed with Donnie and his wife Sada and their kids for six weeks. Donnie had acquired a eight track recorder and board and we started working on an album with his band *Venus*. The band featured a great Hawaiian singer named Ahtim Elenecki, Maka Ala on Bass, Robert Namahoi on Keyboard, Hector and Sundance on percussion and Donnie and I on guitars. It was a different sound like *Santana* does Hawaiian Reggae. Donnie and his brother Bob and I celebrated the finishing of the album with a two day camping trip in Haleakala Crater. A few days later I went wind surfing with my friend surfer Steve Omar, I had a feeling I wasn't going to experience the warm blue Pacific Ocean for a long time. I left again for California and when the plane left the ground and I saw the island of Maui disappearing in the distance I shed a tear thinking about my little Maui Joe I had to leave behind, and prayed he would be alright. I tried to get a deal for the Venus album but I couldn't. Everybody liked the music but Ahtims accent was different than a Jamaican accent and nobody could understand what he was saying.

I hooked up with engineer and drummer Bruce Hively who I worked with at D Town and he was now working at Meridian Movie Studios dubbing music and sound effects to film. Bruce had access to a big twenty four track studio on the movie lot and said, "Lets do an album", we

Maui Lava Field Ruins

started working on a '50s style rock n roll project at night after work. Bruce was doing the drums and I was laying down all the vocals and guitar parts. We had the basic guitar and drum parts done for twelve songs when I got an offer to do a two week northern and central coast tour. My son Tim joined me and my new band that consisted of Tim and I on vocals and

Merrell Meditating In Hospital

guitars, Richard Stephenson on guitar, Jack Baum on bass, Rick Beaumont on keyboard and Jerry Sagouspe on drums. We did several gigs and it was a cookin' band and everybody was having a great time. We were coming back from a gig one night in Paso Robles when Tim looked up at the sky and said, "It will be a full moon tomorrow when we do the concert in Pismo Beach". I said, "Yeah strange things happen on full moon". I didn't know how strange it was going to be.

It was Labor Day week end 1987 and we had a good crowd at the Pismo Beach state park concert. We had a blues band open up for us and they seemed to be draggin' on a little to long, the crowd and my band was kind of restless waiting for us to take the stage. We finally went on and the audience was on their feet and about six songs into the set I noticed my left arm and hand was numb, then I started feeling short of breath and dizzy. I turned to Jerry the drummer and said, "I don't feel good lets take a break". The audience wondered why we quit as everyone was really getting into the music? I went into the bathroom and told my symptoms to a friend named Don who worked at the Arroyo Grande post office, and he said, "I think You're Having a Heart Attack". I said no way I went windsurfing and hiked into Haleakala crater just a few months ago, he convinced me to go to the office and went ahead to call an ambulance. I remember walking in front of the stage and everything started seeming like a far away dream. I barely made it to the office where I passed out and stopped breathing.

The ambulance got there but I was dead with no pulse, they defribulated me several times and gave me oxygen and got a pulse and headed for the hospital with friends and family following. I remember knowing I was dead and I was floating in a sea of darkness and then I saw a white light on the horizon, and the closer it got the better I felt. I wanted to go into the light but every time I got close it went away and I was slammed back into my body. I think this was when they were continuing to shock me as I kept flat lining. I came semi conscious in the ER but kept passing out, I later woke up in ICU with a doctor asking me if I knew my name and what happened to me? I couldn't talk for awhile nor could I comprehend the world I was seeing, it was like a baby being born and everything was new. Later I heard the song *Memphis Tennessee* in my head and I remembered the concert and what had happened.

I was having intense chest pain and going in and out of consciousness, they gave me a drug called streptokinase to thin my blood so my heart didn't have to work so hard. Then I started bleeding from my nose and throwing up blood, I thought that was the end. The doctor didn't think I was going to make it and asked if I wanted my family to come in. I said, "No clean me up after I die, then they can see me". The doctor went to the waiting room and told my family and friends they had done all they could and all we can do now is wait. When the pain would come back in my chest I would meditate and go with it, which actually wasn't good as I wasn't willing myself to stay here. Then I realized I needed to think I was going to make it, and "Think you're going to make it" started going over and over in my mind like a mantra.

Around eleven o'clock in the evening I started improving, and by seven in the morning the pain was starting to subside. The doctor came in and said they were going to transfer me to the cardiac wing at French hospital in San Luis Obispo and do some tests and possibly operate on me. When the doctor left I pushed the elevation button on the bed and raised myself to an upright sitting position and started chanting a Tibetan chant asking for healing energy, "Om Mana Padme Om". I was still on oxygen and had several tubes and wires connected to me, I looked up at my monitor and it looked like a V8 engine running on five cylinders and I hardly had any blood pressure. The more I chanted the more everything came back to normal, a nurse saw this on her monitor in an observation room and was astonished. The doctor came in and said I had made a marked improvement in the last half an hour and they would hold off on moving me for awhile. I was lucky to have one of the best heart doctors on duty at Arroyo Grande hospital when this happened, doctor David Ivans, he looked like a cross between Paul McCartney and actor Jimmy Stewart.

One morning I awoke to a pretty buxom blond nurse who said, "I'm Kathy and I'll be taking care of you", it was great to meet a kind and compassionate lady, and we soon became friends. I steadily improved and chanted and meditated daily and on the tenth day I was released from the hospital and went home to my mom's house to recuperate. Kathy Lambert would come by my mom's house after her shift at the hospital and check on me. As I got stronger and was well enough Kathy and I would go on walks and sometimes have dinner together. I went through months of cardiac rehab at the hospital, exercising with a heart monitor to see how much of a load I could handle. I steadily improved and only had slight chest pain a few times; soon I was lifting weights and jogging on a treadmill.

A year later Doctor Ivans decided to do an angiogram on me and I went to a French hospital for the procedure. They run a wire from your groin area up your main artery and inject dye into the heart arteries, it is then projected on a screen and they can see what part of the heart or arteries is damaged. My left descending artery had a small growth in it that was probably there for years and because I was stressed any blockage at that time could have caused the heart attack. I had already started growing little arteries around the damaged area, I was healing myself! A few months later I did a cardiac stress test on a treadmill and Doctor Ivans said I had made a ninety percent recovery, and it would be hard to tell I ever had a heart attack, even though it damaged thirty percent of my heart muscle.

The world was again fresh and new and I was ready to slowly get back into my music career after over a year off. D Town records had installed a portable eight track recorder and mixing board in a room next to my bedroom at my mom's house so I could get up and record new song ideas when I felt like it. I started slowly writing and recording vocal and guitar parts to a drum machine that would later be replaced by real drums. The subject matter of the songs was all centered around my studies of South American Indian legends and would later come out in 1992 as *Flying To Machu Picchu.*

I decided it was time to put the band back together with future Grammy winner Louie Ortega from *The Texas Tornadoes* on guitar. We did the big 1988 Pismo Beach car show that drew thousands, and many of my old fans came out to cheer me on, I was back!

CHAPTER 18
California Music and Return To MU

I called engineer Bruce Hively in Hollywood and told him I was ready to finish the album we started together. He said he would like to get out of the city and asked if there was a 24 track studio in my area. I said "yes, there's a nice studio called Sutton Sound in Atascadero", a woodsy area just inland and north of Arroyo Grande. We booked time and added Scott Wright on sax, Rick Beaumont and Mark Nelson on piano and some background vocals and mixed the album. I made a deal with Disco Melocoton, a label in Spain and the album came out on vinyl LP as *Back This Way Again* in 1990. It became an immediate collectors item with its gatefold cover and '50s and '60s style music. It was a limited edition on a foreign label and not to many people in America even knew about it.

Around the same time Reckless Records in London got in touch with me about reissuing the two *MU* albums and my 1976 *Maui* album. All the releases got rave reviews and even a mention on MTV but only sold a few thousand copies and disappeared.

In the latter part of 1988 *The Impacts* sax player Joel Rose and *HMS Bounty* guitarist Bill Dodd and I got back together to do some instrumental surf recordings. We had an idea to reform *The Impacts* and release a *Surfing Reunion* kind of album paying homage to our roots. We recorded some songs and lost interest when the rest of the original Impacts didn't want to participate and the songs were put on the shelf.

Kathy Lambert was helping me with organization of my live bookings and taking care of my fan mail that was growing larger everyday, Kathy asked me to move in with her in her little cabin in Pismo Beach. It was great to have some help and support in my life for a change; we would take long walks around town and on the beach. In 1990 my son Tim moved to the central coast from Lancaster California and started playing guitar and singing in my band that sometimes featured guitar wiz Jay Lacey who had played with *The Everly Brothers* and did a movie with Elvis Presley. It was a hot band and we played many memorable concerts. My son Tim was missing his girlfriend Carol from Lancaster and she decided to move to the central coast also. We put Tim and Carol up for six weeks in the little cabin until they found a place to rent. Tim was working as a tile setter and playing with me on the week ends, and Carol got a job at a local grocery store, they later went to Las Vegas and got married. The band started playing three nights a week at a local night spot in Grover Beach called *Burgundy's*. It had a big dance floor and stage, it was a great venue for Tim and I and the band to get tight. We played there the entire summer of 1990 until November. Kathy was getting very good at

Merrell and Nicky Hopkins

Nicky Hopkins, Merrell, Frank Paredes, Art Dougall, Tim Fankhauser

shooting video of the band and after viewing some of her footage I thought it should be on TV. There was a local station on the Arroyo Grande mesa called Route 66 TV, I gave them a call and we started producing a show I called "California Music". The engineer and station owner Marty Scala thought it was good enough to be on satellite and we sent a demo to Channel America in New York. We made a deal and we were on three times a week going to fifteen million viewers! Word soon got out that I was hosting a national TV show and I had many stars from the '60s and '70s on the show, Mike Love of *The Beach Boys*, Eric Burdon, Pete Sears of *Starship*, Ed Cassidy and Randy California of *Spirit* and many others. It was a wonderful event when piano wiz Nicky Hopkins walked on the set of California Music. Nicky's credits read like a *Who's Who* of Rock and Roll music, having played with *The Beatles* and *The Rolling Stones* and everyone in between.

Nicky and I remembered meeting briefly in the late '60s at some large concert with many bands on the bill, we became instant friends. Nicky brought along Pat Benatar's bass player Roger Capps, we got situated on the set and I did interviews with Nicky and Roger and then it was time to play. We did a sound check that immediately turned into a hot jam of our favorite rockabilly songs. It brought back the early years for all three of us when you would just play for fun and see what came out. Nicky enjoyed it so much we made plans after the TV taping to do some recording and concerts together. Kathy and I outgrew the little cabin in Pismo and rented a large three bedroom house in Arroyo Grande so I could set up a recording studio. Nicky and his wife Moira would often spend a few days with Kathy and I when they would be traveling from L.A. to San Francisco. Nicky and I and my band that featured my son Tim on guitar and vocal, Art Dougall on drums, and Frank Paredes on bass and vocal did an outstanding concert at the Vets hall in Pismo Beach June 22,1991. Part of the show was videoed and recorded on a two track recorder and some of the songs would later come out on CD and be shown on TV. Nicky and I also recorded a song together in the Sutton Sound studio titled *Queen MU* that would later be released on my *Return To MU* album. Nicky and I remained friends until his untimely passing from a stomach aneurism in 1994. I was deeply hurt by his passing and Pete Sears and I did a tribute song to him titled *Nicky's Song* that came out on the *Fankhauser Cassidy* album in 1995 with Spirit drummer Ed Cassidy.

One of the musicians I had first met back in the '60s and later in the '70s on Maui, Sky Saxon of *The Seeds*, got in touch with me as he had heard about my California Music TV show. Sky wanted to start a band with me when he came to some of my gigs on Maui back in the '70s. At that time he was living in a van with his two wives, Wings and Lamed, and looked like a homeless refuge from a bygone era; he was still living in the '60s, like time had stopped. We did record a few jams together on Maui and some songs with me playing guitar. I heard later that they came out on a foreign label as *Sky Sunlight Saxon*.

We did an Interview on my "California Music TV show in December of 1991 and he performed his latest song *Flashback 66*. After the show he went to his hotel room with his girlfriend and I got a call in the middle of the night that he was very sick and complaining of abdominal pain. He went to the hospital in San Luis Obispo and they found his gallbladder had ruptured and he was septic and near death. Sky was on a ventilator for ten days, I visited him nearly everyday and fed him ice and water on a sponge, and they said it was a miracle he

Sky Saxon and Merrell

made it when they took him off the ventilator. They moved him out of ICU and into a room and he was still on oxygen. One day I went to visit him and I was amazed he was sitting up and talking like a politician, he took the hose off the oxygen mask and was sucking on it like a hash pipe! Sky leaned over and whispered to me, "Hey man can you get me some buds, if I had some buds I would get well sooner". I said, "Sky you can't smoke in here, with all that oxygen leaking out you could blow this place up!" Sky said, "Oh yeah, wow man, that's heavy". The next morning I got a call from Sky and he says, "Howard Hughes came to me in a dream and said he could get us five million for our combined music catalogs". He wanted to know if I wanted in on the deal and come to the hospital right away and bring my guitar.

When I got to the hospital Sky had chairs stacked around his bed with a sheet going around them in a circle, I said Sky, "What's all this"? He motioned me over and whispered, "A male nurse tried to poison my oxygen last night". Sky wanted me to help him write a song for his doctor who saved him. I hit a 'C' chord on my guitar and Sky starts singing in a Woody Guthrie, Bob Dylan style voice, " Doctor One you saved me and now I can go on", then he picks up a newspaper and sings the headlines, "Woman sues husband for a million in alimony,

Donnie Smith, Merrell and Willie Nelson

The Revels - front row- Sam Eddy, Dean Sorensen, Merrell- back row - Jerry Sagouspe, Jim MacRae, Norm Knowles, Tim Fankhauser

and the Lakers can't score". This went on for about twenty minutes with several nurses looking on. When I left one of the nurses said, "We are glad when you come; you're the only one that calms him down".

After several weeks Sky was released from the hospital and left for Santa Cruz with his girlfriend Terry. I would hear from him once in awhile when he was on the road somewhere and wanted me to wire him money. He managed to get a few independent label releases and gigs that helped support his vagabond life style.

One night I got a call from a friend on Maui who said that Mary Lee had gone off the deep end and was in jail for shooting a gun at a married guy that was going out with her daughter Molly. Mary was sentenced to a year in the women's prison on Oahu and had signed custody of our son Maui Joe over to her daughter Molly. Molly had moved to Santa Rosa California and I did manage to have Maui Joe for about six weeks, we had fun but it was a sad time. Mary got out of prison on good behavior in nine months and Maui Joe went back to live with her on Oahu, and they later moved back to Maui.

I got a surprise call from Norm Knowles and Sam Eddy of *The Revels*, the instrumental band I had played with as a teenager, the band was reforming and they wanted to know if I would like to join. We started doing rehearsals with me and my son Tim on guitars, Jerry Sagouspe on drums and original members, Dean Sorensen on Sax, Norm Knowles on sax, Sam Eddy on keyboard and Jim MacRae on bass. One of our first gigs was at a big club in Bakersfield California backing up one hit wonders Donnie Brooks who had the hit *Mission Bell* and Jewel Aikens who had the hit *The Birds And The Bees.* During Donnie Brooks set he started telling some jokes where he insulted every race and religion known to man. He looked at a black lady sitting in the front row and said, "Excuse me ma'am is that your lips or are you wearing a turtle neck sweater"? Then he decides to pick on a big cowboy a few rows back and says, "You're the guy I saw in the bathroom with the big belt buckle and the little dick!" I thought man we may not make it out of here alive but the show was a big hit and Sunny Tim shined with a great guitar solo in Jewel Aiken's version of *Stormy Monday.* We also played an outstanding show at the Bakersfield fair and the new Revels was going strong again just like the good old days when their song *Church Key* was a hit. We did a great version of *Church Key* and interviews with the original members on my California Music TV show. We went in Sutton Sound recording studio and recorded versions of *Tequila, Wipe Out* and *Lucille* with Tim on lead vocal. All three songs later came out on the French Legend label on a CD called "California Live" with a few songs from the 1991 concert in Pismo Beach with Nicky Hopkins. On September 7, 1992, Tim's wife Carol gave birth to Chelsea Lee Fankhauser, and I was now a grandfather!

The Revels continued playing clubs and concerts for over a year and the reunion ended on a good note at a large concert at the Solano county fair on a huge stage with thousands of people in the audience. The band *Tower Of Power* played earlier before us and there was a thirty minute break and the audience was ready to rock when *The Revels* hit the stage! We started out with *Tequila* and went in to *The Revels'* 1960 hit *Church Key* that immediately got everyone on their feet! Everything was going great and we started a version of Eric Clapton's *Further On Up The Road* with Tim singing lead. We did the intro and when it was time for Tim to come in singing, nothing came out; he just stood there with a blank look on his face. I'm trying to figure out what's wrong and we go into an instrumental and he finally comes in but singing the wrong verse. We just rearranged the song on the fly to fit whatever he sang. What I didn't know was that one of the fans took Tim behind the stage and encouraged him to toke up on a big joint, which he never had done before. Tim had a bunch of teenage girls in front of him screaming and cheering him on, and I had a gang of middle aged women dancing in front of me! Tim kept hiding behind his amp and I told him to get out there and boogie, as the set progressed he came out of his Cannabis time warp and rocked the house! Later we got a good laugh out of it on the drive back home, he promised he would never try weed again.

 Nobody could have imagined that *The Revels* song *Comanche* would be used in the movie *Pulp Fiction* later in 1994. The film would bring many of the old instrumental surf bands back into the spotlight and Del Fi records would even reissue *The Impacts* album *Wipe Out.* Movie and record producer William E. McEuen and I got back in contact and started talking about doing an album together with some new and old songs I had written about my studies of the lost continent of MU. Bill had moved his studio from Aspen Colorado to Santa Barbara just down the coast from me. I played him two of my newer songs *Queen MU* and *Prospectors Moon,* he liked my songs he had heard in the '80s and said he would like to include them in the project also. He found the story about the lost land of Mu very intriguing and started

Ancient Maui Ruins

Maui Ruins and MU map

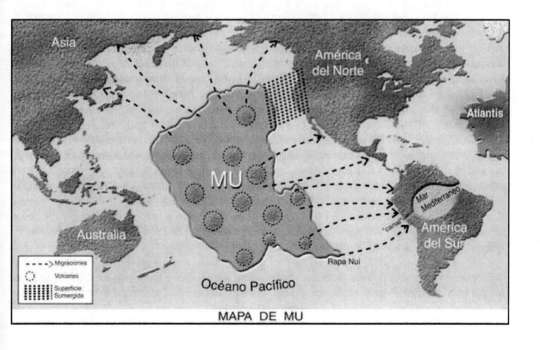

looking for information on it, one day Bill was in an antique book store in Santa Barbara and asked if they had anything on the lost continent of Mu? The old gentleman led him over to an ancient looking trunk that he opened with a very old key and handed him a one hundred and fifty year old book called *Queen Mu*. Bill said the hair stood up on the back of his neck and he felt like he was in a Steven Spielberg movie! Bill called me very excited and said, "You won't believe what I found!" I had never heard of the book and couldn't wait to read it, I wrote the song *"Queen MU"* from some old archeological tablets that told the story of a Queen Mu who came from a sunken civilization in the Pacific ocean and landed in South America and shared her knowledge with the Indians living there. The book was written by a Dutch explorer who had found the writings on tablets and the walls of the Pyramids in the Yucatan. I expressed my frustration to Bill McEuen that I never got to tell the story of Mu the lost continent, Bill said, "Lets do it!" I moved into his studio and in nine months we had the first album done and titled it *Return To MU*. The sessions featured Bill's brother John McEuen of *The Nitty Gritty Dirt Band* on mandolin and John's son Jonathan on guitar, Ed Cassidy, Art Dougall, Jerry Sagouspe, Luis Munoz and Gary Malabar on drums, Randy Tico, Colin Cameron, and Mike Bennett on bass, Jay Ferguson, Bill Cuomo , Dom Carmadella and Nicky Hopkins on piano and keyboard, Bruce Clark on flute and sax. I played guitars, bass , keyboard and sang, and my son Tim and Dean Torrence of *Jan and Dean* did harmony vocals. A stellar cast of outstanding musicians that brought a fantastic sound to this new 'Merrell music'!

Bill McEuen shopped the new album to Warner Brothers Records where he had many albums released previous, but the heads of the company he knew had moved on or were no longer in the business. He then went to BMG and Geffen Records, they liked it but nobody knew how to market it in this new world of changing musical tastes with rap and hip hop. Bill thought we should make it a trilogy and just keep recording until we had three albums, which we did for several years. We took a break near the end of 1994 and flew to Hawaii to do a photo shoot for the CD cover and booklet, Bill has a great eye for photography and we had a lot of fun shooting on the island of Oahu. Then we went over to Maui where my old friend guitarist Donnie Smith offered to drive us out to the ruins in the lava flow I had explored before. Bill and I and Donnie traveled on a trail in his four wheel drive truck to La Perouse bay where we set up Bill's big wide angle camera. I was in my purple robe positioned in front of a strange mound of rocks partially hidden by trees and jungle brush. Midway through the shoot I got an odd feeling as though someone else was there watching us, even though we were in the middle of nowhere. We took a break and I decided to explore around the back of the mound through the jungle, and to my amazement I found stone steps that led to a platform with a fire pit and a stone wall surrounding it. From this vantage point I could see the mound was very pyramid in shape.

When we got the photos back from the professional lab on Oahu there was an oriental lady in a light blue gown with gold ear rings and ancient leather sandals suspended in mid air over my

Dean Torrence and Merrell

Merrell and William E. McEuen

THE IMPACTS

Del Fi Records * D-Town Records * Sundazed Records U.S.A * Gee Dee Records Europe

left shoulder! Bill said, "How can this be, this camera can't do a double exposure!" He took the negatives and photos back to the lab, and they said that was on the photo, we didn't do anything but develop it. Everyone could clearly see the image but nobody had an explanation.

At this time many of my older albums were being reissued on CD, the French label Legend Music released *Doctor Fankhauser* and *The Exiles Early Years* and Sundazed records of New York released *Fapardokly*, *HMS Bounty* and a two CD set on my band *MU*. Del Fi records reissued *The Impacts* album *Wipe Out* and several CD compilations *The Impacts* were on. *The Impacts* steel guitar player, Martin Brown and I got together and started writing some new surf instrumentals to finish the album that had been started with sax player Joel Rose. D Town records put the songs out on CD as *Surfin' 101*.

We did some memorable concerts with the reformed *Impacts* and it seemed the old magic was still there. I had a meeting with Del Fi president Bob Keene and he assured me we would get a new contract and royalties for the CD releases. Del Fi put out a CD that had several songs from the movie *Pulp Fiction* called *Pulp Surfin'* and *The Impacts* started off the CD with "Fort Lauderdale" the song was even used on the popular TV show "Entertainment Tonight". At this time we found out the original contract Del Fi had with our producers Tony Hilder and Norman Knowles back in 1962 was for fifty two years! I had never heard of a record contract that long. Later Joel Rose, Martin Brown and I got together and signed the new contract with Del Fi. It was at this time that I informed Rose and Brown that the twenty eight year copyright that Tony Hilder had on our songs was about to expire and we needed to re copyright and publish the songs in the rightful writers names. I had my publishing company Fankhauser Music ASCAP and I put my songs *Wipe Out, Tandem* and *Sea Horse* in my publishing company. Joel Rose decided he wanted a publishing company and he formed Joel Vernon Rose music. Martin hated paperwork and Joel talked Martin into signing all his songs over to him, Joel didn't write any of the songs on The Impacts *Wipe Out* album. I co wrote *Tears* but was left out of the song in this behind the scenes deal.

Martin Brown came to me later realizing he had made a mistake signing all his songs over to Joel Rose, Martin tried unsuccessfully many times to get his songs back from Joel Rose. Rose distanced him self from us and wouldn't participate or communicate with us. Martin Brown and I decided to forge ahead and recorded two more CD's of instrumental surf music, *Eternal Surf* came out in 1995 on the German Gee Dee label and *Sex Wax And Surf* came out later in 1998 on the Japanese Captain Trip label.

I started doing a radio show called *Surf Beat* on a small FM station in Grover Beach and I was playing vintage instrumental surf music. The movie *Pulp Fiction* had brought back the energetic instrumental surf music in a big way and now there were legions of young bands playing this style of instrumental music, there was no shortage of CD's to play. I started interviewing both old and new bands and did a segment called "Surf Music News" that was quite popular for a few years on about twenty radio stations across the country. One morning I was sitting in my backyard having a cup of tea when a beautiful white dove landed on the fence, I said, "hi dovey" and it stepped on to my hand. The next morning the dove was there again waiting for me, I bought some food for it and made a perch and feeder in an olive tree in my back yard. The dove and I became friends and when the weather got cold I built a small cage and brought it inside to stay warm at night. Ed Cassidy came over one day and was really amazed at my new friend that just flew down out of the sky, Cass and I had a picture taken with the dove. About a year later a neighbors Cat almost got the dove and it flew away never to be seen again, like so many of my friends and loved ones. In 1995 *Spirit* drummer Ed Cassidy and I did some concerts and recorded a blues rock album together titled *On The Blue Road* by The Fankhauser Cassidy Band that came out on D Town records. My son Tim was in the band and did some fine blues lead vocals and guitar, Leroy Richards was on bass, Jim Enos on Piano and Bruce Clark on harmonica and sax. It got great reviews and airplay and was nominated for a blues award.

In 1996 I had a thirteen page article in the popular *Goldmine* music magazine that really opened up a flood of fans that were sending inquires and orders to my post office box daily.

It was overwhelming at first and Kathy Lambert was a great help sorting through the mail and filling the orders, at that point my mail-order business was doing the best it ever had.

Ed Cassidy, Dovey and Merrell

With all the releases and mail-order business I was able to fulfill my life long dream and purchase recording equipment for my studio. *Spirit* and I had an offer from Legend Records in Paris France to do a tour there together and we were negotiating the terms.

Randy California had given me some tapes of some new songs he was working on and wanted me to put some bass and slide guitar on, which I did and later added Cassidy's drums on two songs. They would later come out on a CD titled *California Blues* without any credit for the parts I recorded. Before the French tour Randy went on a vacation with his son Quinn to visit his mother who was now living on the island of Molokai. Randy and Quinn went swimming one day and got caught in some big waves, Quinn managed to make it to shore but Randy didn't and was never found. It was a tragic end to a gifted guitarist and songwriter that was a true innovator in the psychedelic period of Rock and Roll. Cassidy was lost for quite awhile, some musician friends from Colorado tried to get him to start a new *Spirit* band, but without Randy there wasn't any *Spirit*. Cass and I later recorded another eleven songs that came out together with the previous release *On The Blue Road* as a double CD and vinyl LP on the Italian label Akarma Records, titled *Further On Up The Road*. It had an exquisite gatefold cover with beautiful photos and graphics, a real collector's masterpiece. Akarma also released the left over songs from the sessions at Bill McEuen's studio as *The Man From MU,* another collectable gem on both CD and LP. One of the last gigs *The Fankhauser Cassidy Band* would do was a memorable one on a ranch near the beach south of Santa Maria California. It just so happened they were filming a scene at the ranch for the movie *Grumpy Old Men* with Walter Matthau and Jack Lemmon who Ed Cassidy enjoyed meeting. Cassidy and I did a few more gigs together and some recording but Cass decided to semi retire and take it easy for awhile, approaching eighty years old he was the oldest Rock and Roll drummer in history.

In 1997 I made another trip back to Maui and took along my son Tim and drummer Art Dougall and his wife Ferris. We did a gig and had some great spontaneous recordings with Donnie Smith and his band in his studio in Haiku. The songs from the session would come out later on a small East Coast label as *Visitor From 2000 AD.* During the session I went into a trance while Donnie was playing sitar and I wrote *Under A Maui Moon,* a magical song that could have been on my 1968 *HMS Bounty* album. Someone in the band asked, "When did you write that"? I said, "Just now". I brought the song back to the mainland and Bill McEuen liked it so much we overdubbed some keyboard and harmony vocal and added it to the *Return To MU* album.

During the trip to Maui I decided to visit my son Maui Joe who was now living with his mom in the remote village of Hana. I called Mary and she was very vague at first but said I could come and visit Maui Joe. Tim and I made the long beautiful drive through the jungle past glistening waterfalls and spectacular ocean views. We got there about noon and at first Maui Joe just looked at me for awhile and said nothing, and Mary told Maui Joe, "Give your dad a hug". Mary said she needed some things for dinner and would I drive her to the store, I said, "Yes" and we went to the Hana General store and got some food. I was in the check out line with the food and as we approached the counter Mary grabbed a twelve pack of beer and a big bottle of wine. I went "uh oh"; but after everything we went through together it was amazing Mary and I were still even talking. We went back to the house and Mary and Tim started sucking up the beers. I took Tim aside and said, "What are you doing, this could be dangerous". Tim said, "Oh its ok dad just be mellow". Tim had started having a drinking problem while painting guitars at Ernie Ball Music Man. Guitars, it seemed painting and alcohol went hand in hand.

It was getting dark and I just wanted to take Maui Joe back in town to the house we were staying at and have fun for a few days. We ate some fish and rice and Mary put on our 1976 album and said, "I'm sorry I didn't stick with the music, and I'm just an old drunk and please forgive me". It was a very sad moment to see someone who was so talented that I once loved in this state. Tim was passed out and there was no hope of driving the long winding forty five miles of jungle road back to town. Mary went to bed and passed out and I tried to sleep with one eye open on the couch. Sometime during the night she started stumbling through the house looking for beer and fell over an exercise bike. I turned the light on and helped her up and she gave me this wild look and said, "who are you and what are you doing in my house"? I said, "It's me, Merrell". "No this must be a dream" she replied. I helped her back to bed and she fell asleep. Early the next morning I woke Tim and Maui Joe and we started the long drive back to town. Maui Joe pulled out a cigarette, I said, "What, you smoke"? He said, "yeah, I smoke buds and drink beer too!" I said, "Great!"

We went surfing and played pool in the house our host Mike Graham gave us in Kula, and we were having a pretty good time till Tim decided to get drunk with Maui Joe, and Maui threw up. I said," That's it you guys knock it off and go to bed!" The next day Tim was kind of pissed at me and I drove him to the airport to fly back to California and go back to his job at Music Man in San Luis Obispo. The next day I took Maui Joe back to Hana and said an emotional good bye and I drove the long winding road back to town at night in a fierce tropical storm. And again it was a very sad time for me, not knowing when I would next see my young son Maui Joe.

I returned to California and we got an offer from the Japanese label Captain Trip to release the *Return To MU* album, and we also got an offer from Dee Cee records Germany to release it in Europe on vinyl. I sent Sundazed Records in New York a demo of the album in 1998 and told them I wanted to license it to different labels in other country's and they could have the U.S. and Canada rights. I never heard back from Sundazed and we made the deals with the Japanese and German labels to release *Return To MU* in the summer of 2000.

In 1999 I lost my mother Evelyn to cancer and I was very sad and lonely for quite sometime. She was my biggest fan and always enjoyed my music and live performances. I had purchased an older fixer upper house in 1998 in Arroyo Grande and I kept busy working on it and installing my recording equipment. Kathy and I had separated for about six months but she was having a hard time paying bills and was in poor health and not working, so she moved in with me. She went back to school and got a degree in computer and I was very proud of her being able to do that. She got a part time job doing medical transcription at home which can be very tedious and she was smoking like a train.

The cigarette smoking had been a sore spot in our relationship for a long time, and I could never understand how she could be a nurse and smoke, knowing how unhealthy it was.

One day I came home and found her pale as a ghost lying on the couch. She told me she was short of breath and her chest felt tight, I said it sounded like cardiac, but she didn't want to believe it. That night she was very sick and was throwing up, she went to the hospital and they said she was having a heart attack. They operated on her and fixed her clogged arteries but she was very weak for months.

In June of 2000 Just as the *Return To MU* album was coming out on the Japanese label I got a call from Donnie Smith on Maui. Donnie and his band were doing a big benefit concert with Willie Nelson for the Tibetan Dharma center there, and asked If I would like to join them? I already had plans to go to Kauai to help my old friend victor Bailey produce an album on Kauai. The dates worked out so I could do the concert on Maui and then fly to Kauai afterwards. Donnie picked me up at the airport on Maui and we went to Willie's house and discussed what songs we would play at the concert. We decided to do a version of *Wipe Out* with harmony guitars on the end. Willie asked me for a copy of my latest release and I handed him the *Return To MU* CD. The morning of the concert July 15, 2000 was a cloudy and blustery day that looked like rain, since this was a big outdoor event we were concerned. I met Hawaiian legend Willie K., a very versatile musician who could play the sweetest Hawaiian Slack Key and also get down on the meanest blues and Rock N Roll. Don Ho and his band were the opening act and Don came by Willie Nelson's dressing room and said, "Smells good in here" as Willie lit up a big Maui joint !

I quit smoking pot quite a few years before; when Willie passed the joint to me I took a few fake hits and passed it on. Donnie saw that I was faking it and went in the band's dressing room and told them I was pretending to smoke pot with Willie in his dressing room! When I came back to the band's dressing room somebody said, "What does Merrell and Bill Clinton have in common"? They all yelled out, "They both don't inhale!" I was busted!

When we took to the stage the clouds rolled back to clear sunny skies with a very excited audience. We went through several of Willie's hits, and Willie K. did a great version of Stevie Ray Vaughn's *Pride and Joy,* Willie K yelled out in the solo, "Take it brother Merrell", and I made my Telecaster scream! Then we launched into an outstanding version of *Wipe Out* that brought the crowd to its feet as all four of us took turns doing guitar solos. Not many people had ever seen Willie Nelson play electric guitar, but there he was ripping on a Fender Stratocaster doing a solo that sounded like it came from a 1960's surf instrumental! After ten days of jamming, swimming and just having fun on Maui I flew to Kauai.

CHAPTER 19
The Garden Isle

I landed on Kauai at about 11:30am and was met by Victor Bailey and keyboardist Yoriko Hongo and her two young daughters Natalie and Umi. I got in the VW van with Victor who immediately cracked a Budweiser and lit a joint. I met Victor on Maui in 1976 when he came over from Kauai to find me after hearing my Maui album. I helped him make a cassette demo of his original songs in the late '70s. He had some nice ethereal Hawaiian style folk rock songs that he played guitar and banjo on, I figured in all these years his songs must have gotten even better by now. He had a nice upstairs condo with his girlfriend Sarah that had a breathtaking view of the ocean in the little town of Kapaa. I wanted him to play me a song and get to work on the arrangements, but he wanted to get stoned and talk about the good old days. He just kept drinking one beer after another and smoking joints and cigarettes and rambled on for hours. I went to bed in a spare bedroom around 1:00am exhausted. Victor just kept talking and his girlfriend went in the living room and said,"Victor, Merrell's gone to bed". Victor said, "That's OK I just have one more thing I want to say". The next morning was a replay of the night before and nothing much was progressing I had to sit outside on the porch to avoid the smoke while Victor was rambling on inside. Yoriko appeared on the steps and she could tell I was uncomfortable and asked if I would like to stay at her house that was larger with an extra room. I said that sounded fine and we spent a few days going to the beach relaxing and playing some music together. We were waiting for Victor to call us to start rehearsing his songs for the sessions, but several days past without a call. Yoriko worked as a desk clerk from 3:00pm to 11:00pm at a beautiful Hotel on the beach called The Sun Spree Resort. On one of her days off we drove to the end of the road at Hanalei and hiked up to a Heiau at the top of a hill with a fantastic view of the North shore of Kauai. When we walked back down the trail to the car holding hands it felt like we had become one, even though we had never even kissed. She said she felt like she knew me from somewhere before and I felt the same way. In my cosmic hippie mind I was thinking, "This has something to do with the continent of Mu".

Bill McEuen was now living on the north shore of Oahu and had arranged for me to do an interview with reporter Burl Burlingame from the Honolulu Star Bulletin news paper. It came out with a long story about the *Return To MU* album and the concert with Willie Nelson on Maui. It was front page on every news stand in Hawaii, and I was getting recognized everywhere I went. The Japanese Captain Trip label was importing the album to California

Merrell and Yoriko
Hongo

and Hawaii and it was starting to get radio play and had a good buzz going.

Sundazed records of New York said they were interested in *Return To MU* back in 1998, and I had given up on them releasing it, then in late August of 2000 they sent me the contracts. The German Dee Cee Record label was just getting ready to release their shorter version that was going to come out on vinyl LP.

We were supposed to meet Victor and his girlfriend at a park to shoot some video and talk about his recording session. We pulled up at the park and Victor and Sarah were in a big fight and Victor was drunk, and they both had cuts and scrapes. We were upset by this and went back home and talked about what had happened. Yoriko couldn't believe how Victor was so

158

excited for me to come and record and had waited all this time and now he was just falling apart and couldn't even play! A few days later I went to see Victor and got him to play and sing but it was evident that the years of abuse had taken a toll on his voice and musicianship. I didn't think anything productive was going to come of the recording sessions with Victor and it would probably be best if I just went back to California. One night at the hotel while enjoying the music of Kauai legend Larry Rivera, he invited me up on stage and introduced me to the audience who gave me a big round of applause. The next day I had a meeting with the hotel manager in his office and he offered me a gig playing three times a week. I told him I had some previous commitments in California but I could come back and start in November, he agreed and we shook hands. Yoriko said goodbye to me at the airport and gave me a kiss and said she was going to miss me. Something happened between us but I wasn't sure what it was, maybe just the romantic tropical atmosphere I thought?

I watched the beautiful garden isle disappear in the distance and in four hours I was back in California, it all seemed like a dream. Kathy and I had grown apart having once already separated and we hadn't slept in the same room in years. At this point we were more like room mates, although we both still cared about each other. I told Kathy that I had a good offer to play at a beautiful resort on Kauai for possibly six months. We both knew change was in the air as she drove me to the airport and we said good bye. It was a relationship that lasted over ten years and she was the most loyal companion I ever had at that stage of my life.

I returned to Kauai in November of 2000 and Yoriko and I began playing at the Sun Spree Resort as a duo. We became very popular in no time and her Hula dancing was a highlight of the show. She had graduated from the Yamaha School of music with a degree in keyboard and she also had a very good voice. She did need a little coaching with her English and word pronunciation and she was becoming very polished with all the hours we put in performing. She got her desk clerk job at the hotel adjusted to allow us to play on the week ends. It was a very beautiful indoor outdoor stage and one night I was singing *Blue Hawaii*, Yoriko was dancing the Hula and the moonlight was shinning on the water, I really thought I had died and gone to heaven! Yoriko knew the grounds keeper of the old *Co Co Palms Hotel* where the movie *Blue Hawaii* with Elvis Presley had been filmed in 1960. Charlie the groundskeeper gave us a grand tour of the now closed up hotel and showed us the actual canoe still in the canal that was used in the wedding scene with Elvis Presley and Joan Blackman. I was swimming and surfing daily and exploring a Haeiu that had just been uncovered near the hotel. I was shooting video and Yoriko's teen age son Wesley helped out shooting video also.

December of 2000 we did a big release party for my CD *Return To MU* at The Sun Spree Resort on Kauai and Dean Torrence of "Jan and Dean" came over and sang with us. It was a fun show and we had a packed audience, a Japanese couple tipped us $100!

We hired a professional camera man to video us performing some of my songs on the beach that would eventually be part of the half hour television documentary *Return To MU*. We were playing at the Sun Spree Resort one night when we noticed a familiar face sitting in the corner with a base ball hat on and golf clubs. He was having a few beers, smoking a cigar and seemed to be enjoying the music. At the end of the set he tipped us very well, and said," nice music". I told Yoriko "that was Kevin Costner", she thought he looked very short! We later found out they were on Kauai filming the movie *Dragonfly* and they had taken over an entire floor of the hotel with staff and crew.

I got a call one morning that Martin Brown of *The Impacts* had died of cancer, another very talented musician and friend was gone. Kathy Lambert was living in my house in Arroyo Grande and I got a call from her in March 2001 saying that she had decided to move back East, but didn't give me any specifics. I later heard she was living with her mother in Pennsylvania whose health was failing. That was the end of my vacation on Kauai and I told Yoriko I had to return to California. We had gotten close and I saw the sadness in her eyes and she said "she couldn't live without me" and we made plans for her and her daughters Umi now 7 and Natalie now 10, to move to California a month later. Yoriko's son Wesley was in his second year of High School and moved to the northern California town of Antioch to live with his dad and grandparents.

CHAPTER 20
Back Home In Arroyo Grande

picked Yoriko and the girls up at the San Luis Obispo airport on a chilly day in April. I borrowed a truck from Tim to transport all their suitcases and boxes to my house. Yoriko's SUV was being shipped over on a barge and would be in San Pedro south of L.A. in two weeks. She had a hard time adjusting to the change of climate and culture from Hawaii to California and she seemed a little depressed. We had to go down to L.A. to retrieve her car from the docks and I tried to get somebody to help drive her car back as she had never driven on a complicated freeway system before, but nobody was available.

We drove down in my Firebird and as we neared L.A. and the traffic got more intense I saw the frightened look on her face. When we reached the giant bridge that went to Terminal island that was in the movie *True Lies*, she said, "Oh no, we have to go over that"? We found her car in the lot and gave the attendant the paperwork and she got in her car and I said, "Just follow me real close". We made it across the bridge and got on the freeway going north and a car got in between us and I lost her. I slowed down in the slow lane and spotted her and motioned to get off the freeway, we pulled into a gas station and filled both cars. I explained the freeway changes we were going to have to make, and please stay close to me as there was a tricky change coming up to get on the Ventura freeway going north. If she made a mistake she would either end up going east to Bakersfield or south to Hollywood, she was very nervous. I breathed a sigh of relief when she followed me on to the Ventura freeway going north, we stopped at a restaurant in Ventura and had something to eat, she was shaking like a leaf.

I assured her the worst was over and once we got on the other side of Santa Barbara the traffic would thin out. We got home to Arroyo Grande before dark and had dinner and went to bed, around 11:00pm she woke up shaking and complaining she couldn't breathe. I thought she might be having a heart attack, but she was only forty and in great physical shape. We got to the hospital ER and they said she was having an anxiety attack, and had her breath into a bag and gave her some medication to calm her down. The doctor was getting her medical history and asked if she had ever had anxiety or depression before, she said, "Yes, I was in therapy and on depression medication on Kauai". I asked her about it when we got home and she said

Fito De La Parra and Merrell

when she met me she felt so good she quit taking the medication, and that it made her sleepy all the time. She was very uneasy the next day and often felt another attack was coming on so we went to a local clinic. With her medical background the doctor diagnosed her as having depression and prescribed appropriate medication and therapy at a clinic nearby. The medication must have been a strong dose as she slept for a few days and I would wake her up to feed her and give her tea. Meanwhile her daughters Umi and Natalie were very happy and had already made lots of friends at school and felt they were living a rich lifestyle after being poor on a little island.

They changed Yoriko's medication to a lighter dose that she seemed to tolerate better and after many weeks she started to get more alert. I would sometimes go to her therapy sessions and they brought out a lot of problems she had with her mother in Japan who would get very angry and use harsh discipline at times. The girls would also sometimes join the therapy sessions and the therapist thought we had a nice family and that Yoriko had to remember to let Merrell be Merrell, the person you fell in love with and everything would be alright. Our original plan was to record an album together and do gigs as a duo like we were doing on Kauai, but we were getting a slow start. After a few months we started on our album together, a mixture of Hawaiian style originals and standards. She would get up in the morning, have breakfast and record a piano or vocal to one of the tracks I was working on and then go back to bed, I would wake her up for lunch , she would record another part and go back to bed and get up around three thirty when the girls came home from school. It took almost a year to complete the album with Yoriko in and out of bed for eight months, and when I had all the songs mixed and mastered she didn't remember playing or singing the parts! We made a deal with the Japanese Captain Trip records and October of 2002 *Tropical Heat* was released. It got fairly good airplay and sales in California, Hawaii and even Europe. Yoriko was still on a light dose of the medication and miraculously got better; we were enjoying working in the garden planting flowers and tomatoes and laying stone pathways in my large backyard.

I had started work earlier on a *Favorite Oldie's* CD of '50s and '60s songs and I had Yoriko add some keyboard and vocal and the recording was finished in about five months. I printed up 300 of the Oldie's CD on my Ocean Records label to sell at gigs. We started booking gigs with a vengeance and we were getting popular playing up and down the central coast from Morro Bay to Santa Maria. One day as we were walking on the beach I noticed they were remodeling the old fish restaurant that had been there for years. They were decorating it with bamboo and building an outdoor patio with a stage with a Hawaiian style palm leaf roof. I said, "That could be our future local gig!" We applied and got the gig playing Saturday and Sunday afternoons at Fins Restaurant, Grover Beach. It was a perfect venue for our blend of surf, Hawaiian and oldies and again Yoriko's hula dancing was a big hit and the word soon spread and the place was packed.

Charter cable in San Luis Obispo had been re running some of my old California Music TV shows and they wanted me to do a new show, but I just didn't know if I wanted to get back into the grind of doing a regular show again. Years earlier I had bought a seven foot tall Tiki that was standing in my patio, one night I looked at it and said, "Maybe we should do a TV show and call it *Tiki Lounge*"? Yoriko thought it was a good idea, so I called Charter Cable and they immediately gave us three time slots a week. Yoriko had a hard time speaking her lines in front of the camera at first but after a few shows she started to get the hang of it. One of our first shows was a two part live performance at Fin's Restaurant, and I went around on the breaks and interviewed people in the audience. The show went over very well and was good advertisement for the restaurant, Bruce the owner and manager of the restaurant was very pleased. We started getting bookings for luaus and upscale party's and local clubs, one Saturday we played three engagements in a row!

One night while reading the paper I saw that Steve Metz original drummer from *The Impacts* had died of cancer, it was a real shock! A month later his brother Jack of *The Impacts* and bassist of *HMS Bounty* also died of cancer. Then out of the blue after twenty five years I get a call from Jeff Cotton who was now living in Washington State installing ATM machines. He said. "You better sit down, Larry Willey was found shot to death in the desert!" Larry had become addicted to speed and they thought it had something to do with a bad drug deal. Larry got back in touch with me back in 1995 and he and I and Ed Cassidy had recorded a song he wrote called *Just Like Papa Told Me*. It was kind of prophetic as it talked about all the shooting and the stealing that was going down in the city.

 It was pretty scary to look at my wall of photographs and count the people I had played with that were now gone. Jeff Cotton continued to call me at random over the next three months or so, we talked about the good old days and how he liked my new music and was glad I kept going. He said he still played and remembered a lot of the old *MU* songs, I said, "maybe we should get together and play sometime", Jeff said, "you never know". At the same time I got back in touch with *MU* drummer Randy Wimer, who now lived in northern California and was selling water dispensers and filters. Randy had arthritis real bad and had to have both hip sockets replaced but was still able to play drums. He said he would like to get together and play again, I told him I had mentioned it to Cotton but never heard back from him. Randy said, "You might have scared him off". Randy said, "We just never liked what *MU* stood for, the lost continent and all that". I said, "You guys were the ones that got me in to it"? Apparently Wimer and Cotton still had the same quirks that they had back in 1974 when they decided to quit the band.

In 2002 the *Tiki Lounge* TV show and our live performances had gained a huge following on the central coast and we were being recognized every place we went. There was still no word from Sundazed Music in New York as to when they were going to release *Return To MU*, even though the contract had been signed over a year and a half ago. I was disappointed as Bill McEuen and I had spent so much time developing and recording what I thought was my best album ever. The Japanese and German versions were selling and getting a fair amount of airplay but there was no real promotion for it in the U.S.

Rockin Robert Hutchinson a DJ from WAIF in Cincinnati Ohio started playing my song *Calling From A Star* as a tribute to the Columbia astronauts who had died on re-entry to Earth. Several other stations heard it and requested a copy, I made 200 CDs and sent them out and by February 2003 it was on play lists and charts across the U.S. I was honored that they would use my song as a tribute to the astronauts and I even got a thank you card from NASA and The White House! In 2003 the TV show started getting aired on Maui thanks to my old friend Lorelei Bode who sponsored it there. I got a lot of fan mail from people on the island that enjoyed the show. The show also got on a station in Ann Arbor Michigan thanks to video producer Dennis Proffitt who sponsored it there. I enclosed my Hawaiian decorated patio to make shooting easier anytime day or night. I edited in a lot of the footage I had shot on Maui and Kauai, people where surprised the show was produced in Arroyo Grande California. I would interview well known music stars and sometimes we would jam together making musical history.

I received an email from Jeff Cotton in March of 2003 and this time it wasn't friendly. He wanted to know why I never signed a contract they sent to Audrey Franklin's office in 1975 that would give Cotton, Wimer and Parker the rights to everything regarding the band *MU*? Cotton wanted copies of their previous recording agreements and wanted to know why the *MU* albums had been reissued? I emailed Jeff Cotton back that I didn't want to sign away my rights to everything to do with the band *MU*, as he previously stated he wanted to burn all the master tapes! I further stated that Phil Meldman and United Artist Records could license them to whoever thy wanted, and since I rescued the Maui recordings from rotting in the old shack where they were discarded, I owned the rights to those tapes. And I had still never recouped the four thousand dollar loan I paid off for our Acoustic amplifiers that Jeff Parker stole. I told Jeff this was something he should have worked out years ago when he just walked away from the band and said, "It was the Devil's music!" I got a curt reply from him saying, "Thanks for your prompt reply".

Later Jeff Cotton had a lawyer from Seattle send me a threatening letter that Jeff wanted the master tapes back so he could re-copyright the songs he wrote solo and with me. It also stated they wanted a complete accounting of all the sales on various labels, and why hadn't I collected all of Cotton, Wimer and Parker's royalties and sent them to them over the years? Who had appointed me to be their personal accountant? It also stated that Cotton didn't want me to be able to use a few of my songs he had played on that were released on Glenn Records all the way back in 1964! It further stated Jeff Parker wanted royalties for the first *MU* album that he didn't even play on! Wow, they've really gone nuts I thought! I talked to their lawyer on the phone and told him I didn't have an address for Cotton, Wimer or Parker for over thirty years, and Cotton should have kept his ASCAP membership current to get his airplay royalties. I wasn't responsible to keep an accounting for any of the various releases legal or bootlegged of the *MU* albums. I did license the two CD set on Sundazed Music. I agreed to send them a statement for the Sundazed royalties and I signed over the rights to Cotton for the songs he wrote solo without me so he could re-copyright them. I explained the tapes were old and falling apart and they could make copies from records or CD's for copyright purposes. I got Jeff Cotton's address in Bellingham Washington and wrote him a letter stating how I couldn't believe how after I helped him for years, protected him and got him away from Beefheart, that he was now trying to sue me! I asked him if he was going to sue Don Van Vliet for all of his songs he played on? I never heard from Jeff Cotton again.

In May of 2003 I got a call from San Francisco agent Mike "The Fan Man" Somavilla who asked if Yoriko and I would like to appear on the popular Bruce Latimer TV show in Pacifica California near San Francisco? We went on the show June 11th and played a mix of *Return To MU* and *Tropical Heat* songs that went over very well. Richie Unterberger author of the book "Unknown Legends Of Rock And Roll" was also on the show and he talked about the chapter he did on me in the book.

During this time I received an email from Pam Miller the director of programming at Dick Clark productions, saying that they had played *The Impacts* song *Surfin' 101* on Dick's national radio show, and they planned to play more of my music. They even used *Surfin' 101* as background music on their phone answering message at Dick Clark Productions! My songs *Surfin' 101* and *La Perouse,* were both used in a surf movie about old surf board makers called *Shapemakers* by Paul Kraus, and once again like the energizer bunny, instrumental surf music was still going strong! Akarma Records from Italy got in touch with me again and asked if I would like to do a version of *All Along The Watchtower* for a Jimi Hendrix tribute CD that would feature, Robben Ford, Larry Coryell, Steve Lukather and other well known guitarist's? The CD was to be titled *Gypsy Blood Vol 2.* I signed the contract and accepted the $1000 in front to pay for the sessions and musician pay. I did vocal, guitar and bass, and my son Tim did some double lead guitar with me, Art Dougall was on drums and Yoriko did keyboard and background vocals. I sent the tape to the label and they emailed me that they got it and I waited to hear back from them. Then a week or so later I got an email saying that this wasn't a new recording and surely had to be from the '70s and they were not going to put it out! I tried to convince them that the band and I had just recorded the song, I even rented the percussion instrument called a Vibra Slap to put on the intro just like the Hendrix version and I mixed it down to analog two track tape to give it that '60s sound, they were still not convinced that it was a new recording, and said they would not use it!

Meanwhile I was working with a very talented graphics and video editor named Tom Goss on a documentary about my musical history and the making of the album *Return To MU*. It was a long process digging through my old film, video and photographs to put together a pictorial story of my life's work to that point. We were selling plenty *Tropical Heat* and *Favorite Oldies* CD's at our live show and I thought the *Return To MU* documentary DVD would also be a good seller.

I heard from Bill McEuen who was living on Oahu and had just purchased a rambling beach front estate with a main house, several cabins and a swimming pool. He was in the process of refurbishing it and that was his new project. He was slowly pulling out of show business to a mellower life style, as many of his friends like mine were passing on. Finally in June of 2003 I heard from Sundazed Music that they were planning to release *Return To MU* over two years after they signed the contracts! When it came out I got a flood of emails and calls from fans and friends saying the CD had *MU* as the band on the spine of the cover, not Merrell Fankhauser? This created a lot of confusion at retail outlets, magazines and in the music business in general. Every store was filing the CD under "M" instead of "F", the same thing happened on the internet, everybody thought it was by the band *MU* that broke up almost 30 years ago! This was a huge blunder after all the promo we were putting into the release and the TV documentary airing across the country. I immediately called Tim Livingston second in command at Sundazed Music in New York and told him about this big mistake. He said he was sorry and he would get the info changed at their site and every other place he could. I wrote a letter to Sundazed Music president Bob Irwin to reprint the CD back cover and change the spine to my name but I never heard back from him. I continued to promote the release and sent out 300 copies to radio that I made myself with the corrected CD cover. I did several interviews with magazines and online reviewers trying to set the record straight that the *Return To MU* CD was a new solo release by me and not the band *MU*.

Sundazed did little if any promo for the release and the damage had already been done and it appeared it would be another release that would disappear into oblivion, they later discontinued it after only a few years without telling me! Yoriko and I had a very busy summer playing. We would play a Friday night somewhere, then play at noon at Fins, then pack up and play an evening dance or club, and then arrive at noon on Sunday and do another noon to 3:00pm show. It was tiring but very rewarding and we were doing what we had talked about on Kauai, making CD's and playing in California.

One day I got an email from the Jimi Hendrix fan club and magazine saying how much they liked my version of *All Along The Watchtower* on the *Gypsy Blood Vol 2* tribute compilation. I said, "What, they released it"? The fan club sent me a copy and did a nice article and review in their magazine. I immediately emailed Akarma Records in Italy and they said, "Oh yes we decided it was a good track and included it!" I said, "Gee thanks, could you send me a few promos"? They sent me some copies but our relationship seemed a little strained after that and to my surprise they included it on a CD they released by *MU* titled *The Last Album*. I had no idea how they even licensed *MU's* second album, and did they now think the version of *All Along The Watchtower* was recorded by the band *MU*? Many other compilations on foreign labels came out with tracks mixed from other albums that added to the confusion of the origination of different songs.

My friend Bill "The Boogie King" Newell, a local DJ and record collector, ran into Fito De Laparra drummer from *Canned Heat* who was now living in Nipomo, just south of me. Fito had become a fan of Tiki Lounge and watched the show regularly. My band *HMS Bounty* had opened for *Canned Heat* in Bakersfield in 1968, that was the last time I had seen Fito in person. Bill Newell brought Fito over to the Tiki Lounge and we did a great interview about how Fito started playing drums in Mexico City and came across the border and started playing with *Canned Heat*. Fito brought along some old video clips and some unseen footage of *Canned Heat* playing at Woodstock that wasn't in the movie.

My old friend and genius promoter Audrey Franklyn started getting *Tiki Lounge* aired in Hollywood regularly on several channels and we started getting fan mail from the L.A. area. In November Yoriko and I went to Maui for a vacation with our friends Bill and Elanor Seavey. We shot enough video for two half hour shows with beautiful scenery and hula shows. Yoriko and I were not getting along well on the trip and things would just get uneasy, I couldn't understand what she was upset about? The last night on Maui we went out on the town in Lahaina for dinner and dancing and we finally had a good time. We were amazed at how many people recognized us from the TV show on Maui. The island had gotten very busy in the few short years sine I had been there last. We went to visit my old friend Donnie Smith in Haiku, a trip that would normally take less than an hour took three and a half hours in bumper to bumper traffic from Lahaina! What had happened to my mellow island? Reflecting back it was still a beautiful place but it was mellower in Arroyo Grande on the California central coast than it now was on Maui.

We had a big party December 23, 2003 for my 60th birthday. We made a *Tiki Lounge* show out of it with a great live jam that featured Fito De La Parra, Ed Cassidy, and Art Dougall on drums, Mary Ramsey of "10,000 Maniacs" on vocal and violin, Yoriko on vocal and piano, Sean Landers on Bass, Pat Goodrich and Ray Wells on Harmonica, myself and my son Tim on vocals and guitars. Ed Cassidy and Fito hadn't seen each other in years. Fito now had short hair and no beard or moustache. When I took Fito over to where Cassidy was sitting, Cass didn't recognize him. Fito said, "Its me Cass , Fito", Cass said, " Oh I didn't recognize you because you were smiling!" I found out later there was always a riff between *Canned Heat*" and "Spirit" over who got the best dressing room whenever they would play on the same show. It was a standout show, a lot of fun was had by the sixty people that were at the taping. Mary Ramsey and I sang a duet on *You Ain't Goin Nowhere,* and Fito did a great version of *Wipe Out.*

Yoriko was now working as a Teacher's Aid part time at the Arroyo Grande High School, and she was expressing interest in going back to school and getting a teaching degree. After the 9/11 terrorist attacks on the World Trade Center in New York, it was evident America and the world was headed for rough economic times, and there was a feeling of uncertainty in the air.

In January 2004 I began working on a new album of all Hawaiian style music to go with the new *Tiki Lounge* theme song I had written. The entire CD turned out to be a beautiful laid back island style recording with songs I had always wanted to do, *Blue Hawaii, Hanalei Moon, Beautiful Kauai,* and several new originals.

I was getting a lot of requests from fans and DJ's across the country to do another instrumental surf album, but I had some reservations about doing it with most of *The Impacts* gone. I finally gave in and the more I recorded, the more fun it was, I was right back where I started from. I did all the guitars and bass, Art Dougall played drums and Bruce Clark was on sax and flute. Along with new originals we did an instrumental version of *All Along The Watchtower.* Again the Japanese label Captain Trip came through and put out *Rockin And Surfin'* in July of 2004. It got great reviews and substantial airplay across the country in FM niche radio markets, to my surprise Dick Clark played our instrumental version of *All Along The Watchtower* on his national radio show.

My son Tim called one night and unexpectedly said, "They were selling their house in Oceano and moving to Oregon!" They bought a five acre place with a bigger house for a lot less than they sold their central coast house for. Tim and Carol had a big going away party and everybody jammed in Tim's studio that he had just finished a year or so ago.

I once again felt the pain of being away from both of my sons as Tim, Carol and my granddaughter Chelsea left for Oregon.

Chapter 21
Adventures In Merrell's World

*I*n April of 2004 Yoriko and I drove down to Hollywood to do the Audrey Franklyn TV show that aired to over two million viewers in the L.A. area. When we went in the studio we met actor Ed Azner who was just finishing a show. I had been working on my studio and had hit my thumb with a hammer and it was all black and blue. When Ed Azner and I shook hands he asked, "How did you do that to your thumb?" When I told him what had happened, he said, "Stick to guitar playing!" We all got seated on the set and Audrey Franklyn asked Yoriko some interesting questions, and she had good detailed articulate answers. We showed a few of our videos that were shot in Hawaii and Audrey asked us to come back again. The summer of 2004 was again a very busy time for the duo of *Merrell and Yoriko*, and we were booked solid.

One morning when I turned on the computer there was an interesting email from Pati St.John of Neos productions a well established record label on the island of Oahu. They wanted to license my 1976 version of *On Our Way To Hana* to be included on a retro Hawaiian compilation CD titled *Island Summer '60s and '70s.* It featured classic Hawaiian groups *Kalapana, Cecilio* and *Kapono* and *Makaha Sons Of Ni'ihau.* I considered this to be a big honor to be included, and the CD became a top seller in the islands.

One night while reading *Goldmine* magazine I noticed an article that said Del Fi Records had sold its entire catalog to Warner Brothers and they were planning on reissuing Ritchie Valens, Bobby Fuller and The Impacts. And sure enough I started getting emails from Warner Brothers and Collectors Choice Records wanting information for liner notes and a photo of The Impacts. Again it was amazing to me how instrumental surf music was still popular and kept getting released.

Summer was over and Yoriko was now teaching five days a week at Arroyo Grande High School and taking college classes three nights a week, and was teaching a Japanese language class. She was becoming very irritable and hard to get along with, I suspected she was doing too much and might need to go back on medication. She would have occasional bouts of anger and stage fright and it didn't look good in front of the audience. I was doing my best to keep the household running smoothly cooking dinner and making sure the girls got off to school on time. We even had a big birthday party for Yoriko in September and some of her Japanese language students came. I built a special low Japanese style table for the dinner. Yoriko would come home from school and her classes exhausted and would just go straight to bed without saying anything. She would read and drink tea in bed and then just pile the papers and cups in boxes along side her bed till there were no cups left in the cupboard. One day I found a spider nest in the boxes and moldy cups next to her bed and I threw away the boxes and stacks of newspapers and magazines. We had a big argument when she saw what I had done and she told me I was running a military camp, and I was too much of a perfectionist, and she moved into the garage. Only a month before she was planning our wedding, and in a blink of an eye she didn't know if she wanted to be with me? I had helped her when she was sick and paid her car and insurance payments and the household bills, that all seemed to be forgotten. We had a lucrative summer and she saved a few thousand dollars from the gigs and her share of tips and CD sales.

I had an appointment one day in October with an optometrist for a routine eye exam. They used a new advanced machine that examines the inner eye and takes a layered image that comes up on a computer screen. They found what looked like a melanoma tumor in my right eye. I told Yoriko I needed a test to see if it was cancer, and she said, "Don't do it, they're just trying to get money out of you!" I said, "I could lose my eye or die", and she said, "I have no compassion for you!" I was amazed at how cold she had become, almost like I never really knew her. The next few weeks were very uncomfortable as we barely spoke and avoided each other. One day she said, "We're breaking up and I'm moving out!" October 31st Yoriko and the girls moved to an apartment in Grover Beach and I never saw her again, although we had been together for four years.

One day I got a letter from my Washington Mutual bank saying the State Of Hawaii Child support enforcement had taken my entire savings of over $4,000 out of my bank, and the bank was charging me fifty dollars for making the wire transfer! I was never late on any of my child support payments for Maui Joe and I had gotten a letter in 2001 saying he was now eighteen and my payments were over. What I didn't know was they were charging me for Mary's welfare bill she had after we split up and it was over eighteen thousand dollars. It just didn't seem fair that I had to pay this while she was just hanging out drinking, and the Child Support enforcement should have notified me to start making payments instead of just stealing my money! So I resumed sending monthly payments to the state of Hawaii.

I got an email from author Michael Luckman that his book *Alien Rock, The Extraterrestrial Connection* was coming out on VH1 Doubleday publishing June of 2005. It was a book about rockstars that had seen or written songs about UFO's. He interviewed me and used a photo of my *Message To The Universe* album cover in the book, it also featured stories by Mick Jagger, David Bowie and many others.

With the arrival of winter I was alone facing new challenges. My first appointment at the San Luis eye clinic was disturbing, midway through the procedure, with my eye spread wide open and my head in a vise like structure, the doctor exclaimed, "This doesn't look good!" He said I needed to go see the guy who wrote the book on this kind of eye anomalies, Robert Johnson, at the West Coast Retina Center in San Francisco. An appointment was booked for November 24th in San Francisco. My friend singer songwriter T.W. Rush drove me to the appointment which lasted several hours. When I met the doctor I said, "Do you know you have the same name as", I didn't get to finish the sentence and he said, "I know, Robert Johnson the 1930's Delta blues player!" He

Hula Dancer Cynthia, Jane Russell, Hula Dancer Laurie and Merrell

did an exam and said, "This is an easy one, a few blasts from the laser will take care of it". I shook his hand several times and thanked him. I had a patch on my eye for several days, and one morning I removed it and I could see fine, I was just real sensitive to light. I had probably gotten this from years of being on the beach on Maui, being blond and not wearing sunglasses. From that time on I had to wear corrective shaded glasses not only outdoors but in front of the very bright stage and TV lights. I was so happy to be able to see and continue doing what I love, playing music and performing.

I received a call one day from Hula dancer Laurie Vierheilig who had heard Yoriko and I had split up and asked if I needed some dancers? I said, "Yes I do". Laurie and her friend Karen Bright came to my rescue and soon some of Laurie's students learned my songs and we had a new hula troop we called "The Tiki Lounge Dancers" I began playing some casuals with an eighty year old big band singer named Carol Towery who I had produced some CD's for. She had the voice of a forty year old and we quickly became a hit with the older crowd and did a memorable performance at a Christmas dance at the Santa Maria vets auditorium where I had played over forty years ago with The Impacts.

I decided it was time to get back to writing my book that had been put aside for several years and I started writing day and night for a few weeks.

In January 2005 I was performing in actress Jane Russell's night club show at the Radisson hotel in

Santa Maria California. Jane really didn't like Rock and Roll and insisted on all the performers doing 1940's songs. On one occasion everyone started requesting I do *Wipe Out,* I said, "Oh no, Jane wouldn't like that and I might get fired!" One of the older ladies convinced Jane to let me do it; I figured this would be the end of my performing in her show. I did *Wipe Out* and it brought the house down! I walked past Jane's table when I left the stage and she grabbed my arm very tight and said, "That was Hawaiian Rock and I liked it!" I said, "Thanks Jane", and breathed a sigh of relief and went to the bar to get a drink. The bartender noticed my arm was bleeding where Jane's fingernails had been, he gave me a napkin and said, "You better put something on that, you might get cat scratch fever!"

One day I was refilling my water bottles at the local Culligan water store when I was recognized by the attendant in the store, a pleasant outgoing guy named Dave Traughber.

Dave said "Hey Merrell I know who you are, I write songs too, maybe we should get together and collaborate?" I'd heard this before from lots of people and usually the songs just didn't have anything but I agreed to listen to his music. I was pleasantly surprised and he really had a good voice and a knack for early '60s Surf and Hot Rod style songs.

Over the next few months we started writing together and I got the band together and we recorded *"Back In The '60s"*, a song I had previously written as an instrumental that Dave put lyrics to. Then we recorded the other songs we wrote together *"My 40 Ford"*, *"Take It Down"*, *Surfer Susie, "Why Did I let her Go"* and *"The Ocean In Her Eyes"*. They turned out to be very nostalgic catchy songs that could have easily been hits in the early '60s. Dave quickly put a nice color CD cover together and I released *"Back In The '60s"* by *The Mystic Surfers* on my Ocean Records label. We sent the six song CD to about 100 DJ's on my radio list. It got quite a bit of airplay and chart action and even got in the top 10 on some internet radio stations, and we got a few orders in the mail. Sadly Dave passed away a few years later of lung cancer.

In March I flew over to Las Vegas to visit my old friend David Jungclaus and his wife Barbara who were now living there. They sold their house in L.A. and bought a beautiful desert style home in a gated community that had many retired entertainers and movie stars like Tony Curtis. I did an interview with David Jungclaus about UFO research and his book *City Beneath the Bermuda Triangle,* for my *Tiki Lounge* TV show. I also interviewed actress Vatina Marcus who played the Green Lady on the TV show *Lost In Space.* David Jungclaus and I were both fascinated by the tales about Area 51; the secret airbase in the Nevada desert. We made plans to take a trip to the *Little A'le'Inn* bar and restaurant in the tiny town of Rachel where UFO watchers congregated at the edge of the secret base.

We made some sandwiches and left on a cool desert morning headed for the extraterrestrial highway 375. I asked Barbara if she knew how far it was to Rachel and did she have enough gas? She said, "Oh yes, it's just about forty five miles, don't worry". It took quite awhile to get past Vegas and find highway 375, I couldn't believe the Nevada state road sign was actually labeled "The Extraterrestrial Highway" and it had two UFO's on it! We drove for about an hour and it looked like we were on the moon and reminded me of the floor of Haleakala crater, there were no other cars or signs of life for miles. I was looking at a road map and it looked a lot further than forty five miles to the town of Rachel, there was another very small town on the map about halfway there. It was called Alamo. Just then Barbara says, "We're almost out of gas", we all went, "What"? I said, "I hope we can make it to Alamo and there's a gas station there". David started making jokes about how someday they will find our bones out here in the sandy barren desert. We just barely made it to Alamo and there was a general store and gas station, I got out my credit card and filled up the car and we ate our sandwiches.

According to the map we were only half way to Rachel and it still looked like a long way. We went through some beautiful snow caped hills and found a nice place that looked like Mars and we shot some video of me singing my song *Out On The Desert*. It was fun and very surreal; we had to do it quick as the wind was very cold and biting. We jumped back in the car and finally arrived at the *Little A'le'Inn*, which turned out to be about one hundred and seventy five miles from Las Vegas. It looked more like a group of house trailers then a town and the first thing you see is an old tow truck with a ten foot diameter saucer hanging from a boom. We got out and set up the camera and I did an announcement that we had arrived and we were looking for UFO's and maybe some aliens too. There just happened to be one looking out of the window of the bar over my left shoulder. We went inside and we were met by a lady bartender and the owner, who said she didn't want to be on camera. Her husband who had started the bar and restaurant had died not to long ago.

People started coming in from their trailers to see who these new strangers in town were. A guy who was a musician recognized me and said he had seen my California Music show on TV. He said he played there on weekends, and I was thinking he wouldn't get much of a crowd way out here. Just then the door flew open and an older guy and his wife burst in very excited and said, "I saw something it was black and waffling in the wind!" The lady behind the bar said, "You want to talk to the guy with the dark glasses and blond hair". I thought it was interesting that she sent him over to me, neither the bar tender nor the owner wanted to talk about UFO's. The bar was selling numerous trinkets and t shirts with Aliens and UFO's on them; they even had some Alien guitar picks that I bought a handful of. The man and his wife drank a quick beer and off they went into the arid desert, real UFO hunters.

It was starting to get dark and I thought we should be getting back as we had a long desolate three and a half hour drive to get back to civilization. We made it back to Las Vegas and enjoyed a nice dinner in a restaurant and talked about our wild adventure to the edge of Area 51. The trip to the Nevada desert seemed like a time travel dream the next day as I flew back to the beautiful green and blue California coast.

The Tiki Lounge TV show of the trip was one of the current best and we got a lot of response from fans in California and Hawaii. In August of 2006 my son Maui Joe flew over from Maui for a visit, I hadn't seen him since 1997, and it was good to see what a fine twenty one year old guy he had become. I took him to some gigs with me and he helped set up the equipment. At one large venue I introduced him from the stage and he got a big round of applause, being a bit shy he found this both baffling and overwhelming. I even got him to do a segment for the TV show that was later used for a Halloween show. Maui Joe got to spend time with Tim on his ranch in Oregon and really enjoyed hanging out with his older brother and cousin Chelsea. We were all sorry to see him go back to Maui, but he said that he would be back.

I had been working on a kind of fantasy album in my spare time that I called *The Whole Day Ahead Of Us* that had a lot of light hearted fun songs. We did a great magical 3D style video in my back yard with the *Tiki Lounge Dancers* that my sister Linda helped shoot. I did many memorable shows that summer at Fins restaurant with Laurie Vieriligs' Hula troop.

In September 2006 my 1976 *Maui* album was reissued again on the Subliminal Sounds label from Sweden. Ads for the *Maui* CD appeared everywhere on the internet and there seemed to be a renewed interest in my easy laid back Island style music. Around the same time Morning Dew records of Germany reissued the first *MU* album from 1971 on vinyl LP, with a fantastic gatefold cover. The Italian labels had just passed the *MU* albums around without my knowledge and put out different versions on CD and vinyl with great attention to detail making each one very unique, and no royalties were ever received. I even heard *MU* was on a Greek label, it was impossible to keep up with all the releases that I never knew about. There was a bootleg LP of *Fapardokly* out on a U.K. label in the early '80s that I didn't know about for years. There were several compilations of my instrumental surf music and the 1968 *HMS Bounty* era reissues that I was just finding out about also. It was clear there was no way to stop the bootlegs and deals producers and labels made, even if you didn't make any money you just had to accept it. It was amazing how popular the *Fapardokly, HMS Bounty* and *MU* albums had become, *Rolling Stone* magazine in Germany even did an article about my '60s and early '70s records, and also mentioned my *Tiki Lounge* TV show.

The popularity of *Tiki Lounge* was at a high point and was airing to three million people. I decided to write a song called *We Love Tikis*. I released a CD single of the song to my list of radio stations and a video was uploaded of the song to the internet site youtube.com. The song *We Love Tikis* got over four thousand views at youtube.com in a very short time, and was getting played on over two hundred radio stations. The internet was definitely the way of the future for promoting and selling music. The music business had been in a slump for years, department stores like Wal Mart and K Mart were running the smaller mom and pop music stores out of business, and even chain stores like Tower Records closed. Every kid on the block now knew how to find their favorite music on the inter net and download it for free, this was hurting everybody, retail stores, record labels and the bands and artists, it was a new world. Something was happening, and it was very clear in this new fast throw away society that most of the music had dumbed down, radio had dumbed down and the people who were listening had dumbed down! Young people didn't care about a cosmic message from the '60s, they just wanted to listen to their favorite song or beat for a week and go on to the next one. Thanks to Classic Rock and Oldies stations with real DJ's that hadn't been replaced by computers, my music was still getting played. I was convinced by some of these DJ's like Rockin Robert Hutchinson of WAIF in Cincinnati Ohio to keep recording Instrumental surf music.

I started working on the CD *Rockin And Surfin' Vol 2* and it came out on Ocean Records in June of 2007, getting quite a bit of radio play and sales. I made enough money to keep recording more instrumentals for future volume's, I figured I could always release them on Ocean Records and help keep the genre of music alive.

I received an email from Bernd Kunze of JKS World Records Germany, asking if there were any unreleased *Fankhauser Cassidy* band songs? I said, "Yes including the only song Cassidy and I wrote together called *Stolen Guitar Blues*", about *Spirit* guitarist Randy California losing his guitar after a gig. The CD came out as *Stolen Guitar Blues* by *The Fankhauser Cassidy Band,* unfortunately it received minor radio play and didn't sell very well.

My son Tim and his crew had been working on a Merrell Fankhauser signature guitar in his shop in Gold Hill Oregon. It was from a design I did in the late '70s Tim refined it and said they would have a playable proto type in three months. Tim and his crew had built several guitars for *The Ventures* lead guitarist Nokie Edwards, I thought it was very cool Tim was hangin' out with Nokie as he was one of my early influences.

I was having a busy summer again playing shows up and down the coast. I had a full schedule of luaus with the *Tiki Lounge* hula dancers and we played the big five cities Elks luau. I started the season at Fins restaurant in Grover Beach with beautiful weather at the picturesque outdoor venue. The stage covering had succumbed to the harsh weather in winter and the mat and palm frawns were completely gone. There was nothing to block the harmful sun rays from hitting me while I did my three hour show. I asked Fin's owner Bruce if he was going to put a new roof on, and he said yes, "We will do something". We were having a very hot summer and by July it was hitting 100 degrees! One Sunday after playing in the heat I came home very sick, I had 102 degree temperature, and started shaking with chills and fever and I began vomiting! The next day I went to the doctor and he said I had sunstroke and to stay out of the sun at all costs. I was still very sick for a week and couldn't stand the bright TV studio lights or hot water, with any heat the symptoms would come back and I would start shaking.

The following weekend I took some big pieces of cardboard to Fins and tied them to the bamboo structure on the stage roof for shade. When I told Bruce the owner I had sunstroke he didn't seem to believe me and acted like it was a joke, He said, "If you die we will bury you on a sand dune and plant some flowers on you!" It took a few weeks to get over the sunstroke but I still had a few relapses and had to be careful. Due to the extreme hot weather people were finding it hard to sit even under an umbrella on the patio, the restaurant was packed inside, but only the die hard fans would brave the heat outside.

I got a call from Bruce at Fins around the third week in September telling me I was finished for the season and they wouldn't be having me back next year. After six years playing there I was suddenly let go. The end of September I got a call from a popular nightspot in Grover Beach called Mongos. They had quite a few well known '60s bands and artists play there in the past like Leon Russell, *Canned Heat* and *Starship*. I had played there twice back in May and they wanted me for a banquet they were having for some of our wounded soldiers from Iraq. The Surf Rider Foundation had taken them out surfing that weekend and some of the vets had lost legs and arms; it was awesome seeing them actually riding waves. It was a very enthusiastic crowd full of surfers and the local NBC news affiliate KSBY was there. I played Wipe Out and it was broadcast live that night on TV. At the end of the gig a soldier in a wheelchair came up and shook my hand and said it was an honor to meet me and hear me play, it was a very moving experience.

My son Tim phoned me from Oregon and said he was going to have a big musical bash for his 41st birthday in October, and would drummer Jerry Sagouspe and I like to come up and play? He had the new Merrell Fankhauser Signature guitar finished and would present it to me with the crew when I came up.

A few years earlier, Jerry had bought a beautiful vintage 1978 GMC motor home and we set out for Gold Hill Oregon on the 28th of October at 4:00am. I decided this would make a great episode for my *Tiki Lounge* TV show, so I videoed the entire trip and got Mt. Shasta in all its snow covered glory. We arrived at 6:00 in the evening in the beautiful valley where Tim had his new 5 acre ranch complete with a recording studio and guitar factory. We were met by Tim, his wife Carol and my 16 year old granddaughter, Chelsea, who had grown into a beautiful young lady. We had a great time playing some of our old songs, with my son Tim on guitar and vocals, Keith Frasher on Bass and Jerry Sagouspe on drums. A good time was had by all and the crowd enjoyed seeing father and son rocking out! The next day we did a video of the crew at Rock Creek Guitar USA presenting me the new Merrell Fankhauser signature "Impact" guitar, and then we did three music videos; Tim's song *Long Rifle*, the surf instrumental *Monster Swell* and a hot instrumental version of *All Along the Watchtower*.

The following day it was time to record. We just started jamming and right away a great instrumental just popped out in true Fankhauser fashion. We titled it *Indian Summer Surf*, as the valley where Tim lived was surrounded by these fantastic buttes where the Indians had once lived, you could really feel the vibe. The new Fankhauser guitar was beautiful and had an awesome sustain without even being plugged into any effects! The next day I said we need a song to put to video for our trip back, so we started jamming again. Tim came up with this great rhythm guitar part he was playing through a Roland guitar synthesizer that made his guitar sound like a piano, I came in with a dreamy lead part on my new Merrell Fankhauser signature guitar. I imagined us driving through the redwoods in the fog and cruising down the northern California coast.

We finished the song and mixed it but we didn't have a title for it yet, I figured the title would come later. In the morning we left and said goodbye to everyone and started our journey home. Instead of going straight down Highway 5 to California, the way we came up, we cut across the top of Oregon driving along the Rogue River through some beautiful country. Jerry wanted to find a nice RV park somewhere in the Redwoods by a stream where we could spend the night, have dinner and a cocktail and relax, in that order. This was a nostalgic part of the trip for Jerry as his parents had taken him and his brother on this route fifty-one years earlier.

They had taken a picture under a statue of Babe the Blue Ox and Paul Bunyan, and he wanted to recreate this photograph. I thought this sounds like some great video footage for the TV show! First we made a short stop at a Catholic School in Eureka where an old friend of Jerry's was now working. After a tour of the school we said goodbye and got on our way to the Redwoods and the statues in the tiny town of Klamath, California. Jerry decided to get off the main road and explore the inner most parts of the Redwoods, I got some great video of the giant trees with thick fog, just what I had envisioned when we were recording the last song at Tim's. Suddenly we realized we were lost! There was no light, we were under a canopy of giant trees and couldn't tell which way was north or south. I kept feeling Highway 1 was somewhere off to the right, but Jerry wasn't sure. I got the feeling he liked being lost!

Finally after an hour or so of wandering around we found our way back to the highway. We found the statues of Babe the Blue Ox and Paul Bunyan next to a gift shop in the coastal town of Klamath. We got some great video and I took the shots of Jerry under Babe the Blue Ox that matched the one taken with his family years ago. We got back on the road and drove past several RV parks but they just didn't seem right to Jerry, not quite what he had in mind. It was starting to get late and we didn't have much light left. I suggested we find something soon as we didn't want to be driving around looking for a place in the dark, and I was starting to get hungry. But Jerry insisted he had to find just the right place and be able to eat, and then have his cocktail and kick back. It was now dark and we started driving up this steep grade about fifteen miles from Willits. At the top of the grade was a sign that said Cool Valley RV Park, it was three miles down in a canyon. Jerry said lets try; we're getting low on gas anyway. We start down this narrow winding road into this dark canyon and came to what looked like a graveyard for old broken down campers and trailers. We saw a guy come out of a truck with a crumpled up hat and beard looking like somebody out of the movie Deliverance, or Chainsaw Massacre. Jerry said lets get out of here and nervously turned the big beautiful GMC motor home around on this steep narrow road.

The engine started sputtering a little bit going up the steep road, and Jerry said, "I knew I should have brought my shotgun!" Man, we were sure glad when we reached the top of the road; I figured we could at least coast down the other side of the grade if we ran out of gas and make it into Willits. We passed a couple gas stations and Jerry didn't want to stop because the price was a little too high. I said, "Jerry, all those things you wanted to do in that specific order aren't going to happen at all if we don't get gas." Just then a station appeared that Jerry thought had a decent price for gas and we pulled in. We went inside the office and asked if there were any RV parks nearby. The lady said, "Well, there's one back the way you came, about twelve miles at the top of the grade." Jerry and I looked at each other and said, "Oh no that place scared us."

She asked "where are you boys from?" We replied that we were from southern California. She said, "Oh, well there's a Wal-Mart in Ukiah, I think they let people stay in that lot overnight". She gave us the directions, and off we went, it was getting late; we were both starving and afraid all the restaurants might be closing. We were relieved when we saw the Wal-Mart and an Applebee's restaurant just across the parking lot, we were happy campers! We walked in the restaurant and were greeted by this cute blond girl that looked like a *Playboy* Bunny. She had little devil ears on and a little red tail; we had completely forgotten it was Halloween! We sat down and Jerry immediately ordered a cocktail and two beers and we both ordered steak dinners. Jerry was facing the podium where our *Playboy* hostess was and he said, "Merrell, turn around and look at this." I turned and looked to see her wiggling her perfect butt and swishing her devil tail back and forth .Jerry says, "I can't stand it, she's driving me nuts." I said don't look at it, just relax. He's going, "Oh man!"

We finished our dinners and Jerry gets up and goes out ahead of me, and as I walked by this devilish temptress I couldn't resist, I stopped and said, "See that guy, he thought you had the cutest tail he's ever seen". She gave us a big smile and said thanks. When I got out side Jerry asked me, "What did you say to her"? When I told him what I said, he couldn't believe it. We got back to the motor home and Jerry said" maybe we should have invited her to join us". I said, "Yeah we would probably find out she's only seventeen and get surrounded by a swat team telling us to come out with our hands up!" We fell asleep and woke up about 5:30am and decided to leave. As we were driving out of the Wal-Mart parking lot we noticed a sign that read, "It is unlawful to spend the night in this parking lot, no overnight camping allowed".

We wondered how we got away with that? As we approached San Francisco, the early morning traffic had turned into stop and go, so we decided to get off and get some breakfast. After some searching we found a cafeteria style restaurant in an industrial park and had a good breakfast. However we were lost in this industrial area for a half an hour trying to find our way back to 101. I quoted my father when he would sometimes say, "This is a case of the blind leading the blind", Jerry didn't laugh. Jerry wanted to stop at this shop in Hayward that specialized in repairs and parts for his motor home. It was a good break and we both learned something from the owner of the business. We then got back on 101 and I was looking at the map and doing the navigation to keep us on course. I got up and went to the bathroom and when I returned Jerry exclaimed, "Something's wrong, this road doesn't look right!" Just then a sign went by that said Hwy. 17. I said, "We're on our way to Santa Cruz, how did this happen?" Jerry said," I don't know, it just turned into this". We couldn't turn around, so we ended up in Santa Cruz in a parking lot looking at the map and trying to figure out our best way to get back to 101. I saw we could go south towards Monterey and make a left at Castroville and connect with 101 at Salinas. We got to Salinas and somehow became lost again, I kept feeling like we needed to go left. Jerry saw a freeway sign and followed it onto the freeway that was taking us back north to San Francisco. We got off and somehow found our way back on the freeway going south. We found a rest stop about 60 miles north of my house and pulled over and took a nap for about an hour, we finally arrived home just as the sun was setting.

The entire trip seemed like a dream as we reflected back on it that night. Jerry called me up about a week later and asked if I had seen the Fox News? I said no. He said, "You won't believe it, the head of Babe the Blue Ox broke off and fell right where I was standing!" Man talk about timing, if we had been a week later we wouldn't have gotten the shot and you could have been killed! That edition of Tiki Lounge, with the trip to Oregon, got a lot of response from viewers everywhere. I was getting radio play on various songs from my albums all over the world in the U.S., Canada, Japan, Europe, Greece, Spain, Russia, Poland and even Serbia.

In November Ed Cassidy and I did an interview for three central coast newspapers about the new *Stolen Guitar* CD release and my Merrell Fankhauser signature guitar. The reporter wanted a photo of Cass and I playing together for the article, Cass got his old 1947 Ludwig drum kit out of storage and set it up in the Tiki Lounge. We just started jamming for the photo session and came up with a Jazz Rock style instrumental. Cass was excited and said we should try to record the song. The next day after about three takes we had a good track recorded. Cass would drop by every week or so and say we should try to record some more, then he would call a day or so later and say he just didn't feel up to it. He was having balance problems and a lot of lower back pain. He was reading this book about a world traveler who had made this four and a half foot walking stick out of bamboo. Cass had one made and began walking around Arroyo Grande with this big stick getting some strange looks from folks. 2007 was coming to a close with many changes in the music business and the world. The big conglomerate record labels were swallowing up the smaller ones, internet pirating was running rampant, we had global warming and the war in Iraq, and it was indeed a changing world.

2008 started off good with an offer from the German JKS-World Records to release my new album *The Whole Day Ahead of Us*. The music was a '60s style fantasy, where the world was all Peace and Love and everyone was happy. Far from reality as the war in Iraq raged on and the presidential elections had for the first time a woman running, former first lady Hillary Clinton, and a black man named Barack Obama. I thought "What does the future have in store for the United States and the world?" We were having one of the coldest winters on the California central coast I had ever felt, with temperatures going down into the thirty's at night. The snow level was down to the low lying foothills close to what used to be our semi tropical beach. The rest of the country was experiencing the same cold and record snow. They were saying it was global warming, but it felt more like a new Ice Age. It was a good time to stay indoors, record and work on my book. Meanwhile I kept working on more surf instrumentals for *Rockin' And Surfin' Vol 3* and my son Tim came down and recorded a song with me titled *The Good Old Days*. I was also happy to hear Maui Joe was moving over to live with Tim on his ranch in Gold Hill Oregon. Tim got Maui Joe a job driving a fork lift in a food warehouse and my wild jungle boy settled into mainland life.

Next I managed to crank out a country flavored CD titled *Merrell Country*. It had a couple originals *Time To Move Around* and *Lonely Love Blues* co written with *H.M.S Bounty* guitarist Bill Dodd. I also did two of my favorite Hank Williams songs *I Cant Help It* and *Hey Good Lookin'*. In early April of 2008 Ed Cassidy fell while getting out of his car and broke his leg, it required surgery as he had twisted and shattered the bones below his knee on his right leg. He ended up in the same nursing home my mom had been in near my house. I couldn't believe it when I went in to see him, as he was smiling like I hadn't seen him smile in years! He said, "you know Merrell I am so glad this happened and I ended up here, I've met so many nice people to talk to, and they all remember the big band era the way I do". I never thought I would hear someone say they were glad they broke their leg and ended up in a nursing home. After two months Cass was discharged to go home, using a walker. In September of 2008 we were experiencing some of the worst wild fires that had ever been seen up and down the state of California. Then Iowa was flooded like never before and once again the Gulf Coast was hit with a hurricane. I was watching the evening news and they kept saying, "It looks like its time to move to higher ground". A burst of inspiration came over me and in fifteen minutes I wrote a song called *Move To Higher Ground*, everyone said it sounded like a hit! I got the band together and we recorded it in about a half an hour. We did it in an almost bluegrass style, I was playing my Martin acoustic guitar and singing like the good old days on Maui. I had Ray Wells on Harmonica, Julie Beaver on Violin and Art Dougall on drums. I sent a demo of the song to DWM Music a distributor in Iowa , and they said they could get it on the radio and we should sell the CD single and donate a portion of the money to flood relief. I ended up pressing 350 radio promo copies and got the song on nearly 300 stations, and it ended up #1 on about fourteen stations. I got a good news call from my son Tim in Oregon that my son Maui Joe was doing good working at the frozen food plant and Tim gave him an old Ford Maverick he had and Maui Joe fixed it up and had it running in no time. Tim also helped him get a California drivers license and insurance and got his last named legally changed back to Fankhauser. I was very happy to know Maui Joe was now living in Oregon with his half brother Tim, as the island of Maui had turned into a meth casualty among the young people and wasn't a very safe place.

One morning I opened my email to find that DJ "Rockin'" Robert Hutchinson of WAIF Cincinnati, Ohio had died of pancreatic cancer. He was truly one of the biggest supporters of instrumental music and he was a great loss to the genre of music. His loyal friends and DJ's at the station vowed to keep his show going in his memory.

Drummer Dick Lee who had played on the *Fapardokly* album called, and said we should get together and record some songs with Bill Dodd. I told him about the success of the *Move To Higher Ground* song and that I was on a writing jag and recording together sounded like a good idea. We got together for about a week, and recorded *The Ballad Of Fapardokly*, the story of the band playing at the Cove in Pismo Beach, *Maui Wowie* and *Somewhere In My Heart*. I had drummers Art Dougall and Jerry Sagouspe come in and play on the remainder of the songs. Sax man Bob Osborn played on *Love Sick, Bounty's Booty* and *I Landed On The Mainland*. The album ended with an anthem titled *Rock And Roll Fever*. To everyone's astonishment the entire albums worth of new songs were written and recorded in less than two months. I got an email from my old friend Hans Kesteloo in Germany who had been running the Music Maniac record label there for years. I told him about the project and he asked me to send him a demo, and he instantly replied he would like to release it. Another example of how the internet helped in speeding up the process of finalizing a deal. In the old days you would have to send it all by mail waiting for months for the contracts, now it could be done via email in a week! The 12 song CD *Move To Higher Ground* came out worldwide in April of 2009, with a great fold out eco style cover and full color booklet with all the lyrics inside, Hans had done a wonderful job of packaging my latest recorded work.

Hans also began putting my ½ hour TV show *Tiki Lounge* on the internet at his site beyondthebeatgeneration.com. It was amazing how sites like this and youtube.com were making it possible for anyone around the world to view videos and live performances. By June the full length CD *Move To Higher Ground*, was getting good sales and radio play across America. I then got a proposal from Om Om Records of Italy to reissue my 1983 Maui sessions with *Quicksilver Messenger Service* guitarist John Cipolinna and a few songs recorded in California from that time period. The CD *Merrell Fankhauser And Friends Live On Maui and California*, came out in May near the 20th anniversary of John's passing. A DVD movie was in the works about John's musical history and I was filmed talking about the fun sessions we did on Maui back in 1983, it later came out as a beautiful multiple DVD package titled *Recoil*.

I got an interesting email from Warner Rhino Records around this time that they were putting out a 100 song box set CD with the biggest groups from the '60s titled *Where The Action Is: L.A. Nuggets (1965-1968)* and they wanted to include my 1967 song *Tomorrow's Girl* in the line up. The song was originally recorded by *Merrell and the Exiles* but because it ended up on the now famous *Fapardokly* album they were listing the band as *Fapardokly*. I agreed and they sent me the contracts. It was set for a September release, what a surprise to have three releases come out in a year that was marked by the biggest economic recession the country had ever seen since the great depression. I felt very lucky to get anything released. Barack Obama was now the first Afro-American to ever be elected president and he was trying to bring about change by spending more money than any president before him. General Motors had to file bankruptcy, the war in Iraq and Pakistan was still not over and the air of uncertainty was now hovering over the world like a dark cloud..

Bill Dodd and I continued to record in my studio, this time we were working on more instrumental surf songs that really had a different sound. I played a lot of lead and rhythm guitar using my new blue Merrell Fankhauser signature guitar that had a sound that was truly out of this world. Bill Dodd did some fine leads and harmony guitar parts to my leads. I also played bass and keyboard on the tunes and Jerry Sagouspe came in on drums with Bob Osborn on sax. These songs would later become part of *Rockin' And Surfin' Vol 4.*

We were having fun making music just like we did when we first started playing together as teenagers. I got a call around Fathers day that Maui Joe had gotten a raise and promotion at the frozen food plant and he decided to go out and celebrate. He got arrested for drunk driving and his license was suspended for three years, he decided to go back to Maui and left. Tim had noticed Maui Joe had a drinking problem and tried to talk to him about it but he just got defensive. It seemed Maui Joe was plagued with the same problem as his mother and his other half brother Phillip. Tim and I said a prayer together to keep Maui Joe safe. Meanwhile Bill Dodd got mixed up with a gold digger who kept breaking his heart and Bill fell back into a drinking binge and ended up getting arrested twice. He still had talent but it was obvious he was unstable and really couldn't be counted on.

I got a call from Joe Klein who I hadn't heard from in years. Joe was now retired from the music biz and had bought a house in Loflin Nevada where he did a pod cast internet radio show. Joe was going to a convention in San Francisco and said he would stop by for a visit. Joe arrived in the late afternoon about 4:45 and we decided to go to dinner at the local Chinese restaurant, there was a knock at the door and it was Bill Dodd. I introduced Bill to Joe and went to the bedroom to get ready, I overheard Joe trying to make conversation with Bill, but Bill's answers sounded like he was having a completely different conversation! When I went back in the living room I could smell that familiar vodka emanating from Bill, and Joe asked Bill to join us for dinner. Bill said yes and we got into Joe's new Mercedes and headed for the restaurant. Bill was staggering a bit as he got out of the car but had been very quite. As we entered the restaurant several people recognized me and I stopped to sign an autograph and we got seated at a corner booth. All was quite and Bill was sort of mumbling under his breath and all of a sudden he looks at Joe and says "You're not my friend!" Joe said, "Gee dude give me a chance, I just met you fifteen minutes ago". Then Bill yells out "Son Of A Bitch", and everyone in the packed restaurant looks at our table! Kim the waitress comes over and apologizes saying she was sorry they were so busy tonight. We decided to get the food to go to save ourselves from any further embarrassment, and just then Bill yells out "Fuck!"

We got up and I helped Bill to the door and Joe paid for the food. Bill was having a hard time opening the door and had mistakenly locked it, I unlocked it and he stumbled into the grass area in front of the restaurant. Joe and I started walking to the car and it was dark now and Bill couldn't find his way to the car, he kept saying "I can hear you but I cant see you"? We finally got him in the car and on the drive home Bill says to Joe, "So you're a hot shot Hollywood producer"? And Joe says "I've produced a few things". Bill says "Well I can play some blues that will blow your socks off!" When we get out of the car Bill gets aggressive and says he can kick both of our asses, and Joe asks "Is he kidding Mer?"

I instantly grabbed Bill in a choke hold from behind and took him to his car and told him to go home and sleep it off! Joe said "Geez Merrell, you played music with him he's dangerous!" I told

Joe he wasn't always like that and used to be a good guitar player. Joe and I had some good laughs and spent the rest of the evening talking about the good old days and he left the next day for San Francisco.

The next night Bill called and said he wasn't drunk the previous evening and he knew something happened but he couldn't remember what? Bill was living with his mom and he got violent with her one night and she had to call the police. Bill later moved back to Denver Colorado, alcohol had ruined another good musician.

I got an abatement order from the fire department to remove the weeds from the hill in my backyard. I hired a guy to help me and in three days we cleared the hillside and loaded everything into a large green waste container on wheels. What we didn't realize after loading the weeds that contained a lot of dirt clods and sand was that the container weighed over three hundred pounds! The next day I decided to wheel it around to the front of the house to be picked up by the garbage truck. When I got it rolling I noticed how heavy it was and when it hit the lip on the sidewalk it catapulted over knocking me down on my back with the container on my legs and chest! It completely took my breath away and I heard my ankles crunching as it flattened my feet out, then the door opened and the sand started filling up my nose and mouth!

My right hand was trapped under the container and with my left hand I started blocking the sand from suffocating me, I was trapped and couldn't get up and in extreme pain. I managed to clear my nose and mouth and started yelling for help, luckily my next door neighbor heard me and got another neighbor and together they lifted the container up enough to get me out from under it. I was skinned up and had big swollen bruises on both knees and my right ankle was very swollen. I went to a doctor and he said, "You must be very limber, nothing is broken, you only have a sprained right ankle". I started getting arthritis in my fingers years earlier and my right hand and little finger was very sore and swollen, and my back was out and I could barely walk. I got a bandage on my right foot and some pain pills and went home to bed. After a few weeks I was better but very sore and couldn't lift anything. This would have been a perfect video clip for Americas Funniest Videos!

I had a concert coming up at the Grange Hall in San Luis Obispo, it was a challenge and I had some difficulty playing but I made it through it, smiling while in pain. On June 25, 2009 the world was shocked with the sudden death of pop superstar Michael Jackson at the age of fifty of a suspected drug overdose. It was the end of another era that affected everyone the way the death of John F. Kennedy, Elvis Presley and John Lennon did. It was an uncanny day of celebrity deaths as actress Farrah Fawcett and '60s singer Sky Saxon also died on the same day.

I got an email from Bill McEuen who had moved from Hawaii and was now living in the mountains above San Diego. Bill invited Jerry Sagouspe and I down for the weekend at his beautiful spatial house on a hill. Bill was disillusioned with Hollywood and the music business and was in a state of transition. He had a state of the art computer editing suite in his house and was working on a documentary about sail boats and people that sailed them. Many movies had now been shot on high definition video and edited with a Macintosh computer using the professional *Final Cut Pro* program. Film-making was now in the hands of anyone who had the money to buy the equipment and a desire to make a movie. Bill McEuen was now making movies with this new media without the hassle of lawyers, agents and studios. We had a great time talking about the old days and the *Return To MU* album we had produced together. I told him about the new surf instrumentals I was working on and it sparked his interest and he said to send him some tracks and we might collaborate on a video. I hadn't seen Bill in seven years and it was good to see him still being the creative genius that he is.

The August 3rd issue of *New Yorker* magazine had an interesting article about well known author Thomas Pynchon's new book *Inherent Vice* that mentioned my '60s group Fapardokly! The book was about a pot smoking detective on the Sunset Strip in the late '60s and early '70s and *Fapardokly* and my song *Supermarket* were mentioned in the book. Oddly enough the Lost Continent of Mu and Maui was also mentioned in the book! In one paragraph a surfer was being interviewed and he was asked, "which version of Wipe Out came first, the one with the laugh or the one without"? The one without the laugh was *The Impacts* version! I thought, "Who is this guy and how does he know all this stuff? Sundazed Music in New York, who had reissued the *Fapardokly* album on CD, had a description at their web site that read, "*Fapardokly* is the album that will make Merrell Fankhauser a household name! I thought they were nuts at the time, but the *Fapardokly* album seemed to be growing in popularity worldwide.

Around October of 2009 I got a call from Rhino Records producer Andrew Sandovol asking me if I would like to join him and some of the other bands and artists that were on the *Where The Action Is: L.A. Nuggets 1965 – 1968* CD compilation at a big release event at the *Egyptian Theater* in Hollywood on November 1st? I said yes.

I arrived at *The Egyptian Theater* around 2:00pm with camera man Gerald Craig and DJ friend Bill "The Boogie King" Newell. We got situated at the tables in the lobby for autograph signing, and to my surprise I was already getting recognized by a large group of fans and young musicians who were waiting in line.

I sat down and laid an original still-sealed *Fapardokly* album on the table. A young drummer walked up and was aghast when he saw it and asked, "Is this a real *Fapardokly* Album"? "Our band loves this album!" He had a very cute young blond girl with him named Piper, who was elated to have a picture taken with me, of course I was flattered!

Kim Fowley was standing off to the side in a sharp pin striped suit with short grey hair and people kept trying to figure out who he was, as he didn't look anything like his picture in the Rhino box set.

The doors to the theater flung open, and a large throng of fans who had been watching a screening of old *Monkees* TV shows, came out! I was sitting at the autograph signing table next to Billy Hinsche of *Dino, Desi and Billy*, and Johnny Charles of *The Knickerbokers*. Songwriters Van Dyke Parks and Bobby Hart, Mark Tulin of *The Electric Prunes* and Andrew Sandoval the compilations producer were also seated at the table. I did a great on camera interview with Andrew for my *Tiki Lounge* TV show. We talked about the history of '60s music and the clubs on the Sunset Strip and what a special time it was.

Next I interviewed Billy Hinsche and I mentioned I had backed up singer songwriter Joey Cooper in Palm Springs with my group *Merrell And The Exiles* in 1964, just before he wrote *Dino, Desi & Billy's* first hit *'I'm A fool'*. Next I interviewed Mark Tulin of *The Electric Prunes*. He remarked that he was astonished at how young some of the fans were that were coming up to the table! I did try to interview Kim Fowley but he only responded with very short answers and seemed a bit freaked out by it all! Kim had worked with producer Gary S. Paxton on *"Alley Oop"* by *The Hollywood Argyles*. Paxton recorded four of the tracks on my 1967 *Fapardokly* album.

After signing over 400 autographs we went inside the theater for a panel discussion about the '60s scene on the strip. The theater was full and I was introduced by Andrew Sandoval , then writer Dominic Priorie held up my *Fapardokly* album to the cheering crowd like it was some lost Holy Grail of music ! It was very surreal.

I was on the panel seated in front of the screen with Billy Hinsche, Bill Rinhardt of *The Leaves* and Bob Zinner of *The Fields*. They showed slides of various bands, landmarks and clubs like *Pandora's Box* that had long been remodeled or torn down. Billy Hinsche and I talked about the various clubs we played in and how we loved our Rickenbacker 12 string guitars. Billy talked about playing a party for Dean Martin's daughter where *The Byrds* were also playing. When *The Byrds* took a break Billy went over and picked up Roger McGuinn's Rickenbacker 12 string. Feeling a little intimidated just as Roger came back, Billy was in awe of the guitar and got afraid when McGuinn saw him touching it!

Next a picture of my old friend Harry Nilsson came on the screen and I told the story about the time *The Beatles* called him up one night to tell him how they liked his album *Aerial Ballet*. Harry thought it was a prank and hung up on them!

Those days in the sixties were very special indeed and I will never forget all the great times! I was very humbled to be part of the Rhino release party at the Egyptian Theater and that my 1967 song *Tomorrows Girl* was included in the box set. An article appeared in the *Los Angeles Times* on December 1st 2009 edition saying that Del Fi Records founder Bob Keene had died, it was the end of another era.

Chapter 22
Merrell Meets Jane

*I*t was December 2009 and I had been living alone for quite a few years just writing, recording and doing gigs. It was a little lonely when I came home by myself every night to a cold dark house in winter. My video editor at the time kept encouraging me to get out and maybe I should go to one of the singles dinners that he attended? I thought no I don't think I could go to something like that. It was December 21st, two days before my birthday and there was a singles dinner that night and I thought, maybe I should get out.

I got dressed and ready to go and then thought, no I don't want to go, and then I changed my mind and got in the car and drove to the restaurant. I walked in and was greeted by the host who sat me at a table near the door. I was looking at the menu and having small talk with a

few ladies at the table and a beautiful Asian lady walked in and sat down in front of me and said, "Hi my name is Jane". We started talking and she said how she was raised in Peru and I immediately asked her about "Machu Picchu" and other ruins I was very interested in. She had been to all the places I had only dreamt about. We had a nice dinner and conversation and I got up the nerve to ask her for her phone number which she gave me.

We shook hands and said goodbye, but in the confusion I left the number on the table and realized I didn't have it when I got home! A week went by and I was thinking about Jane and to my surprise one morning I got an email from her asking why I hadn't called her? I emailed her right back and said I lost her phone number and would she like to go out after New Years when I finished my gigs and recording sessions? She emailed me back' yes' and we went to a Chinese restaurant the end of the first week in January. We had a great time and I asked her to go out again the following Saturday, she said yes, email me. I had a lot of old email piling up in my computer and one day I decided to dump all my sent emails and trash.

I hadn't entered Jane's email address in my computer and had only been replying to her emails, so her address was not in my computer! I tried emailing her with what I thought was her email, but I got no reply and the emails never came back so I thought, she must be getting them? Several weeks went by and Jane was wondering why I hadn't emailed her? A friend suggested she should email me. I was so happy when I got Jane's email, and we made a date for the following Saturday. We went out for dinner and dancing at a local night spot, and one of the musicians asked, "Is this your wife?" I said "No but I love her". I could tell something was happening as I felt the electricity when I held her hand. We had a lot of fun and she gave me a loaf of banana bread she made and I ate the whole thing in three days and made myself sick! She invited me to her house the following weekend for dinner. That week I had a productive recording session with my old friend violinist Sal Garza who played on my spooky instrumental titled *Shadow People* and we did an eerie video in a four story English style house in San Luis Obispo.

I arrived on a Saturday night at Jane's lovely two story townhouse in Santa Maria where I met her 16 year old son Aaron who was interested in music and played piano. It felt very cozy with the smell of a home cooked dinner and soft music playing in the background. One song kept playing repeatedly with a Latin feel and I asked "What's the title of this song"? And Jane said it's called *Fallen* from the movie *Pretty Woman*, I really like it. It stuck in my head and the next day I looked up the music on the internet and went in the studio and laid down all the instruments myself with a nice classical guitar solo. The next day I added my lead vocal and a harmony, mixed it and made a CD to give Jane for Valentines Day.

She was elated when I played it for her and she cried. That night after dinner we started kissing passionately on the couch and we got carried away, but managed to control ourselves, we were both falling in love. She asked me "Is this a serious relationship"? I said "Yes this is a very serious relationship". Until now I never thought I would fall in love again and I said "You are the woman I could spend the rest of my life with" .My love for Jane inspired me to write a song titled *"When Merrell Met Jane"* and over the next month I recorded an entire album of love songs dedicated to her.

Jane and I became inseparable and we would spend weekends together at her house or mine and she would accompany me to concerts I was performing at. She even started doing acting parts and camera work on my TV show *Tiki Lounge* that still had a large following on the California central coast, Hawaii and Ann Arbor Michigan.

2010 started out on a positive note, I had a good relationship with Jane and my son Tim and I were getting together to do more concerts and recordings. We did a memorable concert on June 4th at the San Luis Obispo Grange auditorium with a host of musicians, Tim and I on guitars and vocals, Keith Frasher on bass, Jerry Sagouspe, Dick Lee and Dennis Dragon on drums and Bob Osborn on Sax. My old friend acoustic musician, Eric Brittain, opened the show. Ed Cassidy was going to play a few songs but his old leg injury was still bothering him and he was still walking with the aid of a walker. We went through a list of classic rock songs from the '50s, '60s and '70s with a few originals; my granddaughter Chelsea even joined us on guitar for a rousing version of *Wipe Out!* The crowd was very enthusiastic and came from as far away as Santa Barbara and L.A. The show was shot by camera man Prez Washington and aired on my TV show *Tiki Lounge*.

It was a fun summer of concerts and I even did - what some said was - the first instrumental Surf version of *The Star Spangled Banner* that was sent out to radio in time for the 4th of July. Around this same time I was contacted by Karl Anderson of the San Francisco based Global Recording Artists label about doing a song for a Sky Saxon tribute compilation CD, I said "let me think about it and I will get back to you". I no sooner put the phone down and I thought about the times I'd spent with Sky and words and melody flowed out and *Two Guys From The '60s* was written in about twenty minutes. I called Ed Cassidy and asked if he would like to play drums on it, and Cass said he'd give it a shot. I also got Eric Brittain to play fiddle on it and I played Dobro, Bass and vocal. It came out a down home Country Blues style that was very catchy. Then we shot the video complete with old photos of me and Sky and video of him on my *California Music* TV show from 1991.

I had been in contact with an interesting and talented young musician named Golly McCry from Germany who was a big fan of my early '60s *Merrell And The Exiles* recordings. He really had a knack for re creating the '60s sound and did an entire album dedicated to me titled *Golly McCry "Shake My Hand": a tribute to Merrell Fankhauser*. The album got quite a bit of radio play and reviews in America and Europe.

Around September I got a call from original *Merrell And The Exiles* keyboardist John Day that he was now living in Tennessee and was planning a trip to California and would like to stop by for a visit. I said great I will get our old *Exiles* drummer Dan Martin who now lives about 45 minutes north of me to also come down and we could do a reunion segment for the TV show. We got together in the Tiki Lounge studio and had a great time talking about the good old days recording in the Glenn Records studio in Palmdale in 1964 and 1965. John and Dan had played on *Send me Your Love* and *Don't Call On Me* and John played organ on *Sorry For Yourself* in 1965, all released as singles on Glenn Records. John remembered one humorous story about us playing a dance one night at large auditorium. We were really rockin' out, when we noticed our bass player Jim Ferguson was hopping around kind of funny and then started slapping his leg; smoke was coming out of his pocket! Jim was the only smoker in the band and apparently a book of matches somehow got lit in his pocket and was burning his leg! How I wish that we'd had video cameras back then! I put together a collage of photos of the band and put our song *Don't Call On Me* to it for the TV show. It was great seeing Dan and John together after over 40 years

October 16th of 2010 found *Merrell Fankhauser And Friends* headlining the annual Clam Festival in Pismo Beach with an audience of seven thousand. The end of the concert was a show stopper with Laurie Vierheilig and *The Tiki Lounge Dancers* doing the Hula to *Wipe Out!* Jane videoed the entire concert for the TV show and it came out very well, considering it was the first concert she shot by herself!

Near the end of November I heard from Rhino Records producer Andrew Sandoval that we had been nominated for a Grammy in the Historical Album category for our CD compilation *Where The Action Is L.A: Nuggets 1965-1968* that included my 1967 song *Tomorrow's Girl* . Andrew said that some outtakes of old *Beatles* songs were also nominated in the same category. I said "Well the air's going to go out of this balloon quickly on February 13th when *The Beatles* win!" It was a great honor and my mind went whirling back to the mid '60s and recording with *The Exiles*, how strange this music business is! 'The Fab Four' won the Grammy, but it was great to be beat by *The Beatles*!

In December I was asked to perform on the Kenny Loggins Unity Christmas TV show in Santa Barbara and I did a version of *Wipe Out* that was aired on a major network. I was doing a lot of radio and press interviews all over the country and getting loads of emails from all over the world. One email was from graphics man Martin Cook from England who said he was a big fan and that he thought a label he worked with might be interested in releasing some of my recordings. I received an email from Rob Ayling of Gonzo Records U.K. asking for a list and description of albums available for licensing. I sent him a detailed list and before I knew it he and his lovely assistant were knocking on my door and we decided on reissuing my *Return To MU* CD with a documentary DVD included as the first release and later a two CD set titled *Merrell Fankhauser "The Best Of*, my first retrospective with songs from 1964 to 2011. Rob also expressed interest in releasing a few volumes of my TV show Tiki Lounge on DVD with a companion CD with songs from each show. I went right to work editing the TV shows and mastering the audio CDs.

2010 was ending on a very good note, I was in love and had many new projects and adventures on the horizon!

Chapter 23
"Message To The Universe And Beyond"

Karl Anderson of Global Recording Artists label got in touch with me again saying he was interested in re issuing my *Message To The Universe* album on CD and possibly later my *Flying To Machu Picchu* album. This was all very good news as the *Message To The Universe* album had only been released on vinyl LP back in 1986 on a U.K label

And *Flying To Machu Picchu* was only released on a French label in 1992 and both albums

Tim Fankhauser, Chuck Negron, Merrell

Merrell Fankhauser And Friends -Rotary Bandstand Arroyo Grande

were long out of print. The reissue of *Return To MU* started getting substantial radio play that was being promoted by East Coast promo man Mack Maloney. Mack did a great job of booking me on several Paranormal/UFO related radio shows across the country. I went over so well that many of the shows had me back for repeat interviews.

Message To The Universe GRA12892 was released in March 2011 and another round of Radio and press interviews started. The song *Alien Talk* from the CD was getting quite a bit of radio play. We did a fun video to *Alien Talk* that opens up at a party with Jane's relatives in Peru and Jane plays an alien at night in the garden.

Meanwhile I continued to write and record surf instrumentals; one titled *Poquito Loquita* was released as a single to radio in May and DJ's were calling it a new classic

In the vein of "Tequila" and "Church Key!" Jane played bass with the band in the video. Next I recorded another instrumental titled "Tiki Jam" and Jane and I were in the video in disguise hanging out at the bar. Nobody realized it was us, we later tried this at a local pub on Halloween but the crowd eventually figured out who we were!

One afternoon the phone rang and when I picked it up to my surprise Yoriko Hongo was on the other end. She said "she had been thinking about me lately and was wondering if I would

Jane Kong performing on Tiki Lounge

like to get together and play some gigs again"? I said "It's been six years and I don't think it would work, that ship sailed a long time ago!" The conversation was polite but uneasy, and we hung up. She later called again and left a message trying to convince me to do a concert with her for aid to Japan after the Tsunami and nuclear tragedy.

The cute little city of Arroyo Grande was celebrating its centennial in July and the organizers asked *Merrell Fankhauser And Friends* to perform July 24th at the Rotary Bandstand in the park. The town has an old west feel with stone buildings going back to the early 1900's. There's a big creek that runs alongside the main street with one of the only cable suspension bridges in California crossing it. It was a beautiful sunny day in the park when we took to the stage and started off with my son Tim's new song *Scrub Ruba Dub*. The audience was immediately singing along with the infectious lyrics and melody. Myself and Tim were on vocals and guitars, Sal Garza on violin, Bob Osborn on Sax, Phil Gross on Bass and Art Dougall on drums. The band was tight and in top form and the audience loved it. The organizers said it was the biggest crowd ever in the park, it really felt good to see a large turnout in our own hometown.

On September 3rd we again took to the stage in a sold out concert at the beautiful state of the art Clark Center auditorium in Arroyo Grande where countless numbers of big stars had performed! It was shot by cameraman Prez Washington for the *Tiki Lounge* TV show and got very good reviews. We took the band in the studio and recorded Tim's songs , *I've Got The Right, Genie Go Down, Pants Are Way Too Baggy* and an electric blues funk version of *I've Got The Right*. I also added some of Tim's earlier songs *Witch Doctor, There Is Peace* and a great version of *Lucille* with me and *The Revels* backing him up! This would be Sunny Tim's first solo album when finished and released; he really had some fun with the Country Delta Blues style songs! My boy had matured into a fine singer/songwriter and guitarist. At this time, Tim had told me he and his wife Carol were getting a divorce, I was actually not surprised. Carol rode Tim pretty hard and really didn't support Tim's music career and he began drinking to much. I had a talk with him about his drinking and he assured me he would be alright after everything was behind him. They sold the ranch in Oregon and both bought separate houses in the town of Medford. Tim also bought an older house he fixed up that my now 19 year old grandaughter Chelsea was living in while going to college and work.

Our next concert was September 23rd down in Santa Maria California for a cancer fundraiser with our old band *The Revels* and *The Sorensen Brothers* and Chuck Negron of *Three Dog Night*. I hadn't seen Chuck in over forty years when he would come in and sing a few songs with *The Impacts* at the *Rose Garden Ballroom* back in 1962! We had a great time talking about the good old days. *Merrell Fankhauser & Friends* opened the show and then my son Tim and I joined *The Revels* for *Church Key* and *Comanche* from the movie *Pulp Fiction*. Then came *The Sorensen Brothers* backing Chuck Negron on several of his hits.

During the concert Chuck said to the audience "You folks will probably remember the words to my songs better than I will, I'm going to have to cheat, well actually I'm going to read", he had a music stand with all the lyrics. Near the end of the show we put all the bands together and did "Joy To The World". I looked out at the front row of people they all had cameras and some of the older couples had tears running down their faces! It was a very special night and the promoters invited us all back to do it again in 2012. Promoter Frank Salazar, who had booked us all at concerts and dances back in the 60's, gave a very touching speech at the end of the show.

I had been communicating with a Dutch writer and DJ named Peter Marinus who was collaborating with me on a complete Merrell Fankhauser discography. Peter had found albums on me in several countries like Poland and Brazil that I didn't even know about! Peter flew in from Holland and I took him over to meet my longtime friend DJ Bill "The Boogie King" Newell. We had a great time talking about music and records, it was fun hearing them telling jokes in Dutch and German. This meeting inspired me to write an instrumental surf style song titled *"The Groovemaster Meets The Boogie King"*. I recorded the basic tracks and got Peter to play bass and we later shot a video for the song that appeared on my *Tiki Lounge* TV show.. Peter and I worked on the discography for seven days going through my archives. With his research we found well over fifty albums counting compilations I was on! Peter did a interview for his radio show with me and Louie Ortega who had played with *"The Sir Douglas Quintet"* and *"The Texas Tornadoes"*. Peter flew back to The Neatherlands and we continued to work on the discography via computer.

I went to work in the studio with my band and we recorded the song *The Groovemaster Meets The Boogie King*. A month later I had all the parts shot for a video that would go with the interview I did with Peter for the *Tiki Lounge* TV show.

Jane's son Aaron was now going to college in Davis California and she decided her big two story four bedroom house in Santa Maria was just not needed and I asked her to move in with me. We started selling furniture and things she no longer needed and gave the house a thorough cleaning and painting. Jane had enough things and clothes to fill up two of my houses but we managed to squeeze everything in to my house and garage and my limited outside covered storage area. We spent about a month interviewing renters and rented her house and Jane and I began life together in Arroyo Grande.

Near the end of the year Gonzo Records U.K., released *Merrell Fankhauser 'The Best Of* 2 CD set with songs from 1964 to 2011 some of which were unreleased. Publicist Billy James at Glass Onyon PR was doing a great job of promoting it and booking me daily doing radio & press interviews. 2011 was closing with another banner year for live shows and releases. I was still working on the Surf Instrumental album *Rockin' And Surfin' Vol 4*. Amazingly Surf music was still popular and in demand and being played by DJ's everywhere!

Chapter 24
"Tiki Lounge Returns to Area 51"

*E*very show on television had a prediction about UFOs and the Mayan calendar and what exactly was going to happen in 2012? Every time you tuned into The History, Discovery or National Geographic channels, the paranormal and UFO mystery was the hot topic. I again was swamped with radio interviews wanting me to talk about UFO's or the Lost Continent of Mu theory. Promoter Mack Maloney came up with a great idea for me to do a special CD aimed at this radio format and audience. I again took the idea in the studio and began cranking out spacey surf style instrumentals with titles and sounds to fit this genre. I sent a demo to Rob Ayling at Gonzo Records and he loved it and gave me the go ahead. In a short time Martin Cook had the artwork done for Merrell Fankhauser's *Area 51 Suite* that would also have a bonus DVD.

In February Gonzo Multimedia released two volumes of my Tiki Lounge TV show on DVD with a companion CD with songs from the various shows in each volume. It was a stunning release with beautiful artwork by Martin Cook. And again publicist Billy James booked me doing lots of radio and press interviews, and the two *Tiki Lounge* volumes were getting reviews online and in magazines around the world !

One of the shows in the DVD set was very timely as it had the *Tiki Lounge* show I did in Rachel, Nevada, on the border of the now legendary secret airbase "Area 51". One day Jane was on the internet and stumbled across a book titled *Merrell Fankhauser* by Terrence Victorino! We were all shocked, what is this? We went to Barnes and Noble and they said it was in stock but was mainly a book that had information taken from magazines, newspaper articles, other books and Wikipedia, and was selling for $49!

There were so many mistakes and misinformation about my history on the internet and in Victorino's book! I started working on my own book more diligently as I knew there would be lots that I would have to clear up! Meanwhile the big promotion and press releases sent out by Billy James for the *Tiki Lounge* DVD sets really started a fire in the media. I started getting even more interview inquires from radio, TV and press.

I got an email from Karl Anderson of Global Recording Artists label that he planned to re issue my album *Flying To Machu Picchu* GRA13002 near the end of May. I felt lucky at this stage of my life to still have so many releases coming out on labels all over the world!

The music world was again shocked February 17th with the untimely death of superstar Whitney Houston. It appeared to be another tragic drug overdose that had taken so many musicians. The Grammy's were set to be televised on Sunday and the entire show was quickly re written to be a tribute to Whitney. It turned out to be one of the most watched shows in many years, under very sad circumstance's the show went on. I was brought to reality when I was doing an interview with "Blues Matters" magazine from the U.K. when the writer said, "You've Been making music for fifty years, your body of work is amazing, but even more amazing is that you're still alive!"

Chapter 25
"Live To Play Another Day"

2012 turned out to be a productive year with several releases and outstanding concerts for *Merrrell Fankhauser And Friends*. I did over 100 radio, TV and press interviews promoting *The Best Of* and the two volumes of *Tiki Lounge* on DVD.

I finished the final mixes on my son Tim's album which was titled *I've Got The Right* and credited to Sunny Tim Fankhauser, and I started sending it out to labels to try to get a deal. I also finished a one hour video documentary and soundtrack CD that I co produced with Steve Omar from Maui titled *Rainbow Bridge Revisited*. It traced the steps actress Pat Hartley took in 1970 from the Sunset Strip in Hollywood to the islands of Oahu and Maui where she met a host of characters, spiritual hippies and ultimately Jimi Hendrix. We interviewed some of the original cast from the 1972 Jimi Hendrix movie *Rainbow Bridge*. It was interesting to hear what they had to say about hanging out with Hendrix making the movie on Maui 40 years ago! Our documentary was filmed in California and Hawaii with beautiful scenery, exciting surfing and music by me, *Omar And The Wave Spies* and *The Space Patrol*. I sent a demo to Rob Ayling at Gonzo Multimedia in England and he immediately signed it for release in June of 2013 on DVD with a soundtrack CD! My *Area 51 Suite* was slated for a March 2013 release date, counting the Sky Saxon tribute CD *Reach For The Sky*, I already had three releases set for the next year.

Around October of 2012, Ed Cassidy was found unconscious on his living room floor and rushed to the hospital. He had been lying on the floor for approximately 16 hours, he said he just didn't have the strength to get up and couldn't reach the phone. He was severely dehydrated. His ex wife Beverley came down from San Jose to take care of him as he was in a wheelchair and wasn't recovering well. She moved him to San Jose where she was living and he died December 6th of prostate cancer, he was 89. I was very sad as Cassidy was a good friend and my musical guru; to be able to keep playing drums till he was in his late '80s was remarkable! Later that day I got a call from a dermatologist about a biopsy I had on a mole on my left shoulder. The doctor said "you have a very serious malignant melanoma tumor", and you need surgery as soon as possible!

Receiving this news and Cassidy's passing the same day hit me like a one two punch!

Merrell with Dean Torrence and Band.

I had the surgery December 20th in the Central Coast Surgical Center with noted surgeon doctor Howard Hayashi. Before the operation Howard said "You didn't bring your guitar"? I said, "I thought you could graft an extra arm on me so I could play while you did the surgery!" Everybody laughed, and I passed out. The tumor turned out to be very large, 3.5 millimeters deep; if it had been 4 millimeters deep it could have spread to my lymph glands and even my brain! I dodged the bullet of death by only .5 of a millimeter!

I was in surgery for over an hour and they also took a biopsy of my lymph node under my left arm, I woke up very sore but felt like I just had a short five minute nap. The lab report came back that my lymph node was ok but there was still some small cancer cells in the fatty tissue around the area. I would find out in February what kind of further treatment I would need? It took over a month to heal and to be able to fully use my left arm. All those years of fun in the sun on Maui took its toll.

New Years Eve was very mellow, we stayed home and fell asleep before midnight as 2013 began, and the world didn't end as some thought the Mayans had predicted.

Near the end of January I got a call from film maker Charlie Booth who told me he was coming out to California from Michigan to work on a project and would like to stop by for a visit. Charlie told me a movie producer friend of his was working on a movie based on the Thomas Pynchon book *Inherent Vice*, and that my *Fapardokly* song *Supermarket* was mentioned in. Charlie and I hadn't seen each other since the mid '90s when he and his dad were working on a documentary in California about old steam engine locomotives. Charlie and his wife Tracey arrived in the afternoon Monday February 4th, and we talked about the good old days for two days straight and even did an interview for *Tiki Lounge* reminiscing about filming on Maui in 1978 and 1983.

Charlie gave me the contact information for his producer friend Paul Steinbroner who was doing some coordinating for the *Inherent Vice* movie. I emailed Paul and got an answer back right away with instructions for me to send him a CD with the song *Supermarket* and any other songs that I thought might be pertinent. I told him how I was amazed that the book's author Thomas Pynchon had mentioned my songs and The Lost Continent of MU, a subject I had studied for years ! I included some of my songs about The Lost Continent of MU on the CD that I sent to Paul.

In a short time I received an email from Paul saying he loved the music and would pass it on to the main producer of the movie and Thomas Pynchon. Warner Brothers later bought the script!

I got an email from my old friend Dean Torrence of *Jan and Dean* asking if I would like to join him and his band for a few songs at their concert at the Clark Center in Arroyo Grande February 9th? I said yes, even though my shoulder and arm wasn't completely healed yet from the recent surgery. The concert was a blast and we brought down the house with an encore doing *Wipe Out, Barbara Ann,* and *Fun Fun Fun!* During *Fun Fun Fun* several ladies rushed the stage dancing and hugging and kissing us! Bill McEuen emailed me from Hawaii when he saw it on YouTube and said it would make a perfect Viagra ad! It was my first gig since the surgery and it felt good to be back on stage, it was just what the doctor ordered!

Dean and I did an interview for my TV show talking about playing together on Kauai eleven years ago, and we both couldn't believe it was twenty years ago that we recorded together at Bill McEuen's studio in Carpenteria! We filmed the concert for my TV show and ended with the video of Dean and I singing my song *Polynesian Dream* that was filmed on the island of Kauai in 2000.

Near the end of February Rob Ayling CEO of the U.K. label Gonzo Multimedia flew over for a meeting with me. He had a brilliant plan to put all of the *Tiki Lounge* TV shows on the internet for 'Pay Per View'! So I started working on making high quality DVD's of fifty shows to be sent to his video editor Harold Houldershaw in England. Who would have ever thought my low budget TV show would go global! .

After a MRI and CT scan I got more good news from doctor Howard Hayshi that I wouldn't need Chemo or radiation on my back area around the surgery, I would just have to have

regular checkups to make sure nothing popped up again. Things were looking good and I could continue on my creative journey doing what I loved, performing and making music!
On June 1st I did a two hour interview on the biggest late night radio show in America *Coast To Coast AM* with host John B Wells. The response was incredible, in three days I got over 600 emails from listeners across the U.S. and even Europe!

Looking back I feel like I've lived several lives and I even died once and got to come back, and had another close call! I am grateful for everything I got to do and experience, every event was a lesson in the book of life. I still look at the sky and marvel at the universe and pray for peace and harmony for all beings on space ship Earth.

I am still "Calling from a Star".

GONZO
Books

There is still such a
thing as alternative
Publishing

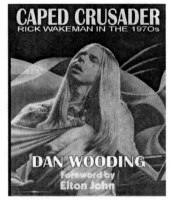

Robert Newton Calvert: Born 9
March 1945, Died 14 August 1988
after suffering a heart attack.
Contributed poetry, lyrics and
vocals to legendary space rock
band Hawkwind intermittently on
five of their most critically
acclaimed albums, including Space
Ritual (1973), Quark, Strangeness
& Charm (1977) and Hawklords
(1978). He also recorded a number
of solo albums in the mid 1970s.
CENTIGRADE 232 was Robert Cal
vert's first collection of poems.

Hype   'And now, for all you speed
ing street smarties out there, the
one you've all been waiting for, the
one that'll pierce your laid back
ears, decoke your sinuses, cut clean
thru the schlock rock,
MOR/crossover, techno flash mind
mush. It's the new Number One with
a bullet ... with a bullet ... It's Tom,
Supernova, Mahler with a pan galac
tic biggie ...' And the Hype goes on.
And on. Hype, an amphetamine hit of
a story by Hawkwind collaborator
Robert Calvert. Who's been there
and made it back again. The
debriefing session starts here.

Rick Wakeman is the world's most
unusual rock star, a genius who has
pushed back the barriers of electronic
rock. He has had some of the world's
top orchestras perform his music, has
owned eight Rolls Royces at one time,
and has broken all the rules of com
posing and horrified his tutors at the
Royal College of Music. Yet he has
delighted his millions of fans. This
frank book, authorised by Wakeman
himself, tells the moving tale of his
larger than life career.

There are nine Henrys, pur
ported to be the world's
first cloned cartoon charac
ter. They live in a strange
lo fi domestic surrealist
world peopled by talking
rock buns and elephants on
wobbly stilts.

They mooch around in their
minimalist universe suffer
ing from an existential
crisis with some genetically
modified humour thrown in.

Marty Wilde on Terry Dene: "Whatever
happened to Terry becomes a great deal
more comprehensible as you read of the
callous way in which he was treated by
people who should have known better
many of whom, frankly, will never know
better of the sad little shadows of
the past who eased themselves into
Terry's life, took everything they
could get and, when it seemed that all
was lost, quietly left him … Dan Wood
ing's book tells it all."

Rick Wakeman: "There have
always been certain 'careers'
that have fascinated the
public, newspapers, and the
media in general. Such
include musicians, actors,
sportsmen, police, and not
surprisingly, the people who
give the police their employ
ment: The criminal. For the
man in the street, all these
careers have one thing in
common: they are seemingly
beyond both his reach and,
in many cases, understanding
and as such, his only associ
ation can be through the
media of newspapers or tele
vision. The police, however,
will always require the ser
vices of the grass, the
squealer, the snitch, (call
him what you will), in order
to assist in their investiga
tions and arrests; and amaz
ingly, this is the area that
seldom gets written about."

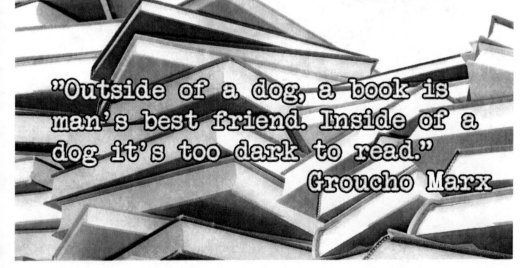

"Outside of a dog, a book is
man's best friend. Inside of a
dog it's too dark to read."
Groucho Marx

Bill Harkleroad joined Captain Beef heart's Magic Band at a time when they were changing from a straight ahead blues band into something completely different. Through the vision of Don Van Vliet (Captain Beefheart) they created a new form of music which many at the time considered atonal and difficult, but which over the years has continued to exert a powerful influence. Beefheart re christened Harkleroad as Zoot Horn Rollo, and they embarked on recording one of the classic rock albums of all time Trout Mask Replica - a work of unequalled daring and inventiveness.

Politics, paganism and ... Vlad the Impaler. Selected stories from CJ Stone from 2003 to the present. Meet Ivor Coles, a British Tommy killed in action in September 1915, lost, and then found again. Visit Mothers Club in Erdington, the best psyche delic music club in the UK in the '60s. Celebrate Robin Hood's Day and find out what a huckle duckle is. Travel to Stonehenge at the Summer Solstice and carouse with the hippies. Find out what a Ranter is, and why CJ Stone thinks that he's one. Take LSD with Dr Lilly, the psychedelic scientist. Meet a headless soldier or the ghost of Elvis Presley in Gabalfa, Cardiff. Journey to Whitstable, to New York, to Malta and to Transylvania, and to many other places, real and imagined, polit ical and spiritual, transcendent and mundane. As The Independent says, Chris is "The best guide to the underground since Charon ferried dead souls across the Styx."

This is is the first in the highly acclaimed vampire novels of the late Mick Farren. Victor Renquist, a surprisingly urbane and likable leader of a colony of vampires which has existed for centuries in New York is faced with both admin istrative and emotional prob lems. And when you are a vampire, administration is not a thing which one takes lightly.

"The person, be it gentleman or lady, who has not pleasure in a good novel, must be intolerably stupid."

Jane Austen